The Freaks Are Winning
The Inner Swine Collection

The Freaks Are Winning

The Inner Swine Collection

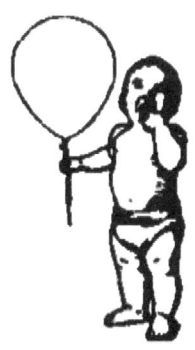

By Jeff Somers

Copyright © 2002 by Jeff Somers except where noted otherwise, dammit.

ISBN: 0-9713719-0-3

The Freaks Are Winning: The Inner Swine *Collection* is a rewarmed collection of stuff that originally appeared in *The Inner Swine* (ISSN: 1527-7704), which is a magazine published March, June, September, and December by Oinking Sow, Inc. (There is no company, really.) Subscription rates and such can be found in the back of this book, in case you're wondering, but stop teasing me, you're never going to order a subscription, *you heartless bastards*. Free trades are absolutely entertained; send me something, and I will mail you treats. Although I have to assume that since you're reading this, you're already a fan, or else why in the world would you pick this book up? Unless it was to call your friends over and have some fun at my expense, saying things like "Look at this piece of shit! How'd *he* get published?"

Still, all submissions or requests for guidelines (there are no guidelines, though) must be accompanied by S.A.S.E. Misty Quinn (left) recently jumped out of an airplane to protest the lack of subscriptions garnered for TIS, she sure did. Misty's always doing little things like that to show that she cares. Any resemblance between this boilerplate and the front matter in Dave Eggers' book is just embarrassing, but I was pressured.

By the way, the characters, places, incidents, and situations in this book are imaginary and have no relation to any person, place, or actual happening. Except for the following people: Jeof Vita, Rob Gala, Ken West, Misty S. Quinn, Danette Knopp, Cassie Carey, Mex Carey, Lauren Strutzel, Loretta Somers, Sean Somers, and Jeff "Captain Fantastic" Somers. Those people are real and should be feared.

Cover art © 2001 by Jeof Vita. We have a picture of Jeof with styrofoam on his head that is very funny, you can see it on page xv.

Printed by Tower Records in the USA

***Friends of the Swine: Mom**, who always encourages me and tolerates the bad language and poor hygiene; **Danette**, whom I love very much and whose boundless energy is the main reason I get anything done, and who worked her ass off helping me prepare this manuscript while I ate chips on the couch and grunted out encouragement; **Jeof**, for always being willing to create an amazing cover for me and for sticking with me despite my ever-increasing uncoolness; **Ken**, who never fails to make me laugh until some liquid squirts out of my nose; **Misty**, on whom I can always count to have a beer with me, or many beers; **Lauren**, whose friendship has always been a blessing and whose presence in these articles is sorely missed; **RA**, whose friendship has been amazingly steady and comforting for a truly startling number of years; **Elizabeth**, who remains in my thoughts despite the distance; **Sean**, who manages to have a kind word for me despite his crippling, insane jealousy; **clint johns**, who truly loves zines and who forced me, at gunpoint, to create this book, which turned out to be not such a bad idea after all.*

Table of Contents

Foreword..xi
Preface..xiii
Dramatis Personae...xv
A Virtual Tour of *The Inner Swine*...xix

Zine Elvis Speaks: Jeff's Deep Thoughts on Zines

ZINE REBEL OR ZINE ELVIS? (OR SOMETHING IN-BETWEEN) 3

MR. MUTE'S GUIDE TO MAKING A ZINE 8

DANCE WITH A HAND IN MY PANTS (HOW I PRODUCE 60 PAGES OF QUALITY
SHIT FOR CHEAP) 13

TEN THINGS THAT ANNOY ME ABOUT MY FELLOW ZINE PUBLISHERS 19

Editorials: My Worldwide Organization of Terror

PIG IN SHIT #10: I FOUND THIS FAKE NUDE PHOTO OF BEA ARTHUR ON THE INTERNET
AND CHRIST AM I DISTURBED: THE GREAT THINGS ABOUT PORNOGRAPHY.....................25

PIG IN SHIT #13: TRAVELING MUSIC FOR THE MENTALLY CHALLENGED: *THE INNER
SWINE* ADVICE COLUMN... 33

PIG IN SHIT #14: THE BEST MEAT'S IN THE RUMP: HOW TECHNOLOGICAL
ADVANCEMENT BRINGS OUT THE ANIMAL IN US ALL.. 39

PIG IN SHIT #18: LET ME TAKE THIS OPPORTUNITY TO WELCOME OUR NEW MASTERS:
I AM READY TO JOIN THE THOUGHT POLICE AND RAT ALL OF YOU OUT 45

PIG IN SHIT #17: CARL SAGAN TAUGHT ME TO MANIPULATE TIME: 'PORK AVENGER'
NEWEST SUPERHERO TO PATROL CITY.. 50

PIG IN SHIT #19: I HAVE ENJOYED SELLING OUT AND CAN'T WAIT TO DO SO AGAIN:
THE INNER SWINE SOLD TO MICROSOFT, INC... 59

PIG IN SHIT #20: *INNER SWINE* AFTER DARK: NOUVEAU RICHE SOMERS SKATING
TOWARDS EARLY GRAVE... 65

American Wedding Confidentials: I Am Disco-Hot

AWC #1: My Weekend With Carla 73

AWC #2: Going Stag in the Age of Couplehood 77

AWC #3: It's A Family Affair 81

AWC #4: It's My Scene, Man, and It Freaks Me Out! 85

AWC #5: My Evening With The Lunatic 89

AWC #6: Touch Me I'm Sick 93

AWC #7: Will The Real Best Man Please Stand Up? 97

AWC #8: Gabba Gabba Hey: "One of Us!" 101

AWC #9: Return of The Gigolo 105

Freaks and Forums: I Am Here to Educate and Make the World a Better Place

Lonely and I'm Cold: Your Gentle Editor's Hang-ups 111

My Friends are Cranky, Mean-Spirited Bastards 115

Like Ma Bell, I Got the Ill Communication: The Weirdness of Communication Today 119

It Takes a Nation of Freaks to Hold Me Back 125

The Inner Swine Forum: Misconnected Dimensions Resulting in Rippling Distortions in the Subatomic Connections of our Visible Universe Causing the Sun to Douse, Planets to Explode, Destruction, Despair, and Eventual...Death. Or: *The Inner Swine* on Relationships 129

The Inner Swine Forum: Anger: Why Resist? Discussing Anger Management and the Universal Can of Whoopass 135

BASTARDS: Specious Arguments and Unsupported Opinions

How I Conquered the Country, Grew Fat on the Blood of my Subjects, Tired of Absolute Power, Abdicated the Throne, and Returned to my Ancestral Home (Or, South Dakota and Back in a Few Short Days).. 143

Cheerios, Taters, and a Big Bowl of Ice: The Single Woman's Guide to Economic Food Shopping (by Karen Accavallo)... 151

The Stink of Wasted Bachelorhood: I Have Seen the Future and It Is Larry from "Three's Company".. 155

Big-Hatted Woman, Where Have You Been All My Life? A Day in the Life of your Editor: The Saint Patrick's Day Parade in Hoboken, New Jersey............ 159

Lies Brandon Tartikoff Told Me: The Subtle Manipulation of TV Sitcoms... 163

You Can Live on Ramen Noodles for $200 a Year: Surviving the Coming Economic Crash.. 171

The Ice Weasels are Living in My Pants: How to Be an Expert at First Glance... 179

Baby Levon Rocks On at the DOT... 185

In the Event of Disaster: I Would Eat My Cat.. 191

Everybody's Talkin' at Me: Reviews, Letters, Legal Threats

Everybody's Talkin' at Me.. 197

The Good... 199

The Bad... 204

The Freaks... 206

Contact Info... 211

Blatant Self-Promotion... 214

FOREWORD

By clint johns, Ph.D.[1]

clint johns just before being removed from Playboy Mansion by security.

I STARTED buying zines for Tower Records in 1998. I wasn't the only buyer at the time. My old boss still held the reins, and I got to search for jewels among the candidate zines he had, for whatever reason, ignored. Or sometimes I looked at new solicitations before he saw them, and either made a recommendation or bought the zine for Tower myself. I'm not complaining, mind you. That's just how it was.

Some time later, in 1999, my boss quit Tower for a simpler life, and I took over Tower's Magazine Division. We call it Mag Hell, ourselves, and if you can't guess why then you should come and look at my office sometime. And then I will call security, because the last thing I need is a steady stream of slack-jawed gawkers hanging out in my doorway.

What I am trying to say is: I see a lot of zines, and a lot of magazines, and a lot of items that don't really look like magazines but are published periodically, thus qualifying as magazines. New titles appear all the time, and titles old and new vanish with equal frequency. It was amid the drifts of paper that I discovered old issues of *The Inner Swine*, still snugly packed in their envelope. The first article I read was "A Virtual Tour Of The Inner Swine." If you read this book straight through, it will be the first article you read, too. If you read this book straight through you may also develop some kind of mental illness, although that is not my central point.

The point is that "Virtual Tour" was an excellent article. It had two things that are always in short supply in every medium: a real voice, and genuine wit. Both ran through the rest of the zine in supply so promising that I really

---

[1] *Mixology*

had no choice but to buy it for Tower's racks. And now, eleven issues later, Tower Records continues to give Jeff Somers money for his scribing. We're selling the bloody thing. In Chicago. In Boston. In San Diego. In Dublin, Ireland (and Jeff has two letters from Irish readers to prove it). The consumer speaks, and finds in the *Swine's* favor. Hence, the book. I happily admit that this was my idea. Unless it doesn't work. Then it was Jeff's idea.

The Freaks Are Winning is a record of the honest work of a real writer. It will, if you let it, entertain you more than any cut-and-paste sitcom on the glass teat. Does it always work? Of course not. We left *that* stuff out of the book. What you've got here is proof that when Jeff is firing on all cylinders his talents are impressive. He'll make you laugh, and when you're not looking he might make you think. Also: reliable reports indicate that many people read *The Inner Swine* on the toilet, a fact many of these people are moved enough to share with Jeff. You might consider that, if you are on the fence about purchasing the *Swine* for your home. Not that I am suggesting anything.

Finally, and most importantly, every copy of *The Freaks Are Winning* sold increases the chance that Jeff will never be homeless, naked and destitute, licking empty ketchup packets for sustenance and living under a bridge somewhere. And we can all agree that we are better off never seeing Jeff naked. So buy the book. Please. That bridge could be near my house. *Or it could be near yours.*

JEFF SEZ: Aside from the fact that I already consume packets of ketchup in my mad desire to continue living, clint's version of events is quite separate from the truth, of which I am the sole, tortured guardian. Like Stanley Kubrick, clint began calling me at odd hours to ask questions like "Do you believe in God?" or "How do you spell 'Reykjavík?'" or "Is it two parts vodka to one part vermouth, or the other way around?" It was actually some months before I realized that he was the new buyer for Tower Magazines. Finally, at 4 AM one evening he called to ask me what the name of Charlton Heston's character was in *Soylent Green,* and I demanded to know if he was ever going to buy any copies of my zine for Tower.

"Uh...sure. Of course! Of course we are. Send me 7,000 next week."

"Seven thousand?"

"Uh, I mean 125. Oh man, I gotta get more sleep."

And that was the beginning of the deal that has made both clint and I very rich, internationally famous playboys who rob banks and get into adventures in our spare time. But that's a story for another sort of book.

PREFACE

CHANCES are that you're a freak. I know this because over the past few years I've been inundated by freaks, and I've come to the conclusion that the freak-to-normal ratio in this world is something like 1,000 to 1, maybe worse. That's okay though, because I'm also convinced that without freaks I'd be nothing, since you freaks are the ones buying my Zine.

My Zine is *The Inner Swine*, and if you've never heard of it, I don't know why you're holding this book right now. TIS started out as a vague idea I shared with Rob Gala (who gave us the name and the general attitude), Jeof Vita (who has done all but two of our covers), and Ken West (whose contributions to this endeavor continue to elude me) back in 1993, and debuted in 1995 as my own personal brainchild. What do you find in a typical issue of TIS? What you find in most magazines, actually: paranoid screeds against my enemies, hallucinatory versions of common everyday events (usually involving an imagined worldwide organization of terror that I personally run, cartoon characters, and aliens), and novella-length run-on sentences exploring the wonder of: Me.

So you can imagine my reaction when clint johns at Tower Magazines suggested that we put together a book of articles from TIS. I demanded to know how much he was going to pay me. He said, nothing. I said, I don't get out of bed for less than $10,000. He said, well don't get out bed then, you moron. I said, wait a second, I think I have a book of articles from TIS under my bed somewhere. Then clint demanded a tribute of meats and cheeses, which I supplied, and the deal was on!

First, I'll take a moment to introduce some of the people that populate most of the articles herein (yes, they really are real people), so you won't be completely confused when you read a sentence like *"Misty turned to me and said 'Did you know you have a piece of bologna on your head?', and then Ken hit me again, shouting 'Loser! LOSER!'"* Well, it can't hurt, anyway. Then I'll take you on a virtual tour of *The Inner Swine*'s production process so you'll understand how easy it is to drool this stuff onto the page and be horrified at what you paid for this book. Then, the real fun begins: a long Bataan Death March of articles from seven years of *The Inner Swine*.

Enjoy!

DRAMATIS PERSONAE

The Inner Swine *Cast of Characters*

MAIL, we get mail. Counting subpoenas, mail bombs, and the *Adam and Eve* catalogue, we get over three pieces of mail a week here at the TIS offices in Hoboken, New Jersey (motto: *"Drink all you want, we'll brew more!"*) and let me tell you, we read and respond to every bit of it. Recently, Jim Evans of Grit, Montana wrote us a nice letter that raised an interesting question:

"This is the third time I've tried to contact you. Please stop sending my family your badly written and unfunny magazine. I have no idea how you got my name and address. I mean, who the hell are all you people and why do you insist on sending me this bizarre publication? Stop, or hear from my lawyer."

Well, Jim, that's a great question. Who the hell are we, anyway? In every issue of this rag you'll read references to all sorts of people, and rarely are their roles and backgrounds explained. In an effort to foster a feeling of family between the TIS Inner Circle (TISIC) and its readers, let me present to you a quick overview of the people you'll find reference to from time to time in this Zine. Of course, it all starts with:

YOUR EDITOR, JEFF SOMERS. My arrogance is why we're all here, bubba. If it weren't for my mad desire to force my ever-deepening sense of disappointment on all of you, none of this would be happening. Several years ago **Ken West, Jeof Vita, Rob Gala** and myself met in the now-infamous windowless kitchen in New Brunswick, NJ and said those magical words to each other: *You know, I've never really liked you.* I believe that mankind is fundamentally selfish, self-interested, and generally full of shit. And that means all of us. What else can I say? I like piña coladas, and getting caught in the rain. I'm not into yoga, and I have half a brain.

Founding Swine JEOF VITA. Aside from being one of the idiots we go drinking with, Mr. Vita usually creates the fantastic covers for our Zine, occasionally writes an article for us, and sometimes bathes, but only after a lot of pressure. An avid fan of comic books, *Star Wars*, and himself, Jeof's charm escapes your Editor here, but has rooted itself firmly in others, especially Misty Quinn, who certainly seems to dig his action. Jeof's art has been published nationally, although his real ambition is to be a Wookie.

Founding Swine KEN WEST. Aside from being someone else who always ends his evenings carrying me out of some local bar, Ken is often referred to in this Zine as our Security Chief. What this means is that when we have troubles, legal or otherwise, we turn Ken loose on them and they...disappear. We don't know how, and we  don't want to know. Ken is actually a Capitalist Oppressor in-training during the day and makes delicious chili. During his free time Ken is attempting to wire his appliances directly into his brain.

 **Founding Swine ROB GALA.** We like to josh about how we drove Rob out of Jersey during our epic struggle for power within *The Inner Swine*. In truth, no one knows why he fled to Seattle and sends me vaguely threatening notes every now and then. No one. You understand? Out west, Rob struggles to save the world through good old fashioned hippieness, which of course we don't want any part of.

DANETTE KNOPP. The most recent person to survive the rigorous TISIC initiation rite, Danette is somewhat scarred psychologically by the experience, which might explain her unreasonable devotion to her native Texas' sports teams. Coming from a long line of rough-and-tumble snake killers, Danette, in her role as TIS Legal Counsel, has taught us all to fear her, which is all we respect, really. The Fear.

 **MISTY QUINN, Esq.** Aside from engaging in disgusting bouts of public affection with Jeof Vita, Misty is an occasional contributor to *The Inner Swine*. One of our favorite people to drink with, Misty is distinguished as being one of the first in a very long line of women who have refused to sleep with me just on general principle. In her real life she is a Dave Mathews fan.

CASSIE CAREY. At various points in TIS's grand history, Cassie has held complete control over us, in the sense that she was our boss and could have fired us for any of the following reasons: Our blatant theft of office supplies, our use of office time to write, lay out, and produce *The Inner Swine*, and all those lies on our resume. She chose instead to encourage our alcohol abuse and changed jobs to avoid the moral quandary. She was lured back into our sphere of influence because she can't stay away from Jeff's disco-hot sense of style. She remains our Publisher to this day.

LAUREN STRUTZEL. Our very own Overall Official Cool Chick has written occasionally for the Swine but more importantly remains an important source of Strutzelosity, of which you cannot have too much. Lauren's support has been invaluable lo these many years. In her real life, Lauren is frighteningly obsessed with dogs.

 **KAREN ACCAVALLO.** Karen is often referred to as 'one crazy chick' in these hallowed pages. Why? One reason is the many times she has threatened our lives. Another is my rich paranoid fantasy life. Either way, Karen is an occasional contributor and has been part of *The Inner Swine* Experience since our first issue back in '95, and has valiantly tried to improve our spelling and grammar, all to no avail. Her failure has made her bitter. In her real life, Karen watches *JAG*.

BABY LEVON. This is our mascot and trademark. We chose a baby for this because babies are the perfect symbol of the self-obsessed human animal. Baby Levon is your way of knowing that something is Official *Inner Swine* Product, our seal of quality. Look for it, or suffer the consequences. Consequences are Ken West's field, by the way.

 **MY BROTHER.** Sean is my elder brother, who has been trying to kill me since Mom brought me home all those years ago. Every now and then we break Sean out of the hospital, like B.A. Barracus in *The A-Team*, so he can write an article for us, but mostly he doesn't do much and we only mention him in ironic and humorous tones. Still, if you see him on the street, please call *The Inner Swine* emergency number: 1-800-PIGGIES and tell us. There's money in it for you.

LEVON SOBIESKI. Levon began his tenure at TIS as a fictional custodian, but quickly ascended to our candidate for President in 2000. After breaking from Jeff Somers' agenda and openly criticizing *Inner Swine* policy, Levon disappeared and has not been heard from since. All references to him in these collected articles have been sanitized for your safety. Since the picture Levon uses to maintain his privacy is a copyrighted one, we can't show it here.

A VIRTUAL TOUR OF *THE INNER SWINE*

Recently I have gotten over two letters requesting information on how *The Inner Swine* is produced. Well, that of course isn't exactly true: One letter was written in crayon and was really just a collection of profanities I interpreted as a request for information of this sort, and the other was a 14-page missive written on *Holiday Inn* stationery requesting naked photos of Misty Quinn, Karen Accavallo, and Ken West. This I also interpreted as a request for information. I have also provided the photos, naturally.

The common reader has no idea how much work and energy goes into a typical issue of *The Inner Swine*. The lazy bastards just sit on their couches at home, fingering the remote and watching *Jerry Springer* reruns until the mail brings an issue to them magically. Then they read it during various visits to the toilet and usually write me nasty e-mails ridiculing my grammar, interests, style, and appearance. They think these issues grow on trees!

Nothing could be further from the truth. There's a lot of blood, sweat, and illegal chemicals in every issue, contributed during a three-month odyssey that begins the day after I mail off the previous issue. This day is known internationally as *Jeff's Day of Binge Drinking* as I celebrate the finale of yet another issue with several dozen rounds of fermented plum juice made at home in my bathtub (that extra special ingredient is me!) followed by realistic hallucinations and my traditional attempt to jam my head into my toilet. Once I actually succeeded. The EMS guys were pretty amused. That is, until I vomited on them.

After *Jeff's Day of Binge Drinking,* the regular production process begins. In order to explain the complex majesty of creating an issue of TIS, let's examine a detailed timeline of how a typical issue, 4(3) September 1998, came into being.

PRODUCTION TIMELINE FOR SEPTEMBER 1998 ISSUE
(OR: *Three Months to Glory!*)

June 2: *Nursing hangover*
June 3: *Nursing hangover*
June 4: *Nursing hangover*
June 5: *No memory of events*

1. THE WRITING PROCESS

June 6: *Purchase supplies for grueling creative hell to come: Twinkies Family Pack, six two-liter bottles of Birch Beer, 12 cartons of cigarettes, two fifths of Jack Daniels, one gallon of distilled water, one box of Depends Adult Undergarments, six randomly selected girlie magazines, one live chicken, and a dictionary of some sort.*

June 7: *Refer to previous issue of* The Inner Swine *to ascertain what ridiculous subject I chose for the next theme and editorial, not that anyone notices, or cares. Scratch head repeatedly wondering what the hell I was thinking when I came up with that dull topic.*

June 8: *Sit down at computer to write editorial. Spend 13 hours playing* Half Life *instead.*

June 9: *Sit down at computer to write editorial. Get distracted by first bottle of Jack Daniels.*

June 11: *Wake up in Rhode Island with someone else's pants on.*

June 12-14: *Nursing hangover.*

June 15-30: *Whereabouts unknown, memory unreliable. I have a matchbook from The Huxton Motor Lodge in Akron. Put this under the heading of "research".*

July 1-6: *Celebrate the Fourth of July with therapeutic cocktails. Write a few brilliant revelations on cocktail napkins for the editorial. Later, suffer temporary blindness from drinking homemade liquor.*

July 7: *Swear off the booze. Spend day shivering.*

July 8-12: *Worms oozing out of walls, flies the size of seagulls invade, have a long conversation with a sewer rat in a smoking jacket.*

July 13: *Take up drinking again in self-defense. Locate cocktail napkins with brilliant ideas. Only one that is legible reads "The cheese is burning!" Decide to start fresh.*

July 14: *Sit down at computer to write editorial. Spend 13 hours playing* Half Life *instead.*

July 15-16: *Wake up at 5AM inspired, sit down and write straight through evening into next day. After 36 hours at keyboard, I have a few hundred pathetic words that amount to a weak, five-page article as my cornerstone for the new issue. I decide it is brilliant.*

July 17: *After getting some honest criticism on the new editorial, I check the Holdover File for old articles rejected from earlier issues. All I find are more cocktail napkins. One has "Socks with eyes!" scrawled on it.*

July 18: *Karen Accavallo calls me and promises to supply at least 30 pages of material for next issue, claiming that she has several brilliant articles mapped out in her head. Half the issue is already full with this contribution, so I head off to happy hour.*

July 21: *Having slept in the Port Authority bus station the night before covered in own sick, I arrive home to find my pockets stuffed with more cocktail napkins. One reads "Vinegar jellybeans!" I soak in a tub of ice water for rest of day and almost drown myself.*

July 22-31: *I go off on spiritual journey into the New Jersey wild, searching for my lost soul. I contract some virus from odd purple berries and become a one-man celebration of bodily fluids. Lost in the wild, I assume I am going to die and decide to write a will and testament. I only have cocktail napkins to write this on.*

August 1: *I am discovered by some teenagers, who inform me that I am only a few hundred feet from the highway. Then they jeer me and steal all my stuff, except my cocktail napkins. As I walk to the highway, I find my last will and testament makes no sense. Apparently I have left Karen Accavallo my collection of go-go boots, but I don't own any go-go boots.*

August 2-4: *Shamed by my recent foibles, I force myself to write an article for the new issue. What results is three pages about why I hate everyone. I decide it's been done, and thank god Karen is supplying me with all that material.*

August 5: *My birthday.*

August 28: *I awaken in my bedroom with no memory of the previous three weeks. My apartment is clean and orderly and all my bills have been paid, my laundry done, and my dishes cleaned and stacked. I am clean-shaven and feeling fit, but have no conscious memory of my birthday or the days that followed. I realize that I have three days to produce the magazine. I check my machine and find a message from Karen, who complains bitterly that I did not give her enough time, so she will not write anything for me.*

August 29-31: *Fueled by coffee, nicotine, black beauties, and pornography, I write for 45 hours straight about anything that enters my mind. I even manage 500 words on pubic hair. By the end I am shaking and sweating, hunched painfully over my keyboard. I estimate that I have just barely 55 pages of material.*

August 31: *I read my stuff again after a bath and a nap. It's terrible. I call an elderly Hungarian man I know and purchase 20,000 words of his psychotic rantings and decide to pass it off as my own. It's worked before. It's how I graduated college.*

2. THE COMPOSITION PROCESS

September 1-3: *In a 72-hour Pagemaker marathon, I finish off the second bottle of Jack Daniels and all my cigarettes, flowing WordPerfect text files. I discover that the issue is only 43 pages long. Another five hours of playing with the leading and kerning brings it up to 60 pages. I crawl into bed and then realize with a start that I'm at work and I've just laid down on the floor of my cubicle. I cannot discern a heartbeat. Apparently I have been fired.*

3. THE MANUFACTURING PROCESS

September 4-5: *After a brief rest period, I break out the trained monkeys and circus midgets.*

4. THE DISTRIBUTION PROCESS

September 6: *I sell a few pints of blood and semen for postage money and mail this fine issue right to your dismal hovel. The postal workers are mean to me. One kicks me in the ass as I exit the post office.*

September 7: *Jeff's Day of Binge Drinking*

As you can see, a lot of work goes into every issue, and aside from the medical and postage costs those monkeys and circus midgets don't come free, which explains why I am always begging people to subscribe to this Zine. The physical demands on your beloved editor are intense, as well; you can't drink as much as the pressure drives me to and live, usually, although I am setting the record anew everyday.

I hope this has answered all those nagging questions my many fans have had concerning how this amazing creation comes to be every three months. If not, at least it has used up four pages in this book, which is certainly just as important. Until next time, keeping buying me drinks!

JEFF SEZ: *The Inner Swine* is lovingly hand-crafted in China from the finest raw materials, and is kept at near-freezing temperatures during its journey from local distribution outlet to your local supermarket. It's freshness is not guaranteed. I'm sleepy.

The Freaks Are Winning
The Inner Swine Collection

Zine Elvis Speaks: Jeff's Deep Thoughts on Zines

EVERY NOW AND THEN, I feel the urge to comment on the world of zines and the people who populate it. Why can only be explained by my immense ego, which manifests as a tiny Leprechaun who stands on my shoulder and whispers in my ear. He is named McEgo, and sometimes he suggests that the world not only needs to hear my thoughts on zines, but that the world will likely be destroyed by fire in zine-related riots unless I speak my mind.

Hence, the following four articles, which I only include here at the urging of several people, who suggested I shouldn't "act all Hollywood" and forget my roots. Whether or not these articles have any actual value I'll leave up to you, anonymous reader who spent money on my book.

"Zine Rebel or Zine Elvis?" was reprinted in **A Reader's Guide to the Underground Press** *in 2001 and on Chip Rowe's web site* **www.zinebook.com**. *By the way.*

The Inner Swine's State-of-Zining Address

ZINE REBEL OR ZINE ELVIS?

Or Something In-Between?

I've been letting myself go a little. So what?

First off, let me thank you for buying this zine and for reading this article. Out of all the articles in this zine, most of which are better, you're reading this one. And of all the other zines out there, you chose mine. Lord knows why. Every issue of this zine is pretty much the same as the last: I ruminate crankily about subjects I know little if anything about, make a few lame jokes, and spruce it all up with stolen fonts and clip art. But, you made some sort of effort to acquire this issue, and then you turned to this page and by god, you're still reading! So, thank you, anonymous reader.

Friends, every now and then I am unfortunately compelled to pull my squinty, mushroom-pale face out of my cavernous (but wondrous!) ass and write about something other than myself. No! Wait! Really! I'm not kidding! Just keep reading, and I'll prove it. Today's subject is Zines, and the wacky personalities that feel compelled to produce them. More specifically, I wonder why good zines die.

Sometimes a zine will come out and it's ambitious, or hilarious, or genius-in-general, and after two issues it disappears. Sometimes a zine will attain a certain level of fame, at least within the zine community, and then, without warning, it disappears. Because I do not shy away from the tough questions, I ask myself: Why? Putting out a zine is never an easy thing, considering the effort, the expense, and the lack of support, so mere obstacles cannot be the sole answer. And zinesters tend to be the most

Appeared in Volume 6, Issue 3, September 2000

arrogant people in the world, convinced that their genius deserves printing, so bad reviews or lackluster response can't be the sole reason either.

After my usual lack of research or preparation, I've come to the conclusion that the main reason good zines die is success.

It seems to me that above the other categories of zines (Review Zines, Punk Zines, etc) you can divide all the ziners out there into three basic categories: **Shock Jocks**, **Movementeers**, and plain old **Writers**. Now, everyone is a beautiful individual snowflake and I can't fit every zine, or every zine publisher, into one of these categories. But I do believe that in general, we're all one of them. Maybe I'm wrong. But that's okay, I'm still filling some empty space in this issue, so it's all good, baby! As with everything in this weakly-written rag, this is all idle speculation on my part, based solely on the issues of zines people have deigned to mail me for free and the ongoing posts in *alt.zines*, where I continue to hang around like that kid who graduated high school three years ago who still shows up at the football games, trying to pick up the cheerleaders.

The Shock Jocks are those amongst our DIY brood who think they're the first people in the world who have dared to use cuss words and scatological humor. They tend to spend their time trying to, well, shock you. I tend to assume most of the purveyors of this sort of zine are teenagers, but that's not necessarily true. In this jaded day and age, of course, the moment any member of your audience detects an attempt to shock, they generally put up their *blasé* attitude and shrug, so it's kind of a futile effort.

This isn't to say that Shock Jocks can't or don't write well, or don't often produce really interesting or funny work. But their main goal is to jolt, to be outrageous. They give their zines titles like **I'd Anally Rape Your Grandmother for Pocket Change** and write articles about the different types of shits they've taken. Then they mail the issues out and sit up at night waiting for someone to tell them how sick and twisted they are, so they can feel smarter than everyone else. Or so it seems to me.

More frightening and usually less entertaining are the Movementeers, who believe that zines are part of some sort of underground revolution. These are the people who happily call you names when you add a UPC to your cover, or agree to be distroed at Tower Records. Their zines are not so much creative efforts as they are propaganda for whatever underground they perceive themselves to be a part of, and as such can be a little dry, and a little cranky, filled with endless railing against people like me who shrug in boredom whenever confronted by their manifestos.

It can be difficult to tell from the outside that a zine is a Movementeer product; they have the same look and feel as any other zine. Certainly if you bought it in a bookstore, chances are it's not, since Movementeers would never sink so low as to be coopted by the System. If the title is too subtle, scan the contents; Movementeer product tends to include at least one screed against a zinester who "betrayed" the underground and DIY ethic either by "selling out" to a distributor or by "buying in" to the mainstream, usually by taking on paying writing jobs. If the zine in question includes articles like that, the chance that you've got Movementeer product is high, and you should put it down unless reading about how lame a sellout someone is entertains you somehow.

Finally, there are Writers, and I put myself into this group. We generally have no interest in shocking people, and we generally don't consider ourselves members of some underground movement or revolution. Oh, we might believe in the DIY spirit, we might detest corporate America, and we might turn down more lucrative sponsorship deals before 9AM than you do all day, but that isn't *why* we're writing, bubba. We write because we like to write, and instead of sitting around waiting to be discovered by the clueless and disinterested literati of the world, we're publishing ourselves and loving it. The main reason our zines exist is to get our writing in typeset form.

The Writers are usually much more concerned with creating new things than with preaching or selling issues or outraging their audience. We may or may not be ambitious about becoming the next David Foster Wallace, we may or may not have grandiose personal visions about where our zine activities are leading, but the main identifying feature is that we write. Our zines are predominantly filled with our material. Each issue is filled with stuff written specifically for that issue, not just leftover college Creative Writing 103 compositions and some random filler like half-assed reviews or pages and pages of clip-art montages rendered unreadable by the magic of Xerox. Not that there's anything wrong with that.

Of course, there are those pesky Review Zines, which exist primarily to review other people's zines. I wouldn't put them in with the Movementeers, because most of them spend their pages reviewing zines, not wheezing on about their political views. They're obviously not Shock Jock product, although I guess there might be some Shock-Review zines out there; I just haven't seen any. Personally, I lump these in with the Writers, because they do fill each issue with their own material. Possibly they deserve their own separate category, but as I am sure the international zine community is *not* waiting breathlessly for this article in order to make its recommendations to the U.N., I'll table that for a later page-eating filler article. Muhahahaha!

So now that I've wasted our time with my own pet theory about zinesters, what was the point again? Mainly, I was musing about how often zines simply disappear, and this three-category theory evolved from there.

Let's face it, almost as soon as a pasty middlebrow white boy like me hears about a famous, wickedly incisive zine, it's ceased publication, and its *wunderkind* author is 34 and working full time for Comedy Central or something. Sure, some zines go on forever, but they are definitely the exceptions. Most zines flash into existence, burn brightly (or not-so-brightly, but I'm not naming names; I've got enough flame wars going on right now. I don't need one more) and then disappear, often before the third issue. Hell, often before the *second* issue.

Of course, some of the reasons for this are easy: A lot of zinesters are teenagers or college students, and their zines are products of that particular period in their lives: the angst, the drugs, the free time. Especially the free time. Times change, they move on to other things, and lots of factors conspire to strangle a zine: Their co-conspirators are no longer down the block or down the hall; their mission in life changes (you can't really do a zine about how badly Harrison High School sucks when you're 22 years old and working full time at the Piggly Wiggly, after all); they very simply don't have as much time to sit around their room smoking pot and writing about how badly it all hurts.

Sometimes, believe it or not, zines actually go big-time. *Wired*, after all, was once considered a zine. Arguments continue about *Bust* and a selection of other titles that now get as much magazine rack space as *Playboy* and accept advertising from Budweiser. I guess when you've got a circulation of 25,000 and you have to actually *hire* people to help you, it just ain't a zine anymore.

Some of it simply has to do with the *why*—which brings us back to our three categories, believe it or not. The motivation behind a zine can be elusive, ephemeral. It's a lot of work to put out something that half the people will be bored by and the other half largely scornful of, and holding onto your motivation can be difficult. The Shock Jocks lose a lot of steam, I think, when they realize that every dirty joke and inflammatory statement they make has been made before, and everyone hits an age when being outrageous starts to lose its appeal, and being taken seriously starts to look good. Or so I've been told. I suspect that the Movementeers get just as easily disillusioned when they discover that so few people want to hear their spiel. Besides, their scorn for 95% of us usually means they don't try very hard to gain us as audience members, and we should probably be thankful for that. The Writers probably get sick and tired of reading about how bad their writing is, or bummed that after five beautiful issues they still have only four people on their mailing lists who aren't blood relations or old friends.

Certainly, *failure* kills zines. But I submit that *success* kills them much more often.

I believe this because putting out a zine is in itself the act of pushing off the weighty ennui of the world. No one puts out a zine imagining that they will have millions of readers, get on TV, and be wildly successful. You spend months working on the damned thing, and when you put it out, the most you get are a few enthusiastic responses and a lot of static. After a while your friends get tired of pretending to care about it. Simply publishing the thing indicates that failure in all of its subtle forms doesn't scare you much.

But consider the ingredients for a zine: You need unequal parts self-centeredness, free time, disposable income, and energy. Success of any kind eats that stuff up. This does not have to be artistic success, although that certainly counts. But it could just as well be career success or academic success. Working 60 hour weeks leaves little energy and time for putting out a zine. And if you do happen to get a writing *career* off the ground and get paid for articles, stories, and books, well, that can leave precious little time, energy, or desire left over for a photocopied zine with a circulation of 75.

We're zinesters. We're *used* to failure, bubba. It's the success that creeps us out.

Now, this is where I speculate on my own future. While I doubt that I am the Faulkner of my generation and am destined for greatness, or even income, as a writer, I do hope to be widely published and reprinted. Why? Certainly not so I can be a Media Whore like Tom Wolfe in his disturbingly white Pimp Wardrobe. Mainly because the more widely my works are distributed, the better my chances are of being remembered after I die. It's that simple. I love to write, too, and if I had an income from writing and could quit my day job, I'd be able to do more writing, yippee! So I do strive for commercial publishing success. What happens if it comes? I've been publishing *The Inner Swine* for more than five years now, and this is issue number 20. If I have a bestseller that gets made into a box office smash, will I stop publishing my zine?

Honestly, I don't think so. I enjoy the freedom too much; I enjoy the ego-stroking. I enjoy forcing myself to come up with these sloppy little articles that are more fun than accurate or well-reasoned. And my Ego will never be satisfied with mere fame and fortune. Where else can I refer to myself as His Royal Highness Jeff Somers?

That's right, nowhere.

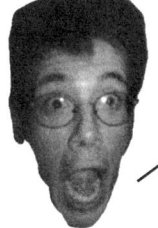

JEFF SEZ: This article got some heated reaction, actually. Some people took offense to having every zine publisher in the Universe placed into three simple categories. Others thought my choice of labels (originally Movementeer, Asthetic, Shock Jock) were condescending, especially since I so humbly called myself an Asthestic. I thought those people had a point so I changed 'Asthetics' to 'Writers' in later versions of the article. Some people actually liked the piece. To be honest, I am not the most disciplined researcher or thinker in the world, and I doubt anyone who's ever read *The Inner Swine* expects deep thinking from my articles, so anyone who took this one too seriously just needs to relax.

Mr. Mute's
GUIDE TO MAKING A ZINE

*Mr. Mute is a silent man who can't stand the sound of your voice. Any of your voices. I invented him in 1998 with the idea that I would draw a comic for each issue of TIS. A quick evening spent drinking Plum Liqueur and doodling him proved that I had all the artistic talent of a pebble, and the **Virtually Artless Comic** was born.*

In each issue of The Inner Swine, *Mr. Mute complains about how much noise you're all making. His essays are accompanied by a spastic drawing of Mr. Mute by yours truly, are laid out in boxes like a comic despite having virtually no art, and generally make little or no sense. Most people can't understand why I think Mr. Mute is so funny. Be happy he's only here once.*

Zine-publishers, as a whole, please me, because they at least have the good sense to put their imbecilic ravings in *writing* instead of bleating them out audibly, thus leaving nothing but the peaceful rustle of paper in their wake. This doesn't mean that zinesters aren't morons. It just means they don't land on my To Do list as often as the rest of you talkative bastards. Of course, that doesn't mean that zinesters don't flout the Laws of Civilized Society, thus earning my wrath. It just takes me longer to realize it, because they aren't SHOUTING their idiocies into my ear. But have no fear, I am well aware that you're a danger to society.

Still, I would rather you all put out zines instead of becoming a street preacher or some such nuisance, which is generally your other career opportunity. Zine Publisher or Street Preacher, that's you, admit it. Towards a more livable world, a world with fewer Street Preachers filling the air with their prattling, I have decided to put my *Campaign for Forcible Silence* on hold and get more of you yokels into zining. So, here's a guide to putting out a zine that anyone can follow, and I certainly hope you all will, instead of talking about not doing it, or talking about doing it, or talking about how people who put out zines are just effete assholes.

HOW TO MAKE A ZINE

1. Decide what kind of zine you're going to put out. Some people would say that there are as many types of zines as there are wonderfully individual people in the world. I wouldn't. There are five. **A. The Perzine.** This is a zine wherein you write about your inner feelings and the events in your life, like a public diary. Don't do it. Perzines are for effete assholes. **B. The Music Zine.** This is a zine that has music, specifically the kind of music you accept and enjoy, as its central theme. This gives you lots of easy material in the form of vapid record reviews and amateurish interviews with bands no one else will ever care about. I don't recommend the Music zines; they're for effete assholes. **C. The Collage Zine.** In this zine, you cut out a lot of clip art and fill every page with various doodles, poems, snatches of text, coffee stains, and inscrutable little shout-outs. Collage zines are like talking with a schizophrenic on the subway. How many times can Bob the fifties man smoking a pipe be used for satiric effect in a zine? The Collage ziners are determined to find out. **D. Poetry Zines.** Jesus, if you're looking for effete assholes, look no further. **E. Review Zines.** These zines primarily review other zines. While lots of zines in the other categories use zine reviews as a way of filling a few pages, or as a nobly-intentioned service to the zine community, Review zines have made this their reason for existing. Before starting a Review zine, ask yourself why anyone should care what an effete asshole like you thinks.

2. Actually create some material. Whether your zine is going to be book-length and cost $15 in stamps, or a single postcard with tiny type, too many zines are quite obviously style over substance. Don't worry about the style of your zine (layout, design, etc.) until you actually have written/drawn whatever it is you want to put in it. You can usually tell a ziner who made this mistake by one of these clues: There are more fonts in the goddamned thing than actual words or cartoons; There are whole articles devoted to the style and design of the fucking zine; The last page(s) of the issue are a big-font, wide-leading exploration of how the authors ran out of material for the issue. If you can't come up with however many pages of reasonably typeset stuff, don't fucking bother to put out issue #1. If it took you a whole year to come up with 1,000 words of stuff for issue #1, why fucking bother? It'll be six years before you come up with issue #2. Might as well go to Business School, asshole.

3. Then, just fucking do it. Got a few pieces of your creative brain on paper? Great, you're a genius, now stop talking about it and do it. I would recommend you don't worry too long about design and layout. You start fucking around with layout and design, and six years later you're still putting the finishing touches on the cover of issue #1. *Some* time spent thinking about layout and design is great: Realizing early on that using 250 different fonts and type sizes, reverse-bleeds, and lots of dim, photocopied photographs is a Bad Thing will move you down to the bottom of my To Do list. For a while. Getting that first issue *out* is much more important than getting that first issue *right*. Get it out, and start working on issue #2. The layout and design will evolve and clarify, unless you're an effete asshole, in which case it will only get worse. As for how to produce your zine, well, thousands of years ago people managed to paint on cave walls. Do you really need an in-depth discussion of Quark vs. Pagemaker? If you have a computer, lay it out in Word Pad, for god's sake. For a photocopied zine, you could type it all on a typewriter, paste it up, and go.

4. Give the fucking thing away. Sure, put a price on the cover, and act all tough about making people pay for it. But then give it away. No one wants it badly enough to pay you, trust me. Maybe five years down the road when you're being celebrated as a genius for a disaffected generation someone will pay you, but for now getting paid should be the last thing on your mind. If you put out a zine in order to make money, you're both evil and dimwitted, and shoot up to #1 on my To Do list. No, give it away. Send it to everyone you know. Send it to every ziner you've heard of. Above all, send it to Review Zines. Good reviews make you feel good, bad reviews might teach you something, and even poorly written or vague reviews can offer you a sense of superiority to the monkey who penned it. Plus, it's free advertising.

5. Stop jerking off on your first issue and put out the second. Nothing sadder than issue #1 out two years ago and issue #2 "still in the planning stages", unless issue #1 sold 500,000 copies.

There. Even dimwitted throwbacks should have little trouble following those steps. While you're busy quietly creating your publication, I will be free to stop supervising you and get back to my real work, reorganizing the world according to my wishes: a quiet, orderly place where no one speaks unless spoken to. Have fun. I'll probably kill you next year.

Dance With a Hand in My Pants

How I Produce 60 Pages of Quality Shit for Cheap

Get caught stealing office supplies and you'll be screwed.

PIGS, this is the zine issue of this zine, a mirror-into-mirror Very Special Episode of *The Inner Swine* that I'm sure will send you all home sniffling back huge, exhaustive emotions drummed up by the nearly-repulsive Baring of My Soul. I assume you all want my soul bared, because you're reading this. Once I decided we needed a Very Special Episode of *The Inner Swine*, I spent a lot of time trying to figure out what the theme for a VSE issue should be, most of that time spent drinking Plum Schnapps in front of Ken West's entertainment center, which is truly a Huge and Frightening collection of technology. Ken now has the ability to pick up reflected television broadcasts from outer space, giving him, in effect, a Time Machine in his living room. This allowed me to make an exhaustive survey of all the Very Special Episodes ever broadcast, throughout time, including the classic *Diff'rent Strokes* episode in which Gary Coleman discovers he was bought solely to amuse Mr. Drummond by dancing, and the eternal *A Christmas Carol*-based *Blossom* episode in which Blossom realizes that being a cute small child too often means being a bizarre-looking and crack-addicted adult. Inspired by these tear-jerking teleplays and Ken's seemingly endless supply of Plum Schnapps, I quickly realized that I was pretty much a bitter poseur bankrupt of ideas and lazily decided the theme for the VSE would be: zines. Summoning the energy to scrawl the word ZINES on my arm in marker, I passed out. As usual when that happens, I woke up in my own kitchen pantsless and covered in red army ants.

Standing in the shower washing ants and various other substances off of my shivering, shriveling body, I thought about my little zine and, as is common in these situations, began to get really angry at all of you who read it, which quickly spilled over into a more generalized rage, which I call Ralph. Ralph usually manifests itself like this: At the apex of my anger, I suddenly go all calm and ceramic, and then Ralph is there, telling me what to do, and I am swept with happy, giddy relief because I no longer have to deal with anything, it's all in Ralph's able hands. Ralph hangs around for a few days and tells me what to do, and then gives me back control. The Bad People keep trying to take Ralph away, but so far we've outwitted them.

All that is neither here nor there, however; the point is that Ralph helped me to realize that the one major issue I could help people with in the zine VSE of *The Inner Swine* is how to put out your zine for (almost) free. How Ralph showed me this is of no concern, although it did involve some property damage.

Let's face it: We're DIY publishers, for god's sake, and we live in a capitalist world, so everything costs money. However, if we had money, ironically enough we would no longer be considered DIY publishers. If we had money, we'd be considered Mega Rich Dilettante Fuckwits, or so is the extent of my comprehension of the issue. Lacking money, we endeavor to publish quality work, manufacture it into a pleasing and accessible shape, and distribute that item to the waiting maws of our greedy, ungrateful fans, all without shelling out a dime, if we can help it. The *No Money and Issues* policy of DIY publishing is one of the more daunting aspects of self-publishing, as we all know: Everything in this fucking world costs money.

Every single person who has ever produced a zine on a regular basis has solved this problem, to a lesser or greater extent, on their own. This is not their solution. As a matter of fact, fuck them if they haven't passed their wisdom along. Ralph and I will be paying them a visit fairly soon. No, what follows is my solution to the cash flow problem, and it boils down to a beautifully simple single command: *Don't pay for anything.* It's easier than it sounds.

First, let's examine the materials needed to assemble an issue of *The Inner Swine*. The materials used for your lame zine may vary from this list. I could not care less what they might be. For each issue of TIS I need: An IBM PC with Windows, a word processor, and Adobe Pagemaker; A quality laser printer; Good letter-sized paper; A quality photocopier; 54-60lb cover stock; Mailing labels; Envelopes; Postage; Several six packs of Raoul's Beefy Beer.

Whew, that's a lot of stuff. And under normal conditions, a lot of expensive stuff, bubba. Happily, I haven't existed under what you'd call "normal conditions" since I was 12, which is when (historians agree) I simultaneously rejected god and accepted my inner UberMensch, who is also, by great coincidence, named Ralph. When you leave normal conditions behind, you enter a shadowy world called Jeff Conditions, and in Jeff Conditions the items listed above are mostly free, with some exceptions. There are actually two possible ways to get all of the above for free: the **Fell Off a Truck** method, which I can't recommend because it involves potential incarceration and prison rape, and then **The Way of Jeff**. In The Way of Jeff, there is no prison rape, at least not that I am personally aware of. There is a rather blatant disregard for laws and the rules of civilized society. But no prison rape. That I can remember, anyway.

THE WAY OF JEFF IN SEVERAL EASY STEPS

Get a Job in Publishing. Maybe you still harbor ludicrous dreams of financial success in the career of your choice. Ha! I giggle girlishly at your dreams. It is an unproven and largely speculative fact that people who self-publish their drivel lack the drive and blandness of personality to be successful in business. If you cared enough to spend 90% of your mental energies on earning money, you certainly wouldn't be publishing a Flintstones fanzine or the like. Therefore, stop thinking about your career and making moolah and land yourself the greatest job known to man, assuming that the man in question is a DIY publisher: low-level shlub in the publishing industry. I did this back in 1994 and it was the best zine decision I ever made. Let's look at the positive side to working in publishing. Want to?

The powerful supercomputers of the future that my office will soon possess will someday enable me to beam The Inner Swine *directly into your brain, probably killing you.*

First off, most publishing companies, as I can personally attest, are confused, disorganized messes. This is due to the nature of publishing, which is an attempt to take the creative process of the human being and streamline it into a profit. It is also due to the fact that the people who choose publishing as a career are 33% DIY publishers more concerned with stealing copier machine codes than with doing their jobs; 33% bored, apathetic people who grew up thinking something would eventually happen to knock them off their sad track but who find themselves now working in publishing; and 33% complete freaks. The last 1% is thought to be made up of men and women who got lost in the bowels of office buildings and wander there to this day, a race of shadowy mole-creatures lost to the sunlit world.

More importantly, publishing companies offer you everything you'll ever need to publish your own scrawled works of art. The day I got my job in publishing, I got a computer with desktop publishing software, laser printers by the dozen, several industrial-strength copy machines, and all the paper I could ever want. Plus, staples. Oh, I also got a boss, an inbox, and a dress code, but shit, man, I inherited someone else's economic strength in the process, and if I have to endure a few conference calls or an occasional employment review, I'll do it.

Free Copies. The best part of having a job in publishing, of course, is the free copies. Free copies are pretty much the holy grail of any zinester, and we'll lie, steal, or cheat to get them. When you work in publishing, free copies are a simple matter of devoting all your thought and energy towards acquiring them. Here are my three basic strategies for getting free copies at work without getting fired and/or beaten up:

1. The Balls of Steel Approach. The simplest but most dangerous way to acquire free copies is to stuff your masters into a folder labeled **HORRIBLE DISGUSTING GROSS PICTURES OF PHLEGM**, march off to the copier of choice, and start brazenly copying. This follows a belief that you can get anyone to believe or do anything simply by applying your massive Ayn-Randish will on them. In this scenario, which I have used successfully under the right conditions, the secret is to **maintain eye contact** with anyone who approaches. The moment I glimpse anyone coming near, I stare at them, fiercely. When they arrive at the copier, they're usually either so freaked out they just hurry by, or are too polite to break eye contact with me. I make no effort to hide what I'm doing. I just keep my eyes locked on theirs until they leave. Men won't look away because of some instinctual competitive drive—they'll challenge you to a fight, but they won't look away, as that would risk becoming known as The Office Nancy, which no man can live with. Office Nancies don't live long, once identified as such. They're usually found about a week later, hanging in the kitchen area.

The BOS technique has resulted in a few conferences with Human Resources, but no firings yet. In Human Resources conferences regarding my staring, I usually manage to break down into tears at least once. Then, a quiet request for our company's employee support hotline, and everyone usually leaves me alone for a few weeks.

2. The George "The Animal" Steel Approach. A more wily but sometimes unpredictable way of scamming free copies is to skulk to the copier of choice and be prepared to cause a diversion if anyone in authority comes nears you. The easiest diversion is to quickly snatch

Normally my job is a heinous maze of suffering. But at least I get free copies.

your materials from the copier (possibly while it's still chugging along) and run; while this is somewhat effective, it often results in burns, ink staining, and my tie caught in the machinery of the copier, with a crowd of people gathered around trying to free me from the copier and picking up scraps of paper and saying, "*What the hell is this?*" At that point it is usually best to feign a seizure of some sort.

A better diversion is to pause the copier discreetly and claim that it's broken. Copiers break down in offices all the time because Americans can't build anything very well and our entire economy is now based on service contracts for shitty crap and licensed use. When the copier is broken, most people just walk away without alerting anyone else or making any attempt, however minor, to fix it themselves. This is because people are dumb and selfish. So turn off the copier, shrug mournfully, complain that you have pages stuck inside and that you'll "be here a while, ha ha ha!", and stare daggers at them as they move on to the next copier. Then turn the copier back on, clear out the paused job, and start over.

A less-than-ideal diversion is to eat inappropriate stuffing materials, like the actual George "The Animal" Steele did.

3. The Nancy-Boy Approach. Come in on a weekend when no one else is around and copy any way you fucking please. Copy in your underwear. Copy with your feet up reading *Penthouse*. Use three copiers at once. Who cares? Once you descend into Nancy-Boy territory you have no worries, and no pride.

Personally, I choose #3. I used to battle my way with #1 or #2, but I'm too tired now. Just call me Nancy.

You may be wondering if The Way of Jeff basically boils down to getting a job in publishing and raping it for every resource it offers. The answer, of course, is: pretty much. If you've already committed to some other career that doesn't offer you free desktop publishing software, free laser printers, and unlimited free copies, well, I'd advise you to reconsider your career choice. Even working part-time at Kinkos would be better, I think, from a pure zine-publisher point of view.

There you have it. My secret: Corporate America is my ally. Rather than railing against the bland, faceless army of Corporate Mongrels, I welcome them with open arms—because each one brings a copy machine with them.

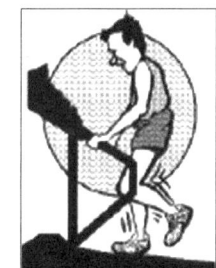

Gotta go back to the endless treadmill of horror that is my job now.

Ten Things That Annoy Me About my Fellow Zine Publishers

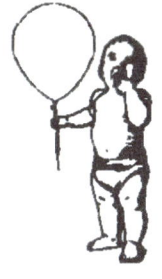

(In No Particular Order)

Sometimes, you just have to be cranky. I will name no names, but there are plenty of annoying people out there publishing zines. I'm sure I'm on other people's lists ("Number three, people who put their disembodied face all over their zine...") but that just makes me feel "big-time".

Ten Things That Annoy Me About my Fellow Zine Publishers

1. When they send me their pathetic zines with nothing but a note (sometimes a *photocopied* note), which says REVIEW ME. The arrogance is breathtaking, as if there were legions of heretofore unknown zine publishers who have nothing better to do. Am I a Review Zine? Nope, and a cursory glance at TIS will reveal that to anyone.

2. When they include a big stack of random advertisements for other people's zines, or when they send me a stack of their own ads and ask me to distribute them to everyone I mail something to. I don't work for anyone but myself, and I am never asked if this is cool before they mail this shit to me, so fuck them.

Appeared in Volume 6, Issue 4, December 2000

3. Spamming the alt.zines newsgroup with what seems like hundreds of postings that merely announce, over and over again, a new issue or updated web site. Certainly, one posting to this effect is fine. Twice earns you a scowl, three times in the span of two days and I'm mailing you a dead rat.

4. The ones who assume that just because I put out a zine, I must be 16 years old.

5. When they bitch and moan about a "bad", "inaccurate", "biased" review in one of the Review Zines out there. Nothing makes me want to read the damn thing less than a bitchy letter in ARGTTUP. Hell, at least someone's *reading* your goddamned zine. Suck it up, silky boy.

6. The ones who e-mail me out of the blue and ask me to link to their web site, without offering to link back, or even hinting that they at some point even read my zine. I'm happy to link with people who either link to me or have given me support of some sort (money, advice, service, genuine criticism) but an e-mail from a complete stranger urging me to up their hit counts? Fuck 'em.

7. The ones who submit stuff to me without asking first. A long time ago in a far-away land, I did implore my readers to submit works to me. This stopped in 1996, when I stopped kidding myself and realized I only had interest in printing *my* works. Since 1996 I've printed a few pieces I didn't write, but all of them were either commissioned by me (translation: I begged a member of *The Inner Swine* Inner Circle to write it) or just randomly caught my fancy. The only indication that TIS entertains submissions is in the *boilerplate* on page 4, which reads in part: "*Address submissions and correspondence to Jeff Somers,* The Inner Swine, *PO Box 3024, Hoboken, NJ 07030, mreditor@innerswine.com. But let's face it, when was the last time we published anything not written by me or one of my cronies? Other people's pimply writing gives me hives. Still, all submissions or requests for Guidelines (there are no guidelines, though) must be accompanied by SASE.*" This is set in 7/8 type at the bottom of the TOC, and I just can't believe anyone reads it. In any event, the statement is not asking people to submit, it is just warning you that if you don't include a SASE with your submission, you'll probably never hear from me. I don't mind the occasional submission, but don't just mail me 65 poems and expect me to care.

8. Their endless, endless first-person navel-gazing. I am rapidly coming to believe that the worst part of zines is when people select any pointless episode in their lives and write about it in painful detail. Why do they assume their rambling, pointless tale about what they did two months ago is interesting in any way? At least have a compelling reason to write about your recent unemployment, or personal crisis, or whatever. And yes, I'm aware of the irony of complaining about this in a first-person narrative, dammit, but at least I'm not telling you a supposedly interesting story about my life.

9. When they gripe at me about some aspect of how I handle my zine that they disagree with. I don't recall signing a membership agreement in some fucking Underground Press Society, and I resent being treated like I did. Don't like bar codes? Fuck you. Don't like poetry? Fuck you. Think I ought to be more active politically? Double fuck you. The beauty of self-publishing is you don't need to care what anyone else thinks.

10. Handwritten zines. It sounds romantic, sure, and I guess when you're 13 you can get away with it. I've had a typewriter since I was 10 years old. No kidding. Is it *that* fucking hard to peck out a few pages of material? Even when your handwriting is legible, it's generally annoying, because it's either filled with hearts-for-dots or little doodles or just *frightening* personality hints. While even in this age of technological wonder some people are still without computer access, typewriters are cheap. Buy one. Handwritten zines blow goats.

Editorials: My Worldwide Organization of Terror

FROM THE BEGINNING OF TIME, there has been an editorial in each issue of The Inner Swine. *There has also been a **theme**, albeit a randomly-chosen and often-ignored one. The editorial usually tries to crystallize the theme into a few pithy pages. These editorials are all called "Pig in Shit" because forcing my opinions on you makes me happy.*

In the first issues of TIS, when I was still putting a lot of time into trying to make Magic really work with the expressed purpose of turning my long list of enemies into small rodents, I took these editorials seriously, and imagined wise people across the planet nodding and stroking their flowing beards while reading my latest, shocking spurt of informed opinion. As time went by, I came to realize that: A) No one was actually reading my magazine and B) I didn't really have any opinions, informed or otherwise. My preferred way of existing is to let life wash over me like an incomprehensible wave while I cower and whimper and beg whatever gods present themselves for salvation.

This was incredibly freeing, since I no longer had to express supportable opinions, or even make much sense, and the editorials slowly mutated into more or less humorous ramblings, most of which described my growing worldwide organization. In reality, my organization consists of me, my collection of pornography, and a Helper Monkey I stole from a disabled veteran, who carries money to the grocery and brings back bottles of beer for me. What follows are some of my favorite entries in the "Pig in Shit" series.

Pig in Shit #10

I FOUND THIS FAKE NUDE PHOTO OF BEA ARTHUR[1] ON THE INTERNET AND CHRIST AM I DISTURBED

The Great Things About Pornography

MANY BOTHANS DIED TO BRING YOU THIS INFORMATION: I am joining the Dark Side. After years of dicking around in the grey soup of the Dagobah System, I'm sticking my light saber as far up Yoda's ass as it'll go and catching the next flight to the *Darth Vader School of Better Living Through Evil*. I will not pass Go, I don't want the 200 bucks. I just want to swear fealty to the Dark Lord of the Sith, kiss the Emperor's ring, and get fitted for my black respirator as soon as possible. As soon as I learn how to strangle people from across the room, the other Jedi had better make travel plans. Dark Lords of the Sith do not take prisoners.

For the smartasses whispering that I joined the Dark Side back in second grade when I pushed Danny Smithson into the mud and he got

---

[1] *The guy who runs the web site I found this at had this to say about it: "It is interesting to speculate on the summit of man's creations. Is our supreme achievement the moon landing? Michelangelo's David? The splitting of the atom? I cast my vote for our first fake of Bea Arthur. The little green men can blow us away now, we've done all we can, and all that can be done."*

Appeared in Volume 4, Issue 1, March 1998

pneumonia and no one ever saw him again, I say: I hear the range on that choking trick is pretty far.

RAGE, DISAPPOINTMENT, DISCO: 1996 was a bloated alcoholic Bataan Death March of a year, convincing me at long last to open wide and accept evil as my personal savior. Which brings me to my subject: sex. Specifically, pornography. I can remember when pornography was a shadowy term that hinted at all sorts of corrupt little pleasures, none of which I experienced on any kind of basis. Those golden days are over, though, people, because we now have the Internet. As far as I can tell, except for the various sports-oriented websites out there, the Internet is really just a big useless wasteland of pornography.

But I'm getting ahead of myself.

A few years ago while wasting a little time in college, a few friends and I attempted to embarrass to death a lovely friend and confidant (who I keep anonymous here because I have learned many things in the intervening years, one of which is to fear the wrath of women). We did this by purchasing for her, without her knowledge, a pair of edible panties. Well, two pair, actually, although the second pair was consumed by Ken West and myself on the ride home (fruit roll-ups by way of latex—ugh) and thus remains lost to history.

This was back in my halcyon days of *grave credit card abuse*, however, and so of course the panties were charged. Ever since then I've gotten some rather strange catalogues in the mail, as my credit info is passed from one greasy outfit to another. Some of the catalogues have been quite eye-opening, to say the least—some have even been educational, in ways I'd rather not discuss. Mostly, it's just been a little embarrassing.

But the look on her face was worth it, pigs. You ask me what keeps a bitter scoundrel like me interested—that look of priceless shock, dismay, and fear is part of it.

My overflowing mailbox o' smut begs the question, however: What's with this pornography shit? This is what the first amendment is protecting—Latex Love Dolls, "Buttman Goes to Panama", toys modeled on Jenna Jameson's vagina (in living plastic!)? Can this kind of filth and degeneration and just plain bad acting be necessary and useful to a healthy society?

The answer, of course, is *yes*.

If, as usual, you find yourself disagreeing with me, I have come prepared—allow me to present to you the **Official *Inner Swine* Great Things About Pornography**. This includes all forms of pornography: printed, filmed, recorded, digitized—imagined. If someone out there is masturbating to it, I'm referring to it—although I am queasily aware of what some of those things might be, considering the quality of reader I usually get.

THE INNER SWINE GREAT THINGS ABOUT PORNOGRAPHY

1. Preservation of Society. I don't believe that pornography or its presence in our society tolls the dying breaths of civilization; in fact, I believe the opposite. I believe that pornography is a healthy aspect of any society, and its continued presence in ours heartens me, for two key reasons the blue-nosed morons usually overlook. One, its presence and subsequent backwatering tells me that there is still *something* in this world considered *pornography*, still something considered so outrageously wrong or strange or sick that it must be labeled. In the same way we need curse words to be a special section of the language, a special type of language that only loses its power and allure when overused, we need pornography to be a special aspect of the intellectual and creative fields (that's right, I used those words with a straight face, and I'll pop anyone in the mouth who makes fun of me). If we no longer considered *something* to be pornography, *that's* when we should get upset and worried, because by that point there's nothing in this culture considered beyond the pale. As long as we have that, as long as there's something out there that, while not strictly illegal, is banished to the margins of our culture, I have hope for my weak-willed fellow humans, whom I meet regularly while purchasing *Swank* magazine at newsstands.

Two, let's face it, pornography provides a much-needed safety valve for the, ahem, male half of the population. It's not our fault we have these raging sex drives and harem fantasies, girls; only a few thousand years ago (or, in terms of evolution's perception of time, three seconds ago) we were hunter-gatherers with an expected lifespan of maybe 30 years, if we were especially agile. Not only did we die young, but our women died young. In order to guarantee that our genes got passed down so that we might live forever, our caveman ancestors developed a strikingly effective technique: They screwed everything that moved and then once more for good measure. This worked well until civilization began and suddenly it was no longer kosher to screw every female you saw whether she was especially fond of you or not. Thus all the complicated rules and regulations (and punishments) of civilized man arose which turned *mating* into *courtship*. For the past few thousand years we men have been forced to rein it in and try our best not to be dirty cheating bastards.

As all men know, and as many women will smugly agree, this is damned difficult. It's not a lesser character or a species-wide personality defect, though, you morons; it's just our nature fighting against the artificial imposition of civilization, and sometimes the battle is a close one. So we have a safety valve. Haunted by visions of your best friend's wife? Rent a movie, masturbate, and *tell no one.*

2. GIVE WOMEN A LEGITIMATE REASON TO FEEL SUPERIOR TO US. Ho ho ho, sometimes my girlfriends amuse me so, especially when they gather together in their Earth Mother robes and smile indulgently when I try to say that men are no worse than women, morals-wise and character-wise. Ah, but the argument that women are just as swinish as men is another article (and one I think I've written several times before) so let's stick to the point: Pornography serves a good purpose in giving these poor chicks something concrete to point to, saying with insane cheer that at least *they* don't rent dirty movies and touch themselves, at least *they* don't support a multibillion dollar flesh industry that turns innocents into crack whores, demons, and, apparently, communists. And if it makes the weaker sex feel better about supporting the multimillion dollar *romance novel* industry, I say it must be a good thing.

3. FAKE PICTURES. Scott Adams, who writes that funny, funny Dilbert comic strip, wrote a book about how he thinks the future will turn out. In this book, he proposes that true virtual reality will be the last invention mankind produces, since once we all have operational Holodecks in our homes we'll never leave again. We'll just roll around our VR rooms screwing Claudia Schiffer or Fabio until we die of starvation or maybe, more appropriately, dehydration. This is true. If you doubt me, take five minutes to really think about it and then come back to this paragraph.

Well, like I said, the future is beginning on the Internet, where one of my more eye-opening discoveries recently is that you can find just about every celebrity you've ever heard of, however obscure, naked. Now, I don't think some of these people ever posed nude. I don't think some of these people ever remove their foundation garments, for Christ's sake. You can find nude pictures of them, because they are faked.

Ah, but that's the boring part—Cindy Crawford's head pasted onto some coke whore's body? Yawn. Even finding something like Hillary Rodham Clinton's head morphed onto some slightly older coke whore's body isn't interesting for very long, once the shock fades. What really amuses me is how creative some of these people are. They don't just paste heads, my pigs, they create complete scenarios, some erotic, some strange, some hilarious. These crude digital artists are changing reality in their own small way, and they are the pioneers of what will be the end of this sick, diseased society. And I applaud them.

Yeah, and I dare you to find a celebrity who *isn't* nude on the Internet. Somewhere, some shut-in geek with a calloused hand has created a fake nude of even the most unknown star. Think of some minor celebrity. Go ahead. Think back to the most boring cocktail party you've ever been to, then isolate the dullest conversation you engaged in or overheard from that party. Recall the name of the incredibly unknown actor or model mentioned in it. As you pass out from re-lived boredom, gasping out the name with a puzzled expression on your face, I'll bet you I can find a fake nude of that person in 24 hours. 18 if you let Ken West help me.

4. IF WE DIDN'T HAVE PORNOGRAPHY, HOW WOULD WE CATCH ALL THE PEDOPHILES? All you hear about these days is how police departments all across America are nabbing pedophiles trying to lure innocent teens into their sick dens of man-boy love. How do they do it? The Internet, which basically translates into pornography, as far as I can tell.

And, on the weirdo flip side of #4:

5. THE EDUCATION OF 11-YEAR-OLDS EVERYWHERE. The funny thing about my sweet earth-mother girlfriends is that they want their Sabrett free from animal by-products, so to speak, but they want gobs of mustard on that dog too. They wrinkle their cute noses in distaste at the very thought of men having sexual fantasies about something as wholesome and American as, say, sheep, and run away in horror if we start discussing the ups and downs of the venerable pornographic film series Swedish Erotica. But they want their men to be James Bond in bed—in charge, in our element, and flawlessly prepared. In other words, they expect us to be able to handle the clutch as well as the gearshift.

I don't know about you, but that little birds-and-bees talk every parent is supposed to have with their kids kind of went by the wayside in my youth. Or else I passed out from terminal embarrassment and don't remember it. Who knows? Point is, if I hadn't seen a few Vanessa Del Rio movies when I was a preteen, I might not know how to do anything. And I would submit without fear that even those of us lucky enough to have their parents explain the fundamental facts of sex rarely graduated to the more advanced courses such as *French kissing, cunnilingus,* or *rubber implements.* Without Ms. Del Rio and her cohorts, where would we men be? That's right, at the mercy of women, which is maybe right where they want us.

And for those of you who don't think the term *rubber implements* is ever going to have any practical concern for your life, I say: *Hey, you never know.*

6. PROVIDING JOBS AND LIVINGS FOR MORONS EVERYWHERE. One fact I doubt anyone will argue is that the performers in your average pornographic endeavor aren't very bright. We're talking well into the sub-human level of intelligence. Okay, everyone needs to make a living. But if the only skill you can pull out of your ass to offer the job market is an *instinct*, something we're all *born to do*—well, there's just something wrong with you. But thank god that an industry exists for such people. I mean, would you want these yokels fondling your fast food or calling you at night on telemarketing cold calls? I think not.

Of course, some of the porno actors did, at one time, have "real" careers. Nina Hartley, who's been making skin flicks for about 75 years now, was once a registered nurse. She gave up that glamorous life in order to pursue her true passion: faking orgasms on screen. This, to me, is somehow worse than mere stupidity. I mean, do we really want people who *freely choose* to be public deviants fondling our fast food or calling us on telemarketing cold calls? I think even *more* not.

Without the gracious pornography industry, these dim bulbs would be forced to undertake some other work, and would most likely end up in occupations similar to their porno jobs anyway: *crack whores.* So if you think about it, pornography is directly responsible for keeping crazed hordes of crack whores off the streets, where they would most likely hunt you down and slit your throat for pocket change.

Remember: Save a life, rent a porno.

7. Marriage Counseling for $3 a Night. One of the more surprising things you find out when you stick your nose into the seamy underbelly of pornography is that one of its largest groups of consumers in this world is couples. After all, it's unreasonable to think that the fires of passion will burn forever without some fanning. After a few years of watching your partner slowly expand and get either hairier or balder, a few years in which your irritation at their various foibles is allowed to ripen and bulge into a really disastrous purple rage, a few years of getting a good look at what this formerly hot and tempting body's gonna look like when they're 50, well—after that it's kind of amazing that anyone has sex after marriage, don't you think? Aside from breeding purposes, of course. During the baby fever stage of any marriage the sex is often and easy, but of course it's also very much like a *job*.

So what are burned-out couples who are slowly learning to loathe each other to do? Specifically, what do they do if they retain some semblance of love and respect for each other through all the back-stabbing and insults? That's right, they rent pornography. Why? For a number of reasons, apparently. As something a little kinky to make sex fresh again. As a tutorial of nasty things they never considered before. Maybe just as a shared experience they can get a hoot out of—after all, maybe their sex life isn't so hot but at least they don't look as ridiculous as the actors in the movies and don't bang like a couple of well-oiled robots. Maybe their lackluster lovelife doesn't look so bad after a few viewings.

Of course, this can often result in middle-aged grown-ups wearing things and doing things that make them look patently ridiculous; all great things bring risk. The point is, pornography isn't always about weirdo men in raincoats skulking around movie theaters. Very often it's part of the glue that holds America's immature couples as one, so they can grow miserable together.

Pornography, far from being a cancer eating away at our society, is often a healthy and necessary outlet for the frustrated (albeit completely natural) abundance of sexual energy shared by humans everywhere. Let's face it: if there were no diseases, if pregnancy was voluntary, if there were no consequences at all to sex besides uncomfortable breakfasts, we'd all probably be having sex as casually as we say hello. Well, maybe not quite *that* casually, but pretty darn casually, I think.

There is a difference, of course, between what I will ironically call "mainstream" pornography and the *fringe evil* that also falls under that umbrella term. As a Swine I enjoy wallowing in the dirt as much as anybody, but there's always a line and anything that is harmful or evil in intent makes even Swines run for cover. After all, one of the main characteristics of "mainstream" pornography is that it's all pretty vapidly vanilla. It is inherently harmless. Harmless in the sense that the participants, on both sides of the transaction, are voluntary and adult.

Because, when you think about the uninspired fantasies that pornography regurgitates, you realize that the industry is not inventing new and destructive filth. It's just using the same filth that's been around since the introduction of the cheerleader uniform. If there's evil in it, well then it's evil that we dragged with us when we hotfooted it out of the Garden of Eden—nothing new, nothing shocking, and nothing we don't carry around with us everyday.

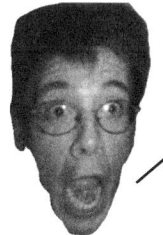

JEFF SEZ: In the early days of *The Inner Swine* I took myself a little too seriously and thought that every article should convey my opinions to the world, which was certainly hungry for them. After the first, oh, ten issues of my zine received nothing but the chill wind of disdain from the world, I began to realize that no one really cared what I thought. Still, my editorials remained more or less straightforward opinion pieces for quite a while, only slowly evolving into the ridiculous displays of egomania they are today—as you'll see later.

The photo included with this editorial drew a lot of letters, and I'll say to you what I've said to everyone else: no, I will not mail you that picture.

31

Pig in Shit #13

TRAVELING MUSIC FOR THE MENTALLY CHALLENGED

The Inner Swine *Advice Column*

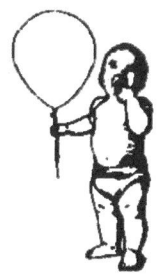

JEFF SOMERS

DEAR JEFF: *In issue 4(3) of* The Inner Swine *you told us that everything in issue 4(4) would be a lie. Is this true? What exactly constitutes a lie these days anyway? And how come you don't print fake nude photos of Bea Arthur anymore?* —**Curious from Evanston**

Dear Curious: No, not everything in this issue is a lie, of course. I was forced on occasion to actually tell the truth. This of course makes that statement from the last issue a lie, which I think makes up for it.

The question of "what is a lie" is very interesting, however. Is a lie simply anything that turns out to be untrue? We at *The Inner Swine Institute of Bizarre Research* disagree. Sometimes people say things they believe to be true, so even if they are not true these people are not liars but rather simple morons (Ronald Reagan comes to mind; with his brain swiss-cheesed from various ailments, he probably did believe all the malarky he spun to us). Lying implies intentional deception, like when Billy Clinton told us he did not have sexual relations with the bimbo intern. Of course, sometimes people are deluded and truly do believe the lies they are telling, which makes them not lies but rather hallucinations. A good example of this is me: I certainly believe that people read this magazine, but that is obviously not true. The fact that I continue to proclaim that it is true doesn't make me a liar or the statement a lie; it makes me a sad, lonely person and the statement a pathetic cry for help.

As for the fake nudes of Bea Arthur, send me a self-addressed stamped envelope, and I'll send you what I have.

DEAR JEFF: *Recently my girlfriend, whom I live with, searched through my pants pockets and found several packs of condoms, some matchbooks with phone numbers on them, and a bottle of Rohypnol tablets. When confronted with this evidence I faked a seizure and locked myself in the bedroom, where I am now e-mailing you from. What should I do? Should I tell the truth and reveal that I've been cheating on her? Or should I lie and tell her I'm holding these items for a friend?* —**Desperate in Hawaii**

Dear Desperate: You fool! You hold the answer right there in your greasy hands! Slip your gal some of them there roofies and then hide the evidence. When she comes to hours later you won't have to admit anything or lie.

This does bring up some interesting territory in the discourse on the lie, however: namely, those moments when the truth can do more harm than good. The main impetus most of us have for telling the truth is, of course, a selfish one: We want to: a) relieve our suffering conscience, and b) minimize anticipated repercussions with the appearance of a sudden conversion to honesty. These are the only reasons most of us would ever admit a lie and come clean, unless we've been nailed red-handed at something.

Instead of giving in to this simpering need to confess and be forgiven, do the unselfish thing and perpetuate the lies you've told. That sounds pretty evil, I suppose, but really, since you'll be suffering from a harping conscience and the terror of being found out for the rest of your days, preserving the false situation, which is keeping everyone else happy, is actually the unselfish and difficult route to take. Confession will make you feel better, but it would cause all sorts of trauma, angst, tears, and regret. Thus, the truth is often more harmful than a delicate web of lies.

DEAR JEFF: *Don't you think it's shameful that our President, the man we trust to run our country's affairs and to represent us on the global stage, not only engaged in such unseemly behavior but lied on countless occasions to cover up these activities?* —**Shocked and Saddened in Omaha**

Dear Shocked: No, I don't, you fucking moron.

Consider the latticework of lies that politicians spin on a daily basis in this country, mostly due to the impossible pressures that our melting pot society puts on them. We have an unreasonable belief that our politicians, not just the ones in our area or locality, but everywhere in the country, should conform to whatever bullshit code of ethics and morals we have managed to cobble together from our brief and tenuous experiences with various religions, codes, and television shows. When you consider the number of people someone like the president has to appeal to just get elected, don't be surprised to learn that they probably lie constantly. Or, if not strictly lie, they will certainly retreat into vague denial and fancy verbal footwork. The truth, in politics, is not noble. The truth will most often get you defeat and disdain.

So, you're Bill Clinton and you've boinked a few interns in your time—no big deal, you figure, it's not like you were whispering security secrets into their white-trash hairdos, right? Ah, but then the bunch of slope-browed conservative subhumans we affectionately call The Republican Party's Ultra-Right get a whiff of stale semen and rumors begin to fly, investigations are launched, pointed questions get asked. Let's take a quick quiz. If you're Mr. Clinton in this situation, do you

A) Admit everything and plea for understanding
B) Admit nothing and attempt to squirm out of it
C) Ask your spiritual advisor for guidance

If you answered "A" or "C" I can only thank whatever god there may be that you weren't elected back in 1996. What kind of an idiot would actually admit something like that to a national audience unless forced to by circumstance? No one smart enough to have gotten themselves elected in the first place, that's for sure. You bet it all on "B" and hope for the best.

And yet, when our President did just that people were outraged and went on endlessly about immorality and shame and lies and such. The President's obviously slippery morals aside, only a weak man would have chosen honesty in that situation. A schmo. A schmuck. And the people who said otherwise were infantile moronic little opportunists who smelled blood in the water and prayed that through this tenuous partnership with the Truth they could accomplish what they had been unable to do over the previous years: oust Clinton. The supposedly sacred truth, to these people, was merely a tool. And I am not referring to a "them" of shadowy power brokers and political movers: I mean all of you small-souled sucks. You mock the concept of truth, and you're too dim to even realize it.

Ahem. Excuse me.

DEAR JEFF: *Recently I discovered that my husband of 23 years—let's call him Rubio—has been wearing my underwear for some time, how long I'm not sure. I first began noticing the stretched-out waistbands and missing brassieres a few years ago, but recently I caught Rubio prancing around like the May Queen in our living room. I retreated into the liquor cabinet before he could see me and so Rubio has no idea that I am aware of his little secret. Our children are grown and attending college. This makes me very uncomfortable. Should I confront Rubio? Should I tell our children? Should I buy Rubio his own wardrobe?* —**Burdened in Berlin**

Dear Burdened: Technically, unless you at some point asked Rubio his feelings on transvestism, this isn't a lie. After all, you probably squat and take a shit everyday but you don't go around telling people; can you be accused of lying to cover up your serial defecation? Probably not, just as Rubio probably has not actually lied about anything. He's maybe guilty of many other things: omission of obviously important personal details, bad fashion sense, etc.—but I doubt he's actually a liar.

We live in increasingly conservative and frighteningly intolerant times; our beloved country's lax immigration policies and supposed love of personal freedom is resulting in a fractured culture of subcultures, each of us eyeing the other suspiciously. Instead of seeking common ground, we're exploiting our differences under the guise of "pride" and multiculturalism—in other words, insular provincial bullshit. And one weapon in this insular bunkerism is to pounce on every supposed moral transgression of the "other". In politics it ain't hard to catch people in lies. Everyone from Ronald Reagan and Newt Gingrich to Al Gore (of all people) have been caught vigorously giving the truth the finger. And in the sensationalistic frenzy of the media-presented reality (woe to anyone who thinks television news doesn't, very subtly, slant everything every single evening) the blurry line between an actual, on-purpose deception and the simple act of not bringing up a potentially embarrassing or harmful fact is easily blurred.

For those who believe that our politicians and leaders should be held to a higher standard of honesty, I give you all the finger. This is the U.S. of A., mis amigos. The people we elect are supposed to represent us. Ask me if I believe any of you shits, or myself for that matter, live up to that sort of gloriously dull moral code. Go ahead, ask me. I'm drooling. Our leaders are dirty little lying shits, kids, because we're dirty little lying shits. In the paraphrased words of Chris Rock: The reason Bill Clinton is so popular is people look at him and say 'Hmmmn. . .wife's a bitch. . .worries a lot about his job, got a lot of pressure. . .bills are piling up'. . .shit, I know Bill Clinton —I *am* Bill Clinton.

DEAR JEFF: *God teaches us not to lie. If more people were to obey God's word, the world would be a happier and better place.* YOU'RE GOING TO BURN IN HELL SOMERS! YOU AND YOUR WEENIE LIBERAL INNER CIRCLE ARE GOING TO MEET GOD SOONER THAN YOU THINK! THE RIGHTEOUS KNOW WHERE YOU LIVE AND WE'RE COMING FOR YOU! —**President, The Coming Army of God's Righteous Children, Atlanta**

Dear Righteous: Well, its been a few decades since I read anything in the Bible, so I'll have to take your word on this interpretation of god's words. If you're right about what god meant, then I'm sorry to say that god was: wrong.

Lies are not just the dark tunnels under the mountain of responsibility, traversed by the weak and slimy amongst us; they are the support wires and pavement of our grand civilization. Take away the lies, my fellow pigs, and you are left with a swiftly collapsing society, borne down by the sudden and unexpected weight of THE FACTS. The facts being that every single human being has lied to cover up something, that we've all engaged in the fine art of bullshit. Eliminate the bullshit, and we once again return to one of *The Inner Swine*'s favorite images: the human race holed up in bunkers, shooting anything that comes near.

See, as onerous as it is for many of us, society has rules. Some of these rules have more to do with ancient tradition than modern necessity (can you say meatless Fridays?). Yet the largely clueless and somewhat superstitious majority of the world's population continues to not only obey these rules but to champion them, as if these outdated concepts and conventions still applied. The rest of us, too smart to skip Friday's cheeseburgers because some demented health official in 1000 B.C. thought the meat was suspect, sometimes ignore these rules and sometimes get caught. The rest of us, the ones who still believe that such traditions and rules still have meaning and value, also sometimes ignore them. Why, if they believe in them? Because people are weak, kiddo. Presidents boink interns, priests abuse altar boys, athletes get addicted to drugs: We all cheat, for one reason or another.

Most of these transgressions, of course, are largely harmless where society is concerned. But if we get caught, that won't matter: The clueless hordes will demand we be punished for mocking their cherished rules. So, we gotta lie sometimes. *No sir, that wasn't me. This won't hurt a bit. Just a glass of wine with dinner, officer. Of course I love you. Was that you? I didn't see you.* The fact of the matter is, if we didn't have lies to fall back on and had to exclusively tell the truth all the time, you'd pretty quickly find out how tenuous our civilization is. Our civilization is supported by a thick network of lies, beginning with the existence of god, running through the concept of freedom in a democratic society, and ending right here in your sweaty little hands at *The Inner Swine*.

DEAR JEFF: *My niece "Jenny" suffers from a variety of physical and mental ailments that cause her to appear as something of a goblin. We love Jenny dearly, however, and try to give her as normal a life as possible. The other day I was out with Jenny in the park getting her a little sun, when a friend of the family came up to us and remarked that Jenny was "dead-dog ugly" and then let out a cackling laugh that went on for almost five minutes. This was very hurtful and rude. How can I let this person know that they were a complete wanker without offending them (they are a very old and dear friend of the family)?* —
Fuming in New Hyde Park

Dear Fuming: Well, I'm always a big fan of breaking out some old magazines and pasting together a nice, luridly threatening letter. Get specific when it comes to body parts. This always works for me.

Your situation does underline an inherent truth in our society (irony alert!): Lying is very often the accepted way of handling social situations. The family friend here obviously expressed their 'true' feelings and reactions to your niece, and yet here the truth was not only unacceptable, but was downright unappreciated. You would prefer that the friend lie their ass off, right?

Telling lies when confronted with polite social interaction is the only way to get by. We all praise creations, feign sympathy, and ask to do lunch when we'd truthfully rather eat dog feces than spend time with this, that, or the other person. Yet these lies are never questioned or denounced—because it's an open secret that we all engage in them. Imagine if we all acted like your friend and just blurted out our actual feelings! My goodness, we'd be in Bunker Country before the year was out!

My Dear Readers: We all lie, in little and big ways, every day of our lives, you know? If you don't think so, you're lying to yourself, and if you really don't, you are one scary motherfucker. We've all squirmed out of a speeding ticket, or called in sick when we're just tired of showing up at work, or told our parents that we have no idea who honked in the bathtub over the weekend while they were away. Our society is both riddled by and supported by deceptions. It's the only way several hundred million people can peacefully coexist in one geographical area, unless you count the introduction of Martial Law, which would probably be just as effective but not nearly as enjoyable. Consider:

Lying is not always the easy way out. Sometimes it's harder and more noble to perpetuate a lie than it is to cleanse your soul and wallow in the shallow pleasure of confession. Lying is often less harmful than the truth. Lying is often the only way you can protect your privacy from invasive and rude people, who are often authority figures. Lying is, finally, almost always the accepted practice of 'polite' interaction; you are, after all, always discouraged from expressing your true views on individuals—and rightfully so. You might think your neighbor is a complete wanker, you might detest your boss' sense of humor, you might dread paying your respects to Aunt Bertha—but you don't say so. You smile, you make small talk, you're polite—in short, you lie. This is how society works.

And we at *The Inner Swine* love it this way—and that's the damned truth.

Pig in Shit #14

THE BEST MEAT'S IN THE RUMP

How Technological Advancement Brings Out the Animal in Us All

SUPREME OINKER JEFFREY SOMERS, HONORARY PRESIDENT AND FOUNDER, *The Inner Swine* **OPENING REMARKS AT SWINECON '98, MOTEL 6 OFF OF ROUTE 9, WOODBRIDGE, NEW JERSEY**

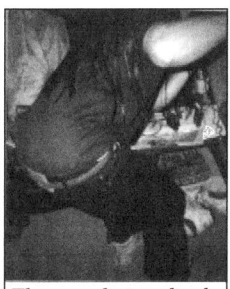

The people involved with TIS are damned proud of their rumps. Just FYI. (Above rump: Jeof Vita)

"Fellow pigs, I'd like to welcome you to—hey, settle down back there—fellow pigs, I'd—HEY! You assholes in the back row SHUT THE FUCK UP!— I'd like to welcome you to—*ALL RIGHT THE NEXT PERSON WHO OPENS THEIR GODDAMN MOUTH GETS BANNED FROM THE OPEN BAR LATER!*

Ahem. That's better.

Fellow pigs, I'd like to welcome you to SwineCon '98, the three hundredth year we Swine have gathered under assumed names to discuss new Swine technology and its impact on our selfish rampage across history. It warms your President's heart to see so many familiar and returning faces out there, but it's even more exciting to see all the newcomers crowding the Gold Room here in lovely Woodbridge. Every year more and more people come to accept their basic evil nature and natural self-centeredness, and that is what SwineCon is all about right? Spreading our message. Everybody?

EVERYONE'S AN ASSHOLE, ESPECIALLY US!!!

Heh, heh, you know, I still get a chill whenever I hear 46 people shout that in unison. Beginning in 1698 when three Italian gamblers gathered in a New Amsterdam brothel to discuss their piggish natures, SwineCon has existed to facilitate communication and debt collection amongst Swines

Appeared in Volume 5, Issue 1, March 1999

worldwide, and much good work has been accomplished at these conferences—why, our flagship publication, *The Inner Swine,* was conceived and chartered at SwineCon '93, held in my kitchen in New Brunswick, New Jersey—making the expense of the requisite liquor bill well worth it.

Recently, however, some of our number have questioned whether, in this age of technological advancement and wonder, we really need to gather in one spot in order to share Swine philosophy, run out on bar bills, and plot once again to overthrow civilization just to see what would happen. After all, through the Internet and cheap long distance calls made secretly from hotel courtesy phones worldwide, we can pretty much hold these sorts of conferences without actually physically holding these sorts of conferences. There are of course a few major flaws in these newfangled ideas. Number one, most of the Swine's electronic communications are closely monitored by the CIA, FBI, NSA, and, most recently (ever since that ill-conceived Presidential assassination threat—whoo, I'll never drink *Jagermeister* again, I'll tell you!) the Secret Service. Number two, none of us have the funds to get such a virtual conference off the ground, since SwineCon '98 also marks the 300th year that you bastards have all failed to mail in your back dues.

(Laughter)

Still, I think the suggestion that technology might somehow alter our role in world events intrigued me, and I think I'll use my time up here to explore it a little—hey, hey, HEY! I told you to settle down or I'll have Security Chief Ken West beat the living shit out of you, okay? Do we understand each other? Alrighty then.

One of the main tenets of *The Inner Swine*, after all, is that man is fundamentally primitive, seeking his own security and advancement above all else no matter what his surface motivations might be. Over the past few hundred years, however, the animal man has experienced an explosion in technology, and in a very, very short period of time we've increased our understanding and control over the forces of the universe a hundredfold just about every other decade. A few hundred years ago we weren't sure how the cosmos was organized, and today we're working on computers that utilize subatomic particles to perform parallel operations a million times faster than IBM's Deep Blue mainframe. Based on my vast knowledge of 70's science fiction films, I can say with complete confidence that the human race is hurtling towards an evolutionary convulsion resulting in a technological society of telekinetic uber-humans, communicating with their thoughts and no longer needing their shriveled, ghoulish mortal bodies. Eventually, you figure, it would be natural that we'd download our minds onto subatomic hard drives and exist as electrical impulses.

I am here to tell you, however, that this concept is flawed, and is not happening. If anything, our race's technological advancements are enhancing our primitive, animalistic tendencies. We're more animal than ever before, and you can thank Bell Labs and Microsoft for it.

WE'RE ALL PART OF A TRIBE. If I were to ask everyone in this room, esteemed Swines all, what the basic feature of man's animalistic nature was, you'd probably all reply that it's his inherent tribalism. Since the dawn of time men have been ganging up with other men to create tribes of like-minded individuals who then crush any dissenters through their combined might. Certainly, if I ever looked out into the crowd of Swines and saw something that might be legitimately defined as "combined might" instead of 46 slightly employed agitators with FBI files, I wouldn't hesitate to give the order to crush the rest of society and remake it in our image. Forming tribes and hating anyone not a part of that tribe with the white hot intensity of a thousand suns is pretty much what people *do*. It's a primal reaction to fear, and it lives on even in today's enlightened times.

TECHNOLOGY ISOLATES. Increasingly we are telecommuters, living in gated communities, shopping via phone lines, communicating via e-mails, paying to have the real world piped into us over cable lines. There was once a time when you *had* to interact with your community. The only way to get anything done or have your interests considered was to get to know your neighbors—your tribe—and be known by them. Now, none of that is necessary. People live in suburban developments where their neighbors remain shadowy figures behind minivans and shrubbery; they communicate anonymously in Internet chat rooms. Technology creates firewalls that humans have never had to deal with before. Isolation is scary. No one likes to feel like they are alone in the world, against the elements. Everyone likes to have a few buddies around them in the Big Bar Fight of Life, right? Of course they do. The need for a tribe is increased by the isolation of technology, and everyone tags up into teams, instinctively seeking protection in numbers.

You see it everyday on the Internet, the ultimate in isolating technology, where everyone uses a pseudonym and getting flamed is as easy as expressing an opinion. People join newsgroups, Internet relay chat (IRC) lines, or ICQ lists, and "Holy Wars" arguing the merits of a particular computer system or application or philosophy are pretty common and easy to start. In one sense, the people who swear by their PC and who argue with the people who live and die by their Macs are tribes. They support each other, attack their enemies, and protect their cherished ideas. Instead of being a huge bastion of individuality, the Internet is actually a Thunderdome of warring tribes. If you ever need evidence that we're not as advanced and civilized as we'd like to think, just lurk in some Internet newsgroups and watch the feces fly.

WE WORSHIP GOLDEN CALVES. What else defines primitive man? Not only are we social animals who gather into tribes for comfort and defense, we're also very superstitious and are easily fooled into believing the most ridiculous things through a combination of clever marketing and state-of-the-art special effects. Normally when I say something like that I'm referring to Christianity—or any religion, really—but today some would say that technology is eroding that primitive instinct to believe in higher powers. After all, most modern people don't believe there are water gods or tree nymphs, right? While most people seem to buy into the concept of a supreme being, there are plenty of relatively intelligent arguments in favor of a supreme being. Just because they're all wrong doesn't mean they're not intelligent, after all.

All right, everyone calm down. Don't make me ask Corporal Punishment to step in here.

As I was saying, in these modern times our willingness to believe that ridiculous icons can lead us to some sort of salvation or wisdom hasn't dimmed, it's just been conscripted by the supreme forces of marketing. The fact is, people buy cars, invest monies, choose all manner of products simply because we're told to by our modern gods: celebrities. Doubt me? Millions of lowing morons who would normally rather suck a tailpipe than read a book without glossy pictures ran out to buy books just because Oprah told them to. *Someone* out there is watching a putrid television show called *V.I.P.* simply because Pamela Anderson stars in it. Sure, we're not examining some virgin's internal organs for hints regarding the right date to harvest the grain, but we *are* sort of looking for guidance on how to attain success and happiness. . .and if Jonathan Pryce tells us we'd be wise to purchase a Lexus or an Infiniti or whatever piece of shit luxury car he hawks. . .well, a lot of us listen.

We have sex goddesses and gods, we have war gods and goddesses, we have gods and goddesses for everything in our overburdened modern lives. Technology has allowed us to have an icon for the smallest and most minutely defined aspects of life—whereas in the past, humans had to settle for the major stuff like death and the moon and fertility. Today we have icons for all that and more, because technology makes it possible. Polytheism is alive and well and thriving on the E! Entertainment Network and The Home Shopping Channel. Instead of making us less superstitious and less willing to believe in the magical aspects of our universe, technology has made us more so, with millions believing in alien abduction, with hundreds of urban legends spreading like scripture everyday, with clothing and style trends popping up everyday like bushmen worshiping Coke bottles. Our gods are movie stars, their scripture and legend are *Titanic* and *Gone With the Wind* and *Star Wars*, and our religious icons are the diet cola they hawk on television. Blessed are we in the light.

WE'RE STILL ALL BAD MOTHERFUCKERS. If anyone in this room here today has never been the recipient of a restraining order, raise your hand. (Laughter) Obviously we've all had a few violent blackouts after a night of dangerous binge drinking. Everyone's crashed a car into an enemy's house, everyone's smashed a few windows. Everyone's accidentally picked a fight with off-duty cops. I mean, who hasn't?

Yet, in all the bad science fiction movies I saw on television as a kid while waiting for my parents to go to bed (so I could attempt to watch free porno on scrambled cable channels) the future was always presented as a triumph over violence. Technology, it was hinted, would make unnecessary all our base instincts. Ever see a barroom brawl on *Star Trek*? Except for those episodes where the evil Captain Kirk infects everyone with a virus that unleashes their deeply buried id, no, of course not. The whole idea was that in a world where machinery and computers had solved all of our social problems, mankind would be free to turn their attention to advanced civilization topics like *Group Sex* and *Soylent Green*.

This isn't happening, pigs. It's obvious to anyone with a brain that our technology is frighteningly weapons-based: Not only is the greatest amount of money and effort put into our military forces and nuclear programs, many of the great technological advancements of today have stemmed from military research projects. Just like ancient man hurling bigger and bigger rocks at each other whenever tribal skirmishes erupted (over water rights or hunting grounds or a lack of available women), we still seek the security of mighty weapons. Our primitive notions of security and defense haven't changed all that much (our anxieties being focussed on the survival of our genetic material and organized against the *other*, the differing tribe of weirdos we detest and imagine detest us in turn) and technological advances have simply granted us destructive power beyond our minor understanding. The machinery of war has bloated into something frightening. The motivations behind it languish in our DNA, written millions of years ago for a set of circumstances which have receded into the dustbin of history.

Let's face it, technology hasn't stopped us from murdering each other. Modern technology of the last few hundred years or so has gifted us with the gun, after all. Instead of frightening us into sensible pacifism, this neato invention (I can see many of our brother pigs waving their nickel-plated Glocks around now—uh, please don't make me call security *again*) has inspired us to greater and greater feats of homicide—the USA, gun paradise that it is, has yearly homicide numbers that just make your head spin. New York City had less than a thousand murders in 1998 and this was actually reason to *celebrate* there. Meanwhile, backwards countries that don't allow every mentally challenged house monkey within their borders to purchase a firearm have murder rates in just about the single digits. Murder there is, like, *murder*, you know? People get excited when murder occurs. Here in the USA, you get murdered, people yawn, medical examiners eat lunch while eviscerating you, cats play with your toe tags.

Even in the virtual world where technology is really all there is, there's a frightening amount of anger and violence in effect. People spam us. They send us e-mail bombs. They slip viruses and trojans into our downloads. They hack our passwords and wreak havoc. We need firewalls, antivirus software, and constant vigilance to fend them off, and it don't take much to get targeted by these snot-nosed little wusses. The death and destruction they cause isn't *real*; it doesn't necessarily kill anyone. But it's still death and destruction, neither tempered nor prevented by our technological mastery. In fact, since a lot of the malcontents and social pariahs who make up the ranks of these cyber-asses probably have a personal intimidation factor of zero, technology gives them a chance to be violent that they probably wouldn't have been able to indulge, otherwise. Very simply, technology gives us more chances to *be* violent.

Now, while my private staff moves through the audience waking up dozing members, I'd like to thank the SwineCon '98 organizers for a swell job. We're all impressed with the free porno on the televisions in everyone's room, though I would like to remind everyone that SwineCon is *not* going to cover the honor bar expenses—and I can see by the white-faced reactions out there that some people were counting on a last-minute change of heart on that matter.

Now, Legal Counsel Danette Knopp has a few announcements related to the subject of room furniture damage, but before I yield the microphone I'd like to sum up my message here today: The technological and industrial development of the human race has, in universal terms, been sudden and *fast*. Biologically, genetically, and instinctively, we haven't even begun to catch up. We're still pretty much the same apes who were hurling feces at our enemies a few thousand years ago. As a result, our technology isn't necessarily making us *less* violent and animalistic—it actually amplifies those primal urges towards the primitive and the feral.

As Swines, of course, we love this. Nothing warms our bellies more than the daily territorial pissings and Mexican standoffs we witness in daily life that define our feral nature. These dark instincts are what make us human, and we for one celebrate it instead of burying it beneath perfume and Brooks Brothers suits, which is what most people do, the fuckers.

Oh well, I can see by the arrival of my lawyers that the time has come for me to return to my yacht in international waters to evade United States treasury officials. Remember, we're all assholes, and linked in that glorious Swine tradition, I call upon your brotherhood to deny having seen me here, and to answer no questions unless forced by circumstance or legal remedy. Thank you all, and may SwineCon '98 be a smashing success! Ms. Knopp, the floor is yours."

[Applause]

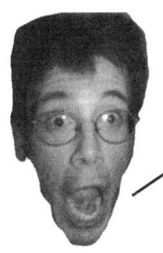

JEFF SEZ: One of the earliest times I envisioned my Worldwide Organization of Terror, and all the traditional parts are there: me as alcoholic dictator, Ken West as dangerously violent Security Chief, supposed conspiracy of swines. Since this editorial I've expanded the concept quite a bit.

The title doesn't really mean anything, so don't think too hard about it. I think I got it from a cartoon.

Pig in Shit #18

LET ME TAKE THIS OPPORTUNITY TO WELCOME OUR NEW MASTERS

I Am Ready to Join the Thought Police and Rat All of You Out

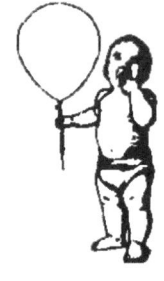

Questions Are a Burden, and Answers a Prison for Oneself, Natch.

MY PIGS, in the past I have hinted at the Great Change, the coming Inner Swine Pogrom that would remake the world in my own image. I have ruthlessly implied all sorts of violence and upheaval in order to intimidate all of you into giving me tribute, usually in the form of free drinks or dates with your sisters. I have been proudly detailing my anticipated despotic reign, getting so specific and repetitive that some wisenheimers have lately been wondering aloud if there really ever will be a Swine Revolution, or if it's all just been a complex and bizarre ruse. The answer is yes and no. No, it wasn't intended to be a bizarre ruse, but, thanks to new intelligence brought to me by a badly injured Chief of Security Ken West, I now realize there will not be a Grand Swine Revolution. Why? Because another organization, many times the size of my own and much better equipped, is set to spark their own revolution very soon.

All I can say to these shadowy men and women who will soon rule our planet is, I welcome my new masters with open arms, and humbly suggest I would make an excellent and photogenic mouthpiece-cum-lackey. I am

Appeared in Volume 6, Issue 1, March 2000

ready and willing, in other words, to become Chief of their Thought Police.

How do I know there'll be a Thought Police for me to lead against the rest of you? Simple: There's *always* a Thought Police. It's the oldest law enforcement organization in existence. There's one now, actively working to maintain society as it sees fit. Chances are, you're a member in good standing, unless you got this zine by stuffing it into your pocket and casually walking out the front door. The only thing the Thought Police lack right now are nifty uniforms and an official leader, which, given the go-ahead by our future oppressors and a decent budget, I'll be glad to take care of.

You see, civilization is a precarious balance. It exists only because the bulk of the population self-polices; if we witness a crime, most of us are likely to report it; if we're involved in a crime, we're likely to report it. Civilization exists because of this implied partnership between citizens and police, but the implication is deeper: Because of this partnership, the police are obvious and apart from the rest of us, for the most part. They are uniformed, carry badges. Their cars are clearly marked, and even their private vehicles bear stickers proudly. We know, or can easily find out, who they are, and this enables your friends, family, neighbors, bosses and vague strangers you've never met before to easily rat you out if you attempt something that goes against the grain of society, that in any way poisons their particular pond. In short, society exists in part because, on some level, we're all ready and willing to betray each other. We're Pigs, after all. Not only are we fundamentally self-interested, dishonest, and cruel, we're more than willing to rat the other guy out if there's profit in it—and for most people, there's definite profit in maintaining order.

This is a Good Thing, believe it or not. People who state that the world would be a better place without an army of police out there in riot gear have no fucking clue, have no idea what kind of chaos lurks just beyond that fork in the road. This is a Good Thing because the moment we stop policing ourselves, the cops will melt into the crowd, and become Thought Police too.

Okay, but if there's always *been* a Thought Police, why does this matter so much? Well, no one said the Thought Police are particularly good at their jobs right now. It's one thing to be a good worker bee and be willing to turn people in for crimes, to scream for help when witnessing a mugging, to exert some reasonable effort to avert a murder, a robbery, a rape—it's quite another to translate that instinctual, trained impulse and contact a representative of law enforcement, and even then there is the bulky mechanism of arrest: the search for the suspect, the onus of probable cause, the Miranda reading, the processing, paperwork, and writ of habeas corpus, as weightless as that often turns out to be. All this clutter and bureaucracy serves as a buffer between the Law and us, and gives us the comforting illusion of privacy and freedom.

If we stop policing ourselves, then having a visible and easily identifiable police force becomes useless. If no one *calls* the cops, then you're relying on the random chance that they'll witness crimes, which is not an effective way to manage a society. Once that occurs, the cops go under, pull on their regular folk skins, and you won't know you're sitting next to one until they point at you, open their mouths, and emit a screeching wail. And next to them, smiling nervously, will be your best friend, who's just happy it wasn't them this time. And above their left shoulder, on a poster hanging on the subway car wall, will be my smiling face, because I intend to be the Chief of the Thought Police.

Just in case The Coming Powers That Be are reading this (or that their advanced Echelon technologies are sifting through this electronically) I might as well make my case for why I should be Chief of the Thought Police. Trust me when I say you don't want to be anything else once the boot comes down on humanity's neck; life's gonna suck for anyone not part of the ruthless system. Think about it: Think about all the minor and apparently unimportant laws you break on a regular basis, relying on your friends, neighbors, and even complete strangers to keep your confidence. Do you park overnight in bus stops? Do you steal interesting pint glasses from bars? Do you cheat on your taxes? Scalp tickets? Purchase any kind of illegal substance? Since I know that most people are all a bunch of indolent, violent morons (naturally, when I say "you are" I don't mean *you*, I mean the rest of you, the lowing crowd of shiftless bastards) I know I am not alone in the breaking of small and apparently unimportant laws. We've all got an unwritten rap sheet. Now imagine that all the people you rely on to keep your confidence were potentially Thought Police, who would be happy to rat you out, at a moment's notice, in order to keep the spotlight off of themselves.

That's right. You'd be screwed. And guess what? You'd start ratting people out in self-defense.

That's the secret of a Thought Police, of course: There really are no Thought Police. Or, perhaps more accurately, there are only a small number of them, and while not wearing a uniform or carrying a badge they are well known to the community. Word gets to them, filtered through the population, but the foot soldiers of the Cops, the enforcers, are everybody, the entire population. Mister X witnesses you putting slugs into a washing machine. He tells Mister Y all about it. Mister Y seeks out Mister Z, who is known to be a Government Informer. Next thing you know, I'm at your doorstep, smiling, looking resplendent in my jackboots and uniform.

And why should it be me? Just like everything else I'm involved in, my main contribution is always razzle-dazzle®. I bring the razzle-dazzle® to everything I try, of course, as is well known in the publishing, pornography, and criminal justice spheres. Razzle-dazzle®, of course, is an umbrella term describing all sorts of personality and style considerations, so let me detail what, exactly, I'd bring to the position of Chief of Your Thought Police.

Impeccable Fashion Sense.

My fashion exploits are well-documented in the annals of history:

```
The Kurt Cobain druggie-look I
modeled in 1980 for my fourth-
grade school photo.

The powder-blue bell-bottomed
tuxedo at the prom.

The red and white flannel shirt
I've been wearing constantly
```
since 1990.

```
The all-black Converse Chucks I
now wear as "dress shoes".
```

In an official capacity, with a budget for uniforms, I would bring back the elegance and dramatic lines of fascist regimes throughout history, using none other than the jolly, obscene Hermann Goering as my fashion model. Sure, the Nazis of the Third Reich were reprehensible and are likely dancing jigs of horror and torment on the lake of fire as we speak, but they were snazzy dressers, and I intend to bring black leather overcoats and monocles back into style.

A Willingness to Completely Betray My Fellow Humans.

No danger of a weak-kneed bout of remorse, or any dull-witted mercy from me. I'll industriously enforce the Illuminati's laws and efficiently liquidate the remaining population as per instructions. If you doubt my complete inability to empathize with my fellow humans, please feel free to read past issues of *The Inner Swine*.

My Cult of Personality.

I already have a sizable organization of desperate losers willing to give up their lives for me and my cause—which can just as easily be *your* cause. Rather than go against me, and spend countless hours and dollars chasing me down to my bunkers and rooting me out of your new empire by sheer force, why not buy me off and absorb my organization? It's a Win Win, after all; I get to live and indulge my selfish desire to exist, and you'll get an Enforcement branch ready-made. No one loses. Except, of course, the millions of the unlucky oppressed, about which I do not care.

Well, there you have it. The funny thing about our police forces is that they are, compared to the truly oppressive organizations known throughout history, a weak and ineffective group, making those who complain of their fascism and oppression amusing, at best. As long as we continue to police ourselves, as a sort of Thought Police Lite, we're pretty safe from true oppression. People who think we're being systematically oppressed by a few instances of random if regrettable violence have no idea what true oppression is. To these whiners anything which even vaguely and distantly threatens their immense wealth of comfort and ease is oppression.

The fact is, we've got it easy, and we have it easy because we're willing to do some law enforcement ourselves, and be complicit with the cops, at least occasionally, at least when it really matters.

Thus, as our eventual conquerors can see, this will all have to be upset and rearranged if they're going to squeeze the newly enslaved human race for every drop of sweat available—there's way too much freedom-causing wiggle-room as it stands (believe me, I know). A true Thought Police will have to be installed to make sure that all these fundamentally dishonest humans are kept under the thumb—and I am eminently qualified to be Chief of the Thought Police. I welcome my new masters with open arms, and urge them to take me on—you can trust me, lads, and that's the truth.

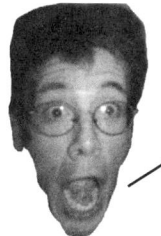

JEFF SEZ: Ever have the haunting feeling something better should have been in this space? I do quite often. This editorial was blatantly inspired by an episode of *The Simpsons*, wherein Homer is sent into space and releases some ants from their cage. The ants, floating around the space shuttle, appear grotesquely huge due to camera distortion, and Kent Brockman the new anchor assumes that huge alien ants have invaded earth. Immediately, there is a graphic of an ant alien whipping a human slave, and Kent launches into an impromptu oath of servitude to his new ant masters. Hee hee! You gotta wonder just how much of this zine is just regurgitated television shows. Conservative estimate: 65%.

Pig in Shit #17

Carl Sagan Taught Me to Manipulate Time

'Pork Avenger' Newest Superhero to Patrol City

By J. Jonah Jameson

Pork Avenger, defender of justice, eater of bacon. And lots of it, by the looks of things.

SUPERHEROES are in short supply these days, and those that remain are getting long in the tooth. Superman, that staunchest defender of justice, is now pushing 70 and has lost a step or two. Spiderman now only appears in public to endorse his line of products or on his speaking tour. The Incredible Hulk, sadly, died last year of a brain tumor resulting from years of apparent steroid abuse. And the list goes on: superheroes felled by age, advancing criminal technology, or their own reckless ways.

And there are precious few emerging to take their places. Despite an increasing instability due to a mental state that would land a less renowned (and less wealthy) man in an asylum, we still rely on Batman to fight crime and maintain order simply because there is no one else. The city would love to ask these old geezers to step down, as they are increasingly a threat to the public as much as to the criminal elite—last week Wonder Woman, in pursuit of a horde of rampaging Bog Men under the command of Die Fuhrer of Filth, killed 13 innocent bystanders when she became lightheaded and crashed her invisible plane into a shopping mall. While the wondrous lady recovered and did indeed capture the Bog Men and defeated Die Fuhrer of Filth, the damage to the shopping mall in both money and human lives was almost three times as much as the Bog Men had inflicted on the city in their six-week reign of terror. But with a police force comprised of only 12 middle-aged men who are paid mainly to do the paperwork that legalizes the superheroes' actions, the city cannot afford to retire its spandexed crimefighters. Thus, the Mayor has been stepping up efforts to recruit new aliens, mutants, and mentally unstable millionaires to take on the challenge of fighting crime in the city.

Response has not been good. The Mayor stated at a recent state dinner honoring Shazam (wheeled onto the stage by his nurse and signifying his acceptance of a gold plaque by waggling one eyebrow) that "...due to modern techniques of genetic splicing and psychiatric therapy we're not getting the level of mutants and psychopaths we had in the 'golden ages' of 1930-1960. And what with Krypton being destroyed and all, there haven't been many superhuman aliens in the past decades." The only candidates for superheroship, the Mayor went on to say, have been regular men and women "with a dream. I'm the Mayor, it's not my job to destroy someone's dreams, but dreams aren't going to defeat Dr. Lava's evil plans to construct an artificial volcano in Central Park on July 4th, submerging the city in molten lava."

Recently, however, a new figure has emerged on the crimefighting scene. Bypassing all the normal avenues of application and interview for a crimefighting position, this valiant defender of justice has simply begun fighting crime, anonymously. Wearing a pig's nose and a shimmering suit made of aluminum foil and, apparently, pipe cleaners, this new superhero calls himself "The Pork Avenger" and has caused quite a stir within City Hall and both the superhero and supervillian circles. He was called a "poseur" by Superman in one interview and a "cursed bane on my existence" by the evil Mr. Ragin' Cajun, The Pork Avenger has been a mystery and a rebel from the moment he stepped on the crimefighting stage. Until now. For, in an exclusive here at the Daily Planet, the identity of The Pork Avenger has been unearthed, and the first authorized interview with this new superhero is presented here. As you'll see, the city may be running short on mutants and aliens, but there is at least one more mentally unstable millionaire ready to take a bite out of crime.

[BEGIN TRANSCRIPT]

DP: Do you mind if we identify you, Mr. Somers?
TPA: Uh....you just kinda did. I'd like to remain anonymous. Without my pig suit, I'm just a slightly paunchy man with poor hand-eye coordination. If my enemies knew who I was, I could be targeted by criminal cabals for assassination when I was in my civvies, you see. So you could cut that part where you said my name out loud.

DP: Right, so we won't say that you're Jeff Somers, world famous millionaire publisher of *The Inner Swine* and several collected works of pornography.

TPA: I'd appreciate it.

DP: Let's get started then, Mr. Somers. When did you decide to become a superhero?

TPA: You just said my name again.

DP: Don't worry, we'll edit it all out when this prints.

TPA: Uh, okay. You sure?

DP: You're kinda wimpy for a superhero, ain't you?

TPA: I'm not wearing my pig suit.

DP: Right. So, when did you decide—

TPA: I got mugged by the Wee Willie Gang last year.

DP: The gang of midget evil geniuses that Batman put in jail a few months ago?

TPA: Yeah. It was very embarrassing, but there were, like, seven of them, and they're very strong for their size, and they overpowered me. But it was embarrassing, and I suffered a lot of mental anguish about it. I kind of went into left field for a while, walked around the mansion in my bathrobe. For a while I wouldn't let anyone shorter than me into the place. My butler had to wear huge platform shoes.

DP: So you became mentally unbalanced.

TPA: You could say that, certainly. Then one night I was inspired: Why hide from crime? I vowed never to hide again. I figured I would take the fight to them, and right then and there got my research team out of bed and set them to making a superhero suit for me. I vowed to make the streets safe for me again.

DP: How much did the suit cost?

TPA: Eleven million dollars, plus catering costs. It's worth it though.

DP: What powers does the suit give you?

TPA: Well. . ..none, actually. The money was mostly spent on developing a type of aluminum foil that wouldn't tear. The first suit was made of Reynolds Wrap and every time I bent a limb it just tore apart.

DP: Uh, so what powers *do* you have?

TPA: Oh, *powers*. Only one, but it's a doozy. You see, Carl Sagan taught me to manipulate time.

DP: Uh. . .isn't Carl Sagan dead?

TPA: Yeah. But he taught me years and years ago, only I didn't realize it until last year. Here's the story: Remember that show he hosted, *Cosmos*?

DP: Sure.

TPA: Well, there was this one episode I saw when I was about 10. In it, Carl Sagan was explaining the concept of relativity, and he did this by saying,

"Let's suppose for a moment that the speed of light is 35 miles per hour". Then he hopped on a motorbike and went 35 miles per hour, explaining that if that really was the speed of light, he'd be experiencing time dilation as he drove. Everything would seem normal to him, but the world around him would be stuck in normal time. He might go for, oh, a three-week vacation in the Alps, and come back to find that millions of years had gone by, because his sense of *three weeks* was now incredibly speeded up. In other words, it's all relative.

DP: Understanding a simplified concept of relativity isn't a *power* so much—

TPA: No, but it inspired me to wire time circuits into my pig suit. When I want, I accelerate my personal time zone to the speed of light. This means that to me, the world seems to stop still, and this lets me manipulate situations to my advantage, then return to normal time and kick ass. For example, when confronted with a gang of irreverent youths bent on relieving me of my wallet, I go into Light Speed Mode. Because they are experiencing time so much more slowly than myself, I relieve *them* of their weapons and wallets, tie their shoelaces together, and then return to normal time, victorious.

DP: Amazing! How did you develop the time circuits?

TPA: We don't know. Someone was trying to run *Duke Nukem 3D* on a Microsoft NT 4.0 machine and it crashed and a little grey smoke came out, and suddenly, there were the plans. We quickly made notes and The Pork Avenger was born! There was, I must admit, some argument about which one of us would get to be the superhero and what the name should be. Happily, I own everything and everyone is contractually obligated to me.

DP: So this is a form of time travel, then?

TPA: Sort of. If I were to go into Light Speed Mode and sit in a room for a year, and went back into real time, I'd emerge into the future, since all of you would have gone on without me, in real time. You see, *I'm* not moving any faster, really, my perception of *time* is. It's taught me a lot about time and our relationship to it, you know.

DP: Like what?

TPA: The most striking thing about people is the shocking amount of time they waste. They don't think they are, but they are—it's because so many of our priorities are fucked up, in serious ways. What we *think* is a wise way to spend our time usually isn't. It's like an epidemic of wasted time, because most of what we do is based on the ridiculous assumption that we're going to live forever.

DP: Now, that's an arrogant assumption—

TPA: Is it, goatboy? Let me ask you this: Why are you conducting this interview?

DP: Uh, it's my job.

TPA: Uh-huh. It's a waste of time. Most jobs are. You don't give a ripe fuck about me, or most of the things you do for money. You do it anyway, and at the end of the day there's a few more hours you'll never get back. Pretty unfortunate, ain't it? When you die weeks and weeks of this will flash before your eyes, endless pointless conversations with people like me. A shame.

DP: I don't—

TPA: Maybe you'd like to be my sidekick, The Squealer? I have a keen cape you'd get to wear. Of course, you'd be captured and tortured by my evil enemies about twice monthly, but there's a good health plan in it.

DP: Uh, no.

TPA: Sure, go ahead and waste your life, then. Think about it: eight hours a day, sleeping, rounding out to about a third of your life. One third! My god! Eight hours a day working, if you're lucky. Another third. All right, let's assume you eat your Nietzsche Pops every morning, sipping the hot cup of life's possibilities, and you only sleep four hours a night and you spend half your time at work doing your own thing and thinking grand thoughts. You're back down to one third of your life, a complete and utter waste.

DP: You can't *not* sleep. And most of us have to work. Can you waste time you don't have any other options for?

TPA: Good question. Sure you don't want to be the Squealer? You're sharp.

DP: Uh, once again, *no*.

TPA: Someday you'll want the snout, my friend, and it will be denied you, you know. As for your question, doesn't it all come down to elevators?

DP: Elevators? I suspect I've lost control of this interview.

TPA: Don't be silly; you never had any. Elevators: I've spent several of my minutes observing you people in elevators. You know what you do? You stand and stare straight ahead. You let the time wash over you as an unobserved wave, you waste it. From my point of view, people do this an alarming amount of time: on lines, on public transportation, everywhere. And then BAM! You're dead, and visions of elevator doors flash before your eyes.

DP: What are we supposed to do in elevators, for god's sake?

TPA: I dunno. But isn't it ironic? People everywhere running around screeching that they have no time. People say that to me all the time: *I have no time, as soon as I get the time, when things calm down a little and I have some time*—come on! Obviously we have oodles of time. We're just using it to stand in elevators, to ride buses, to watch commercials. It's not that you don't *have* time, is it—it's that you've *misplaced* time.

DP: Interesting—but what does any of this have to do with being a crime-fighting superhero?

TPA: Nothing. But it's an important lesson. If you added up all the time you've spent unwisely, you'd have enough there to work a second job, maintain a second family, write books, sculpt busts, foment revolution. It completely invalidates the statement that you *don't have time*. Why, if everyone reclaimed just five minutes of Lost Time and spent it crimefighting instead, I'd have nothing to do. If everyone reclaimed 10 minutes of Lost Time a day, pretty easy to do, we'd all have an average of one month extra time over an average lifespan. One month—think of what you could accomplish if you actually applied yourself for a month.

DP: The mind boggles.

TPA: Sarcasm, eh? The final refuge of the weak minded. All I know is, give me 30 really productive days and I could write a fucking book, build a house, bring war criminals to justice. One good month. Problem is, of course, you rarely string together 30 gangbuster days of real productivity, mostly because there's always those moments of Lost Time to contend with.

DP: So. . .what can you do, then?

TPA: The only choice you have is to at least use your Lost Time better, reclaim it as best you can. Every moment you're standing around with your thumb up your ass is a Lost Moment: Don't let it happen. Read books on the bus, on line, in waiting rooms. Bring a notepad with you and make notes, write poems, draw sketches. Plan carefully. Pay attention. *Don't* just stand and stare, sit and stare, wait and stare.

DP: Or, in your case, fight crime and defend life, liberty, and the pursuit of justice.

TPA: Um. . ..if I agreed to that it could be shown in a court of law that I endorsed that phrase, which is property and trademark of Superman's Supermania Industries, and I could be sued. That guy's lawyer spends all day writing cease and desist letters, you know. Let's just say I use my misplaced time to make the world a better place when I'm not publishing a vanity publication or soft core pornography. You know, for kids.

There you have it, Metropolis: our newest superhero, The Pork Avenger, with his shimmering aluminum foil pig suit, which grants him the ability to shift into an alternate relationship with space-time. Aside from making him extremely long-winded and negatively punctual (explaining sheepishly that when you can move at the speed of light appointments become vague and difficult to keep; "After all, to me your time is monstrously slow. I pop off to have a cigarette and when I get back, hundreds of years have gone by and you're dead. What's a guy to do?") it has given him the power to halt crime in its tracks.

He also has a powerful message about the nature of time and its lack in our lives: Stop wasting it! As he is fond of obnoxiously pointing out, most of

EDITORIALS: Pig in Shit #17

us waste lots of time everyday, often without even realizing it. Instead of letting time wash over you like an incomprehensible wave of events, pay attention and use your time wisely, or at least as wisely as you're able.

Unfortunately, The Pork Avenger faces many challenges in both his crimefighting efforts and the dissemination of his message: his shocking personal hygiene, which this reporter can unfortunately personally attest. Until this superhero learns to literally clean up his act, he might be successful in battling evil (probably by overwhelming them with his superhero halitosis) but he'll never convince people to listen to his message. Or have lunch with him.

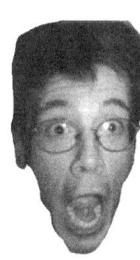

JEFF SEZ: The picture of The Pork Avenger was, er, *modeled* on Arthur from *The Tick*. That's supposed to be me in that costume, after all, so a traditional superhero with rippling muscles just wouldn't do.

Concepts of relativity are presented as I understand them, and are not meant to be necessarily reliable or accurate. Use them to build time machines and whatnot at your own risk.

Pig In Shit #19

I HAVE ENJOYED SELLING OUT AND CAN'T WAIT TO DO SO AGAIN

The Inner Swine *Sold to Microsoft, Inc.*

Somers: Very Rich but Soulless Now.

FRIENDS, I am happy to report that after months of delicate negotiations, I have sold *The Inner Swine* and its parent company, Oinking Sow, Incorporated, to Microsoft in a deal worth $17.5 billion in cash, Microsoft stock options, and fifths of Wild Turkey. I know all of you are sharing in my joy and excitement, even if none of you will ever see so much as a bent dime out of the deal.

Over the past 20 years or so, a fundamental shift has occurred in our society, culminating in our current world wherein everything has been boiled down to mere commodity, even thoughts, ideas, and sentiments. In a world where the Hallmark corporation uses our most tender emotions to sell greeting cards, where even the most idealistic people form corporations and launch their IPO almost before the office furniture has arrived, where everything is potential advertising space—well, in such a world it isn't long before even slow people like myself come to the conclusion that everything we have, from our thoughts and feelings to our bodies and abilities, are just commodities. So when Microsoft asked me if I'd be willing to sell the intellectual property that represents my thoughts, beliefs, and personal style, my only question was: How much, bubba?

The rest of it was just haggling.

While I will continue in my capacity as Editor-in-Chief, managing the day-to-day operation of the magazine, Microsoft CEO Bill Gates will be

Appeared in Volume 6, Issue 2, June 2000

stepping in as our newly created 'Content Tsar' and will guide TIS to even greater glory than its current readership of over 17 people across this grand country. As everyone knows, Mr. Gates took some of the slim resources at hand (secondhand C code, some old-money family connections, a half-completed Harvard education, and a complete lack of morals) and built the world's largest corporation. Think what he can do with my proven talent! That's right: just about anything he wants. He owns us now.

Mr. Gates' plan for the future of TIS is grand in scale and breathtaking in vision, and is outlined below. First, though, I'd like to anticipate the hate mail and personal attacks that no doubt will follow the publication of this, the final issue of TIS overseen exclusively by Your Humble Editor. Let me answer some of the obvious questions and get some of the unpleasantness out of the way. Want to?

HOW CAN YOU SELL SUCH A PERSONAL PROJECT AND WATCH IT BE TURNED INTO CORPORATE DRIVEL? It was remarkably easy once I saw the trucks pulling up to deliver the cash (I demanded it be paid in 5- and 10-dollar bills) and bottles of bourbon. But everything's a commodity, don't you see? In this instance I sold my attitude and limp-wristed writing. But every day for the past 10 years or so I've been selling my *time*, my very *existence*—so this really wasn't so bad. Sure, for the rest of my life Microsoft is going to be pumping out propaganda in my name, ruining my legacy. But I'll probably be too drunk to notice.

HOW MUCH CONTROL WILL MICROSOFT AND MR. GATES HAVE OVER THE EDITORIAL CONTENT OF TIS? Complete, 100%, as-if-I-were-a-puppet-on-a-string control, baby. I sold it all. I can't even use the TIS office bathrooms without a pass from Mr. Gates. He'll return margined notes on all my articles and will have final approval before we go to press. He'll probably ghostwrite a lot of it too. Actually, all I have to do is provide a clear, non-pornographic photo of myself for byline purposes and stay out of everyone's way. They'll just put my name on everything. Also, I have to get a Microsoft tattoo on my left arm.

IN OTHER WORDS, JUST FOR CLARITY'S SAKE, YOU JUST SOLD YOUR SOUL. Yes.

DOESN'T THAT HORRIFY YOU? Nope. I am wrapped in a warm money blanket and filled with whiskey-love. Let's face it: People sell their intimate stories and personal experiences to television on a daily basis. Slept with someone famous? They'll pay you to describe the sex on national TV. Killed a few small children for fun? There's some cash waiting for you over at some tabloid's offices. Got a terrible secret and some minor celebrity? Oprah or Rickie or someone will be willing to slither some money your way and you can share it with the horrified studio audience. I don't see much difference—at least I'm not telling you about my battle with pills or the way my old scoutmaster used to touch me. Count your blessings.

EDITORIALS: Pig in Shit #19

To put it all the best way I can, piggies, I sold the only commodity that I have left to sell, and this makes me no different from anyone else in our day and age, the Age of the New Materialism. No longer do we value objects over more important matters in order to qualify as materialistic. Now it means that we regard everything—including our inner lives—*as* objects. Welcome! Please affix a price tag to yourself before taking your seats. The bidding will begin in a few moments.

THE NEW MS-TIS®[1] : As I said, Bill Gates as our new Content Tsar has a bold plan to make TIS the cutting edge in sarcastic perzines. Bringing the same innovative spirit, which has created such computerized triumphs as that little animated paperclip, Mr. Gates and the TIS Development Team will overhaul the current TIS paradigm, building on its strongest parts and replacing the rest with pure Microsoft goodness. I had very little input on this operation, since shortly after the process began I became lost in my new 117-room mansion and could not be reached for several weeks. Hey, it wasn't funny. I almost starved to death. In the end I was rescued by some vagrants who had squatted in my garages. It *still* isn't funny.

The five-step plan that the Microsoft Development Team came up with follows in all its simple beauty. I recently had my pool drained and filled with dimes. I heartily endorse this new direction, reflecting concepts and ideas that are "outside the box". I have a car made entirely out of gold. It burns sixteen gallons of gas to go around the block. In the final analysis, I'm sure that all my readers will agree that the new MS-TIS® will be better than, funnier than, and, most importantly, more expensive than the old, crufty, DOS-based TIS, with an electronic subscription going for about $55. Also, I recently bought Iowa and am too busy printing up eviction notices to care. Here's the memo they sent me:

MS-TIS®: BETTER THAN JUST TIS!

Notes from the MS-TIS Development Team:

1. No More Paper. This is the Internet age, morons—why are you bothering with a printed magazine? Print is dead. No one under fifty reads newspapers and the coming generations are only interested in web content, and XML and VRML are gaining acceptance and will soon make HTML look like COBOL. So MS-TIS® will only be published on the web, using

---

[1] *MS-TIS is a registered trademark of Microsoft, Inc., and is protected by national and international copyrights. We will send someone to pull your eyelids off with a pair of rusty pliers if you so much as whisper it without mailing us $5 cash.*

MS Frontpage Proprietary Extensions, of course, so only people using at least Internet Explorer 6 will be able to access the pages, and then only if they let us set a cookie, and then only if they fill out three pages of forms asking for personal 'marketing information'. That's why the web is better than print: control!

2. Color! What's with this black and white shit? Ever since Ted Turner colorized the world and led us from the black and white era, some print-based delivery modules have insisted on relying on an outdated protocol. Sure, almost every pair of eyes in the world can process black and white information—but it's a new millennium, babe, and color is how professional, A-list entities express themselves. We have chosen yellow and purple as our base colors, and the entire issue of MS-TIS® will be printed purple on yellow. You're welcome.

3. Security! In order to embrace and extend MS-TIS® and make it proprietary, the entire issue will be in code. Subscribers who successfully fill out our personal info forms and configure their PCs to read our MS-TIS® web page will also have to memorize a complex algorithmic code to be able to read the text. This will keep unscrupulous thieves from stealing our content. This makes your MS-TIS® experience more secure and protects your personal information, which we will of course store as plain-text cookies on your hard drive. It's a feature, dammit.

It looks like you're not laughing at this issue's editorial. Would you like some help comprehending it, you poor dim-witted sucker? Because as you know, there are no refunds.

4. TIS Assistant! We're proud to announce the addition of the MS-TIS® Assistant, which will be an animated Ken West that will pop up from some unspecified region of hell to offer MS-TIS® readers assistance. Ken will, of course, speak no English, but will grunt and gesture angrily in an attempt to communicate to our dullard customers what they are doing wrong. After a few minutes if the problem has not been resolved, Assistant Ken will throw up his animated hands in disgust and reboot your computer without warning.

5. Constant Upgrades! We on the MS-TIS® development team were horrified when we realized that TIS had not had a major upgrade *since its inception* in 1995!! At Microsoft, Inc., we're committed to making previous versions obsolete within a minimum of three years, and MS-TIS® will be no different. We'll refer to the 2000 version of MS-TIS® as Version 2.0, and by 4.0 we expect all previous editions of TIS to be unreadable. When we brought this issue to The Editor, he said that in many peoples' opinions TIS has always been unreadable, and then laughed heartily until something bright and shiny caught his attention, but none of us knew what that meant. Of course, every time a new upgrade becomes available all subscribers will have to purchase new code algorithms and subscriptions.

You gotta like the way these stock-optioned kids think. Well, I gotta; they paid for my good opinion, after all. The final barriers between commerce and the rest of our lives has been thrown down and nowadays everything is for sale, all the time—why should I be the only one who doesn't cash in? Our private stories: material for cheap television shows with an endless need for new and more outrageous stories. Our pain and suffering: now considered consumer demographics for pharmaceutical companies that run cheerful advertisements for their drugs to an ignorant and reactionary public, duped into pressuring their doctors into prescribing drugs. Our private space: now just another advertising palette, as if seeing ads on urinal grates, buses, coffee cups, and every available flat space on the street weren't enough, now they reach you in the home and school, through television, radio, web pages, spam e-mail, junk snail mail—everywhere.

Everything's a commodity, pigs. Start selling.

Me, I recently used $117 million to wallpaper my study. Later on today I'll be paying $75 million to clone a brontosaurus just to slaughter it and have a bronto steak for lunch. And I'll be launching my new zine, *The Hidden Bastard*, with a $200 million advertising kickoff next week on NBC, CBS, ABC, and FOX, running prime-time infomercials starring various Playboy bunnies. See you there! And start selling!

Pig in Shit # 20

INNER SWINE AFTER DARK

Nouveau Riche Somers Skating Towards Early Grave

By Sherry Ann Markie

Reprinted from *US Weekly*, July 15th-29th issue.

Man drink like that and don't eat, man is going to die.

JERSEY CITY, NJ—*You might think a man well-known for his egocentrism would be an easy score for an interview, but when my editors at* US Weekly *assigned me the task of tracking down Jeff Somers, founder and Editor-in-Chief of* The Inner Swine, *six long months filled with legal battles, bizarre messages from Mr. Somers on my answering machine, and at least one frightening moment where I believe my life was directly threatened by people working on Mr. Somers' orders followed.*

It started out normally enough; I contacted Mr. Somers' legal representative, Danette Knopp, and left a message requesting an interview. I was in turn contacted by Misty Quinn and informed that Mr. Somers (whom she referred to as "The Shithead") would be more than happy to sit down with me for an interview, and that he would contact me directly with details. Then, some time passed. After a few weeks, I contacted Ms. Quinn and was met with nothing but voicemails and unreturned phone calls. After a month had gone by, my phone started ringing in the middle of the night, from an unlisted number. Whenever I answered, I was hung up on.

About two months after my initial contact, I received a postcard from Mr. Somers, postmarked Bermuda and signed "AM ENJOYING THE INTERVIEW PLEASE BEAM MORE QUESTIONS DIRECTLY INTO MY BRAIN, LOVE, JEFF". As I was standing in my living room reading this, the phone rang. It was Danette Knopp.

"Burn that," she advised grimly. "If you show it to anyone, we'll

Appeared in Volume 6, Issue 3, September 2000

drown your cats." Then she hung up on me.

The next week, two legal documents arrived from The Inner Swine corporate offices: The first was a cease-and-desist order compelling me to stop "beaming telepathic questions directly to Jeff Somers' brain", and the second was a release form in anticipation of the interview. Completely perplexed, I signed the release and couriered it back to Oinking Sow, Inc., a subsidiary of Microsoft.

That night, and every night thereafter for about three weeks, Jeff Somers called me at odd hours. He always seemed out of breath. He ignored anything I said, and merely talked, on and on, long monologues, which often made no sense. At the end of every call, Danette Knopp broke in on the line and advised me that the preceding was a private communication and I would be sued humorlessly if I repeated any of it, not to mention the horrible torture my cats would have to endure. Then, suddenly, the phone calls stopped. About five days after that, I awoke in the middle of the night to find about six men and women in skintight black catsuits standing around me in the bedroom, holding guns. They argued about killing me. One hissed that her orders had come from "The Big Pig himself" while another kept insisting that if they "whacked" a "civilian" without West's (TIS Security Chief Ken West, I assumed) written authorization, they would all find themselves taking the dirt nap.

"But The Big Pig told me personally."

"Lauren, he probably got into the Demerol again," another whispered. "He says a lot of things."

I watched in palpitating horror as they slipped out of my bedroom, silently. The next day, a courier arrived bearing a signed agreement to be interviewed, along with a list of restricted questions that I wouldn't be allowed to ask. I signed wearily and then didn't hear anything for almost another month.

In the end, I had to attend a party in order to get Mr. Somers' attention. Not just any party, but a party which, legend has it, has been going on uninterrupted for almost a year now, ever since Jeff Somers sold The Inner Swine and its corporate owner Oinking Sow, Inc. to Microsoft for a reported $17-plus billion. Jeff then purchased a tract of land on the outskirts of Jersey City and spent heavenly amounts of money to build his "Pig Manor": a huge mansion with 117 rooms and a staff of almost one hundred. Upon its completion in February 2000, Mr. Somers announced a party and invited all manner of friends, family, politicians, and celebrities. The party has gone on uninterrupted since.

The following is from my log of the day: At the gate, where the ornate iron grillwork depicts pigs cavorting around the stylized initials of Mr. Somers, I am frisked roughly and thoroughly by two hulking guards in black paramilitary uniforms. At first they insist they must

EDITORIALS: Pig in Shit #20

confiscate and destroy my tape recorder, but upon my insistence that Mr. Somers himself gave me explicit permission to bring it inside, they appeal to their boss, Ken West, via radio. A few moments later Mr. West himself arrives driving a black jeep, wearing a similar uniform. A .45 caliber semiautomatic rides on his hip and a well-chewed cigar rests comfortably in one corner of his mouth. The large black man steps out of the jeep and extends a hand to me.

"Ms. Markie," he says in a pleasant baritone, "forgive my men. They're not trained to be polite." He shakes his head as we climb into the jeep. "I gave up a good job for this shit." he sighs.

The drive to the manse takes about five minutes at top speed, which sends us flying over bumps and into the air several times. Mr. West cackles rather insanely each time the jeep crashes back to the ground. At one point he looks over at me. "Someday I won't make it back, if god's good as they say!"

At the front door, with the low throb of music from within, Mr. West wishes me luck and tears off in his jeep. I am frisked again, slightly more politely, by two women guarding the entrance, and then escorted inside, where I am met by Mr. Somers in the foyer. He is wearing pajamas and a silk smoking jacket. He's unshaven and a little wild-eyed. He is wearing what appears to be red converse chucks without socks. He strides towards me with a hand out, flushed, breathing hard, and you can feel his body heat like a wave of humidity when he's still a few feet away. I am instantly terrified. I look around, trying to locate an exit, but am engulfed in a hug before inspiration strikes me.

"Katie, so glad you could finally make it. I feel like we already know everything there is to know about each other," he whispers into my ear. I decide not to point out that my name is not Katie. He breaks away from me and takes my hand. "Come, let me show you around."

We enter the ballroom, and if I wasn't being pushed gently along by Mr. Somers' hand on my back, I would have stopped cold to gawk. It's bedlam, with a healthy dose of ancient Rome. It was the world's largest disco, filled with people, many of them celebrities. I must confess that this reporter was shocked, for a moment, at the sheer size and spectacle of this never-ending party.

"We have supplies trucked in everyday, and I've actually created a whole company to handle the waste products—you'd be amazed how much waste is generated!" Somers slurred, waving to seemingly nobody and everybody at once. He leaned in close. "Especially the celebrities. They're uniformly disgusting."

I had prepared a list of questions, of course, and pulled them out to begin my interview. Somers sat me down in a sumptuous leather chair and sat across from me, looking around carefully to see who was nearby. Only a dazed Hugh Grant, looking glassy-eyed and nauseated, shared our little space, and he certainly didn't seem likely to remember anything.

"Don't mind him. I doubt he'll make it through the evening." Somers said casually. "Please, ask your questions."

US: Is it true that this party has been going on for almost a year now?

JS: About eight months, if I recall correctly—which I may not, my last sober day having been a frightening Sunday some time ago when I got locked in the upstairs bathroom for a while.

US: It looks like half of Hollywood is here, and most of them seem to be breaking one law or another.

JS: (leaning forward) Do you know why I keep inviting the celebs? Because I hate them. They're wastes of my time and your time and skin in general. This is just the easiest way to get rid of them. I'm doing god's work.

US: Uh, God's work?

JS: Look, I'm not actually murdering anyone. I'm just letting these arrogant, self-involved, talentless little fucks commit pleasant, slow suicide. When a celebrity dies here, we then process the body into pâté and serve it to the guests remaining alive.

US: I don't understand...

JS: Okay, listen. Let's take an example. See over there by Mount Cocaine?

(Across the vast ballroom was a literal pile of white powder, about six or seven feet high. A large crowd of people was gathered around it, most mildly famous.)

US: You mean Jesse Camp? What was he, a DJ or something?

JS: A VJ on MTV, actually, by virtue of winning a contest. Completely untalented, obnoxious, and so full of himself he actually released an album. Can you believe it?? Yet somehow attention is paid to him, simply because he was on television. So, he's invited here. He's allowed to do whatever he wants, except leave. Oh, we don't exactly detain anybody. We just don't make the exits real obvious. Eventually, he'll choke on his own vomit, or OD on something, or slip and fall and crack his head open. Then my security and legal teams document the scene, and we'll all be eating Jesse Camp on crackers later!

US: That's...horrible.

JS: Not as horrible as the thought of another album from that guy. It's a public service, really. I mean, these people are not our talented celebrities. They're not the writers and directors, actors or singers with talent, who might leave behind something that makes their otherwise grotesque existences worth our attention. No, these are the idiots who are pretty much famous simply because they're famous.

US: So you...murder them?

JS: Murder? Absolutely not. These assholes are killing themselves everyday. The problem is, in the outside world no one just lets them die. Inevitably, someone calls 911 and their lives are saved. They get a lot of press because of their close calls and they publicly clean up their acts, until the next time. Or, it's covered up, and their publicists come up with insulting cover stories. Here, the only difference is, no one is going to call 911. If some asshole drinks himself into a coma, we leave him lying on the bathroom floor until the end comes. And then (whooping like an Indian) PÂTÉ CITY, BABY!

(At this point a group of lingerie models giggled their way near us and had to be gently turned away by Mr. Somers' security staff.)

JS: Models. The more of them I manage to trap in here, the better the world is.

US: Really? I find that a little surprising, coming from a male.

JS: I'll ignore the obvious insult to my gender and explain that models are the absolute lowest of the low. Here are people who are famous, well-paid, and afforded respect simply because they adhere to a certain physical standard. Getting that level of attention simply for the random arrangement of your genes is evil, plain and simple. We encourage our models to go bulimic here. We've had several starve to death already.

US: So, basically, you just want all celebrities to die.

JS: You're not paying attention. I don't have a problem with celebrity—I just believe in a celebrity of talent. If you do something special, or do something better than most people, or somehow, in some small way, improve the world—then by all means, get rich, be interviewed by Entertainment Tonight. I fully support that. But to stand around in someone else's underwear? For that you should get a quick kick in the ass and bus fare home. That instead you get rich and famous is an imbalance in the universe, and it makes me very, very angry.

US: Isn't that arrogance of the worst sort, to think you're in charge of fixing everything? Isn't it the same sort of arrogance that spurred on people like Jim Jones and the Unabomber?

JS: Hey, you're good! But the difference is, I've been given a sign by god. I was made a billionaire by Bill Gates. Neither of your examples were. Besides, if you think about it, all I'm doing is providing a venue for the self destruction that vapid celebrity breeds. These idiots are mostly morons. Pretty morons, but morons. They kill themselves by accident, you know? Suicide is one thing. It's tragic, it's bewildering, it's one of the great mysteries of our existence, the fact that someone could be so depressed that they'd stop their own consciousness. On purpose. But these assholes are barely conscious themselves. They die puking on my bathroom floors thinking, *this can't happen, I'm famous!*

US: Don't they deserve a chance to grow, to learn, to earn their notoriety?

JS: Nope.

US: *Nope?*

JS: Nope. Sorry. They have a chance everyday. They blow it, they blow it. I'm just here to grind them up into a tasty meat paste and serve them to their eager replacements. Besides, that train of thought is part of the problem. The assumption that they must have some intrinsic value just because they're famous. We don't sit around waiting for our siblings or friends to suddenly deserve fame and fortune. But just because (his eyes roam the room) Britney Spears over there is rich and famous for singing songs other people wrote, and singing them badly, we're supposed to hold our breath for the next fifty years, waiting for her to "deserve" her fame and fortune? I'm sorry, no.

US: You're going to let Britney Spears die here?

JS: Actually, she's a little brighter than expected, and persistent, too. I think sometime soon she's going to make it out of here. We, um, might have a lawsuit on our hands.

US: That would be a shame.

JS: Sure, that's okay, you don't understand the deep anger that injustice inspires in me. But that's okay. You don't have to. Thanks to our recent sale to Microsoft, I have the means and the motivation to rid this world of useless famous people, and I will.

US: And what would you say to the suggestion that perhaps you're one of these useless celebrities, now, Mr. Somers?

JS: (smiling) Well, I'd say throw your own goddamn party.

American Wedding Confidentials: I Am Disco-Hot

BETWEEN THE YEARS 1994 and 2001, I personally attended almost 20 weddings. I attended these weddings as both invited guest and in my role as Wedding Man, available gigolo-date for single female friends. Over the years, my wedding experiences have left me pudgy from thousands of appetizers, bleary from thousands of watery cocktails, and something of an expert on that peculiar and frightening American institution: the big wedding.

Always desperate for material with which to fill the yawning white space in every issue, I hit upon the idea of writing short essays about the weddings I'd been to. I can't recall how I convinced myself that anyone would want to read these essays. However I managed that, it probably involved quite a few cocktails, after which I am usually willing to believe you people will read anything.

In this section I've included every American Wedding Confidential written to date. Number seven was nominated for inclusion in The Zine Yearbook, *but did not make it in, because you're all against me.*

American Wedding Confidential #1

My Weekend With Carla

I showed up at Carla's around 2:30 PM shaved, showered, and pressed into uncomfortable shoes, which I do not wear for just anybody. I also smelled good, which anyone who knows me well will attest is not such a common occurrence. I was buffed, shined, and ready to boogie. As I stepped into Carla's apartment it became obvious that she was not: The place was littered with underwear, recently purchased shoes, and trash. Carla was in the throes of typical chick-like lateness, rushing about applying last-minute makeup, brushing her lustrous hair, and vacuuming herself into rubber underwear, all for my benefit (hubba hubba).

I tried to make myself at home, but anytime I tried to leave the living room I encountered a pile of underwear and Carla, screeching that I couldn't go in there. Eventually I found that I was only welcomed to sit in an uncomfortable chair in a shadowed area of the living room, and there I stayed.

Carla finally emerged ready to go, and I witnessed the first of many transformations for my wedding date, this one from Crazy Girl to Normal Girl. In her nice dress and with her hair combed, she appeared almost normal. We got into her chariot and drove to pick up her friend, Dorothy. Here I grew worried, as Carla seemed to have little idea where her friend lived and appeared content to just drive around in circles and hum to herself. Adding to my desperation was the fact that Carla kept one finger mashed on the 'lock' button so I could not give in to my urge to leap from the moving vehicle. We were saved by the sight of Dorothy waving at us from her front porch.

We got out and Dorothy told us to beware of snipers; apparently some local outpatient had been shooting at her trees just moments before. Carla

Appeared in Volume 3, Issue 1, May 1997

seemed interested in this story, and I began to think her friend would have a calming effect, when Carla suddenly noticed that the dress Dorothy was wearing was strikingly similar to her own, and a cat-fight broke out on the front lawn. I was able to save Dorothy only by pointing out to Carla that since the offending dress was now stained green and red with grass and blood, it no longer resembled her own. I carried the unconscious Dorothy gently to the car and we were off.

    At the wedding, Carla developed an unseemly fascination with the bald head of the man seated in front of us. This was actually a good thing, as it kept her relatively quiet throughout the ceremony, except when she loudly informed me that I would be blasted by lightning for my sins, and the several times she asked me if I was interested in any of her girlfriends, all of whom, she asserted, had "big bazooms". With the aid of several burly ushers I was able to rush her from the church before being identified.

    We arrived triumphantly at the hotel for the reception, and Carla lost little time digging into the rum supply, double-fisting it for most of the evening. Her transformation from Normal Girl to Drunk Girl was seamless, as was her almost unnoticed transformation from Drunk Girl to DANCING QUEEN. I'd had no idea I was the official non-threatening male guest of the DANCING QUEEN, but my education was quick and brutal. She danced the Twist, which is to say she danced the Twist to every song that the band played, often by herself on the dance floor with a hot spotlight following, and once with a dozen tuxedoed men clapping time and hooting.

    As the hour grew late, I was pulled aside by Wedding Officials and asked to remove her from the dance floor so the older couples could dance safely, without fear of being smacked or trampled by the rampaging DANCING QUEEN. I donned my fatigues and hustled her off to the bar, where she loudly berated the bartender for trying to give her drinks in plastic cups instead of glassware. As he hustled off to take care of this, she leaned over and breathed into my ear.

    "My rubber underwear has cut off my circulation," she said, "I think my feet are numb."

    Around one in the morning we all admitted weariness and retired to the room we had rented for the evening. Here Carla instructed me to strip and lay down in the tub, but I refused, knowing better. I wrapped myself up in a bolt of fabric in order to protect myself from Carla and from the corrosive cold of the air conditioner, which the other denizens of the room had insisted on activating. We implored Carla to change out of her dress and remove her rubber underwear, fearing permanent brain damage from the lack of circulation, but Carla became irrational at this point and seemed to feel threatened by this piece of good advice, curling up defensively on the couch and growling at anyone who came near her, accusing several of her friends of attempted sodomy. In a bizarre moment, her friends made up a taunting song, which included the words "finger" and "crack", and sang it over and over again until poor Carla wept. At this point I fell asleep, and so cannot detail Carla's undoubtedly agonizing transformation from Drunk Girl to Hungover Girl.

In the morning Carla announced several times that she felt like a "whore" but still refused to change clothes, planning instead to hang around the lobby of the hotel in the hopes of getting into another wedding reception, and at yet another rum supply. I enlisted several of her big-bosomed friends to help me force her into the car, wherein she grew grim and drove me home in silence, complaining that her underwear was up around her neck.

THE END

American Wedding Confidential #2

Going Stag in the Age of Couplehood

All I can say is, never attend a wedding as a freewheeling bachelor. Never never never. Families abhor bachelors, and the rutting-fevered atmosphere of the pagan marriage ceremony brings this sentiment out in spades. It gets ugly.

My friend, Madge, was getting married and had scheduled her wedding very inconveniently for my rent-a-date purposes; every woman who owed me a favor or who might conceivably enjoy dressing up and drinking watery drinks with me for several hours was otherwise engaged, usually with a sudden vacation to some exotic port. If I'd been a less secure individual, I might have thought all my friends were avoiding my wedding invite, but of course, that couldn't be. So, in a moment of whimsical affection for my friend Madge, I doomed myself by deciding that, what the hell, I'd go alone.

I don't know what, exactly, I imagined the wedding reception would be like. I guess I had some disco-fueled sex fantasy involving available and drunkenly wanton bridesmaids (forgetting in my f ever that Madge had no friends who could accurately be described as *drunkenly wanton*) and me ending up the evening like Sammy Davis, Jr.: on stage with the band, tie undone, microphone and cocktail in hand, calling everybody "baby" and singing Barbara Streisand's "People Who Need People" while the bride and groom slow danced. This was never, ever going to happen, not even for a second. If you believe in alternate universes, there was never even an alternate universe where that was a slight *possibility*. Frankly, I didn't take a lot of different things into consideration: a) the awesome instinct to matchmake in the modern catholic female, b) the sheer horror uncoupled bachelors inspire in the hearts of catholic matrons, and c) how uncomfortable suits make me (so binding).

Appeared in Volume 3, Issue 2, September 1997

Still, for whatever reason, I somehow convinced myself that attending Madge's union ceremony *Solamente Jeff* was a good idea. I even went out and bought a new suit for the occasion, because I was feeling lucky. Under the fascist-shopping guidance of the infamous and gorgeous Elizabeth Augoustinatos, I picked out a dignified dark-green number that artfully accentuated my beer gut and brought out the somber color of the bags under my eyes. In a shopping mood, I also went in search of an odd and unique wedding gift. I didn't want to give in to conformist tradition and buy Madge something she actually *wanted*; I'm an artist, after all, and had to find something symbolic and beautiful but patently useless.

I won't tell you what I bought, though I will say that I succeeded. While Madge will protest her undying affection for my gift because it came from *me* (and thus will likely be worth money someday), I doubt it has ever seen the light of her living room. I should also mention that my choice of gift was ungainly and large, and I packed it into an even larger box, wrapped it garishly, and brought it with me to the wedding, I suppose so I could set it on the seat next to me and not feel so lonely.

The wedding itself was normal: The groom had the glassy-eyed stare of muscle relaxants, Madge was a vision in white and guarded by security professionals so no one would have the opportunity to smudge her makeup. In the middle of the ceremony, she put the ring on the wrong finger, couldn't get it off to fix the mistake, and dissolved into giggles while the groom, completely numb from sedatives, stared at her in mute horror. I lurked in the background trying not to absorb any of the holiness going on around me. The two families could sense that I was a wolf among the flock and they steered clear, leaving empty seats around me for a two pew radius.

At the reception, I lugged my huge present around with me like the Ancient Mariner with his pet albatross until a very Italian woman took pity on me and told me where I could put it down safely. She then had me sit with her family, introducing me to her beautiful daughters with a degree of pity that instantly made me bitter and resentful. I spent a great deal of the cocktail hour smoking cigarettes, muttering to myself.

When we were all seated for the ridiculously intricate introduction and Bridal Awards Ceremony, I spent a few quality moments trying to figure out the demographics of my table. Wedding veterans will tell you: Every table tells a story, baby. There's always the Single Friends table, the Obligatory Coworkers table, and the Never-Talked-To Childhood Friends table. I was none of those, and I slowly came to realize, to my horror, that I was seated at that nightmare scenario known as the *Dateless* table.

Without warning, I'd been bitten by the despised monster and been transformed into one of *The Dateless*.

I had also been carefully placed next to Madge's colorful cousin who had a sunny personality, a bountiful bosom, and a complete lack of attraction either to or for yours truly. I'm not saying that Madge was trying to match us up, but I am saying that she figured she'd seat us together and see what happened. I was learning that nature abhors a bachelor and the wise women of our tribes will always try and find you the sort of happiness they have found, the sort of happiness which results in a 113% divorce rate in this country. The sunny and bountiful cousin, however, also had something akin to Attention Deficit Disorder, and she dashed around the reception like a lemur spooked from the brush, which was doing nothing to attract me.

Defeated, I left the reception at the appropriate time. The bride and groom were liquored up and weary and had no energy to pity me as I exited alone, determined to never attend another wedding dateless. Or to wear that suit ever again.

THE END

American Wedding Confidential #3

It's A Family Affair

The hardest part about attending my cousin's wedding was finding a suitable fake name for her so I could eventually write about the event. Being from your prototypical Irish-Catholic family, I have several thousand cousins, not to mention hundreds other less-defined relations, plus the weird hangers-on who aren't even related to me but who are always at these family functions. Finding a name that no other member of my clan was currently using, so as to avoid the usual libel threats my family throws at me on a daily basis, was the most difficult and research-intensive task I've had to perform recently. After months of deep thought and careful searching through the bars and taverns of the tri-state area (the best source of Irish-Catholic wisdom in the country) I've come up with a winner: I'll call my cousin Smilla. I do happen to have a three-month-old, second-cousin Smilla, but she's too young to have been the subject of this essay, so it's okay.

I asked my gorgeous friend Elizabeth to be my date at this event, which was partly due to the deep and abiding friendship we have developed over the years and partly due to the fact that Elizabeth can cause car wrecks when wearing certain dresses. Attending family weddings is like going to a high school reunion for me: It's a bunch of people I haven't seen in a while who are dying to dig into the steaming pile of gossip I represent. Naturally, you want to make a big impression in these situations, and Elizabeth also kept everyone's eyes off me and my sadly neglected physique. Little did I know that the evening would be a slow, tortuous dance of humiliations.

Elizabeth drove us to the chapel-cum-reception hall somewhere in the uncharted wilderness of New Jersey's strip mall hell, and we arrived in time to glad hand a few aunts and uncles (some of whom attempted to glad-hand Elizabeth, causing a few early shouting matches) and take our seats to watch the ceremony. Smilla was marrying a Jewish man who looked vaguely Italian and so the ceremony was a mix of Catholic and Jewish. Having been to a few weddings, I can tell you now that both sides of that coin are equally boring. Elizabeth slipped a stiletto heel off of her graceful foot to jab me in the side every time my snoring threatened to become an embarrassment.

When the wedding huddle broke up, we had some time to wander the halls during the cocktail hour while they readied the reception hall. We found ourselves trapped, along with my mother and brother, with the craziest of my crazy uncles, who relaxed in a plush chair with a scotch on the rocks telling us about Jesus, who apparently speaks to him on an almost constant basis. Every time my Crazy Uncle's eyes fell on me, I was afraid he was going to denounce me as a witch. At the first break in my Crazy Uncle's nearly seamless soliloquy I grabbed Elizabeth and demanded that we go outside for a cigarette. My brother, no fool, tagged along despite the fact that cigarettes make him turn green.

HUMILIATION #1: Freed from insane relatives, the three of us prowled the corridors curiously and were having such an enjoyable conversation that we were late getting to the reception hall. The wedding party was gathered at the doors, ready to make their big entrance, and Smilla spied the three of us waiting politely to sneak in after them. My cousin insisted we sneak in before the wedding party, and we burst into the room amidst cheers and music meant for the bride and groom. I stopped to grin and wave like a superstar, until Elizabeth manhandled me to a nearby table, which, I must admit, I kind of enjoyed.

HUMILIATION #2: The table we'd found ourselves sitting at wasn't the table we were supposed to be sitting at, but rather one of the kids' tables. It was Elizabeth, me, and several 10-year-olds who were rather belligerent towards us. Often I had to use violence to defend myself. The fact that several of my aunts and uncles no longer speak to me can be directly traced to my actions, words, and attitudes at this table.

HUMILIATION #3: After the pandemonium had settled down a little, I went to the bar for a much-needed stiff drink, whereupon I was promptly carded. At my own cousin's wedding. I have always been cursed with a cherubic and innocent face, which is why I get away with copping free drinks and cheap feels from my friends on a constant basis, but this was too much. I took our drinks, grabbed Elizabeth, and once again demanded we go out for a cigarette.

When we returned from prowling the halls once again, my family in general had boozed itself into a frenzy, with fights, romances, and general silliness breaking out all around us in record numbers. The groom, well-oiled with liquor through the evening, was hoisted up on a chair along with his bride and a handkerchief for what appeared to be some sort of traditional religious nonsense, and promptly fell off the chair. They hoisted him up again, and he promptly fell off again, killing several people. One of my uncles is a cop, though, so it was all made right in the end.

Finally, Elizabeth's friendship had been strained enough, and we made our way through the EMS workers, police, and wounded to say good night to the bride and groom. The bride eyed us with the traditional Catholic-matron marriage eye and thanked me for coming, the groom thought my name was Steve and seemed to be still standing only because he was too drunk to fall down.

In the car, with the wind screaming past us and Elizabeth's perfume in the car, I pondered the horror of the family wedding and decided that it was definitely better to be a rent-a-date than the relation. As a rent-a-date I can get really drunk and make a pig of myself at both the buffet and the bridesmaids' receiving line, and my mother never has to hear about it.

THE END

American Wedding Confidential #4

 It's My Scene, Man, and It Freaks Me Out!

The best types of weddings to get invited to, the uninhibited bachelor soon realizes, are the ones wherein you're no longer very close with the person or persons inviting you. Obviously some remnant of affection or intimacy or whatever remains to get you invited in the first place, but if his first response to the invitation is surprise, the enterprising bachelor knows he's onto something big.

When my friend Deidre invited me to her wedding, it was perfect. I was not close enough to be intimately involved with the plans, had met the groom only once (and that in a crowded smoky place he would never remember me from) and knew only a limited number of her other close friends. The reason this was exciting was simple: Weddings are filled with drunken, relaxed women in tight, revealing, but uncomfortable clothes who have been whipped into a mating frenzy by the sheer romance and primal procreative mood of the ceremony. After a few too many glasses of white wine and just the right number of love songs, any man with no perceivable limps or skin diseases starts to look attractive, as long as he seems vaguely like marriage material.

"Marriage Material" is a tricky term that means, basically, that there is no reason the poor slob couldn't be goaded into exchanging vows should a relationship blossom and the idea of living with him and bearing his children not bring images of prescription drugs dancing into the poor gal's head. Not all men fall into this category, for a variety of reasons: the aforementioned limps and skin diseases, an existing marriage, baleful personality, halitosis, and an alarmingly long list of character defects that range from a wandering

Appeared in Volume 4, Issue 1, March 1998

dick to an inability to stand up to her father. The exact prerequisites of "Marriage Material" vary from girl to girl, and are difficult to pin down, but every lean and hungry bachelor knows that he has to look it to have any chance of being the real Best Man of the reception.

There are two ways to acquire this mysterious veneer.

The first is to do whatever is necessary to appear honestly distressed at your single status, to achieve a delicate balance of machismo and sensitivity, to try and project the sort of manly sadness stemming from your loneliness that will set women's hearts a-pounding and knees a-buckling and make you look like the third-rate Heath Ledger sensitive hunk you know you could be.

The other, more attractive to lazy bachelors, is simply to show up with a good trophy date and not tell anyone she's your platonic friend or your best friend's sister or your cousin Ruth. Because the one true law of "Marriage Material" is that if some other woman is willing to appear in public as your girlfriend, you must be it.

I asked my gorgeous friend and confidant Misty S. Quinn to be my Trophy Date for this one, for a variety of reasons: She can drink like a sailor, she's a good choice of people to talk to for hours and hours, and she's good-looking enough to blind when the mood takes her to wear skintight black evening dresses. Also, since Misty regards my own libido as an amusing if unimportant detail of my existence, there was no chance of me losing sight of my real objectives and getting distracted. She was perfect for Trophy Date status.

I was ready. With the lovely Ms. Quinn on my arm and my own dashing lack of any discernible deformities, I knew I had "Marriage Material" stamped on my forehead.

And then, we got lost.

And I mean *lost*. We got lost on the way to the ceremony, although not too badly, and managed to sneak in with only a deafening amount of squeaking hinges and muffled giggles. Then we got lost on the way to the reception, in a big way. Well, in all honesty I should say that *I* got lost. Misty just sort of sat in the front seat staring out the window in a saintly display of tolerance. But then, Misty's known me for years now and if she hasn't come to terms with my general incompetence she never will.

Being lost in New Jersey, however, means never being too far away from a major highway, and we did make it to the last half of the cocktail hour after being on the road for almost four hours. We were starving, and all the food had been gnawed down to the bones by the other guests, who resembled army-ants or piranhas in their greasy-lipped frenzy. I settled for a stiff cocktail and some sushi, while Misty trembled and wept because all the good foods had been devoured. I held her gently in my arms as she cried, forlorn at the lost *hors d'oeuvres*.

At the actual reception, we were both so burned from the ride down that it took many glasses of liquor before we felt relaxed enough to enjoy ourselves, and by then I suppose I had lost my appetite for meaningless romantic entanglements with booze-flushed floozies in the coatroom. Besides, my pickings were slim: The women at our table (the official "old friends we don't know what to do with" table) were vague little sorority moppets more interested in discussing the details of every wedding they'd ever seen, heard of, or imagined in their narrow lives, and none of the other women were drinking enough. So I settled in, talked to Misty, snuck out with her to watch Game 4 of the World Series on the hotel lounge TV, and eventually got shit-faced enough to dance.

And there my careful veneer of Marriage Material vanished, like ice on a July afternoon.

Dancing is not a male activity. Men who dance well are not men (although men who avoid dancing are cowards), so most of us flail about with an unseemly awkward motion, endangering our friends and dates and ruining our cool exteriors. In self-defense, most sensible men have adopted a sedate white-man's overbite type of dancing that is neither exciting nor embarrassing, it is simply dull. Not me. In my self-defense, I get as goofy as I can, dancing as if I were in a Bill Murray movie. I make my dancing into a big joke. This is fine if you're dancing in front of good friends who already don't respect you, but in front of strangers. . .sometimes it is a mistake.

It didn't matter, really; we had a good time, made it up to our room after several hours of dancing, and had sweated all the alcohol out of my body. Luckily, I was too tired to be humiliated and hit the sheets immediately upon entering the room; Misty unfortunately changed into frumpy sweatpants and a T-shirt. The next day I happily drank coffee, clogged the tub drain, and ate a complimentary breakfast of greasy sausages and buttery eggs. . .

. . .and promptly got lost on the way home. Misty, tired of all this bullshit, finally took charge and directed me home. As I dropped her off I considered the whole night to have been a rousing success, even if I had wasted a great Trophy Date opportunity. Oh well, one thing I know in this crazy life: There is always another wedding waiting for me.

THE END

American Wedding Confidential #5

My Evening With The Lunatic

AND THEN THE RAINS CAME: Whenever I get the chance, I celebrate the various benefits and joys of being a wasted bachelor at a wedding, especially if you're just the rent-a-date for the evening, bearding some lesbian or doing a favor for a between-boyfriends lady pal. Singing happy paeans to buffets, open bars, and easy chicks in tight formal wear, I may have forgotten to explore an equally important facet of the swinging gigolo's wedding experience: the dark side.

Oh, it's there. I didn't think so myself until a few years ago. Behind the free booze, between the drunkenly wanton bridesmaids, hidden by the blinding light of the camera capturing the *Locomotion* forever, eternally, winks the grinning leer of **The Darkness**, waiting for some sucker in a bad suit like me to innocently wander in. I started my long, slow walk into **The Darkness** when Insane Coworker #23 invited me to her friend's wedding one day. This was about five minutes after she'd told me she liked me a whole lot and I'd blithely given her the memorized and oft-used (believe it or not) "we're better off being friends, but I will always be there for you" speech. Usually when I give that speech I mean it, and I meant it at that moment; even though I am running the other way as fast as I can whenever someone wants to date me, I usually do want to be friends.

I hadn't yet realized that Insane Coworker #23 was, well, *insane*.

Perhaps the timing of her invite should have been a clue. After someone cries a little and tells you how shitty their lives are and then hints that maybe you could be a ray of light in that mess, and after you've replied with the aforementioned "I'd rather eat cat feces than date you, but I will always be there for you as a platonic friend who refuses to give you his home phone number" speech, who in their right mind could then refuse an earnest

Appeared in Volume 4, Issue 2, June 1998

invitation to a wedding? Maybe the sort of bastards I wish I were more like could manage it, but I am far too afraid of my own evil to do it. So I gave in to the manipulative bullshit and said, yes, of course I would go to the wedding with her.

And there's **The Darkness**, pigs: When you start showing up at weddings willy-nilly, eating and drinking and flirting with abandon, inevitably you're going to get nailed. People know you like to go to weddings. They know you encourage the practice of inviting you. So when someone like Insane Coworker #23 slithers up and invites you, you have no excuses. You're Wedding Man. As the months went by between her ambush and the wedding, I realized with slow, dawning horror two simple facts: Insane Coworker #23 was not putting her feelings for me behind her as quickly as I would have wished her to, and *this wedding was already the longest night of my life and it hadn't even started yet.*

The day of the wedding dawned gray and stormy: A Noreaster had floated into town and the world was a quick fox-trot from a tropical storm. I was driving. Driving being an optimistic term for what was really 93% floating. I set out bravely, asking my mom to take care of my stuff and leaving behind sealed envelopes for all of my friends to open in the event of my death, or mental breakdown. I went and got #23, who wore something that probably would have been irresistible on a woman I had some vague interest in. I was already counting the hours; she had just begun the seduction.

The wedding itself was a miracle of perseverance. As the soaked and unamused guests arrived at the drafty and cavernous church, an angry-mob atmosphere started to form like a cloud around us. I sat with #23 as quietly as I could, feeling the pulse of **The Darkness** all around us. She chattered cheerfully about how great weddings were and how beautiful her friend was. I chewed my nails and once again spent an unsatisfying few minutes trying to figure out what, exactly, was attractive about me.

Between the ceremony and the reception we had what amounted to 30,000 years of free time, and I pondered worriedly what #23 and I would do to pass the time. She got us invited back to the bride's grandparent's house, which sounded good until we got there and realized that we were the only people invited. I quickly accepted a stiff drink and locked myself in the bathroom with it for a few moments, contemplating either crawling out the window or drowning myself in the toilet. In the end I had the guts to do neither, so I emerged and sat down next to #23. She sat close to me, letting me smell her, which is a favorite trick of girls that I usually don't mind at all.

But this time all I could smell was: **The Darkness**.

The reception was fairly big and energetic and I began drinking immediately. So did #23, which I tried to subtly discourage. After two hours, however, #23 was fairly blitzed and dragged me onto the dance floor for some dirty dancing, grinding against me with what she imagined was seductive fervor. Hell, maybe it was. I couldn't tell with all that Darkness ringing in my ears. I danced my Bill Murray dances with the wide-eyed look of deer in headlights and brain surgery malpractice plaintiffs, feeling her smear **The Darkness** all over me with every disco beat.

At one point the band mercifully played "I Will Survive" and I was able to convince #23 that it wasn't appropriate for me to dance with her to that one. She found her friend the bride and I spent a few soul-muting moments sitting at our table with the other men, smoking a cigarette and wondering how it had all come down to this. The other men didn't give a shit.

When we finally escaped the reception, we found the entire Eastern Seaboard submerged under water. I drove grimly into the flood. I spent a grueling two hours driving her home, balked at several moments by immense lakes of water where there had once been roads. The citizens were out looting and burning civilization down and I could see the Nazgûl circling overhead waiting for the car to give out and strand me as **The Darkness** summoned its minions and prepared for its triumph. I would not be stopped. Against all reason, all hope, all rationality, I kept driving, often in reverse for several minutes at a time, until I sat idling outside her apartment, hands white-knuckled on the wheel, panting.

#23 still thought the night had gone well and, more disturbingly, thought the night was young. She chatted for a few minutes about a good time this and a fun night that, and then invited me up. I had looked down the hairy maw of **The Darkness**, however, and such simple horrors no longer held any pain for me. I still had my good-guy fetish, however, and told her sincerely that I had to get up early, I was tired—girls, you've heard it all before, albeit usually after the sex. She seemed to accept this and said good night, but as I leaned over to give her a parting peck on the cheek, I could see her positioning herself, giving me ample view of her neckline, ample opportunity to let my aim drift a bit and perhaps reconsider the soft sound of her stockings rubbing together, the rain, the perfume in my car.

Around me, I heard **The Darkness** laughing.

Hastily, I pecked her on the cheek, reached around her seductively, unlatched the door, and pushed it open, grinning madly as she stumbled out with the table centerpiece and a look of shock on her face. I waved, slammed the door, and sped off, leaving #23 and **The Darkness** standing there in the rain.

THE END

American Wedding Confidential #6
Touch Me I'm Sick

Weddings are ridiculous affairs. Putting aside the obvious hilarity of two people in this day and age claiming to not only know themselves but also a completely different person well enough to make a reasonable lifetime commitment, there's also the issue of the sheer gluttonous spectacle of it all. The wedding business is huge, weddings are incredibly expensive...and why? So you can invite a bunch of mean-spirited relatives, greedy ravenous friends you haven't spoken to in a few years, and all of their anonymous and bottomless girlfriends, boyfriends, domestic partners, wives, husbands, and who knows what else, and then stuff them senseless? I don't mind getting filled to the brim with watered liquor, rubber chicken and stuffed mushrooms three or four times a year, but ask me if it's necessary.

And you can't blame us, the lowing stampeding herd of guests you've invited. The human race isn't very complex: Put a feed in front of us and most of us are like Boggies, we eat until we're swallowed by an unexpected cloud of unconsciousness and rushed to the hospital. You resent the fact that you spend $20,000 just so I can draw a face on my beer gut and dance shirtless on a table while eating clams and chugging champagne (all the while being cheered on by everyone except my sobbing, red-faced date)? Then *stop inviting me.*

Ahem.

Earlier this year I was once again asked to pull out the old forest green suit and cut a rug at a wedding, this time being a rent-a-date for my friend Laura, who lives in South Carolina now and whom I don't see nearly often enough, mostly due to my failure to travel south. A childhood friend of hers was getting hitched over in Staten Island and, as is often the case with our lost generation, she needed a date. After exhausting her other options, she settled for me.

I'm well known in the wedding business now, and upon learning that I was to attend, the reception hall hired three extra security people and restocked the bar. Such is my power.

Laura warned me that there was going to be no expense spared at this soirée, so I broke down and invested in a haircut a week before the festivities, to show my good faith. Of course, this was one of Italo the Barber's (who has been cutting my hair since I was four with a maintenance of style and skill you've got to respect) $9 specials, which is to say: invariably a disaster. So I showed up at Laura's house shined up like a new penny, except for my hair, which seemed to be prepared for a different experience altogether (possibly a rectal exam, possibly a murder attempt—who knows what my hair was thinking?).

Laura didn't notice, however, as she was recovering from a bout of stomach virus so disastrous she'd been on IV fluids just the day before, which is to say she was still too busy vomiting to notice whether I looked good or not. I suggested that perhaps she was too ill to attend, but as she delicately locked herself into the bathroom she waved me off and insisted that everything was fine. I shrugged and went outside to spread plastic drop cloths over my car's upholstery, just in case.

The wedding revived Laura somewhat, what with the brisk fresh air and the spirited drive over (I think my driving is spirited because so many people are moved to pray whilst in the car with me) and she greeted old friends enthusiastically, and finally took notice of my disastrous haircut. She politely ignored it, and me, for the rest of the ceremony, which was pretty long and dull as weddings go, and involved an odd spot wherein the bride and groom wandered off somewhere else entirely and left us all standing there in silence, wondering what the hell was going on. I imagine the couple got quite a hoot out of that, the bastards.

The reception, however, was Laura's undoing, as you might expect: It's hard to be at a well-catered reception and not eat until you pass out, and Laura continued to help herself to treats despite the mounting evidence that she shouldn't. I was driving, and so only had one drink, which actually does nothing to improve my surly and combative nature. Upon our arrival we discovered that a nefarious couple had taken two seats at our table, meaning that we wouldn't be able to sit with Laura's brother and sister and their respective dates, with whom we had forged a strong bond over stiff drinks and appetizers during the cocktail hour. We wanted the couple to go sit at their own table, but nobody wanted a scene. We men stood around with our hands in our pockets, unsure of what to do, while Laura stalked off and caused a scene anyway. The offending couple were sentenced to a less prominent table and glared at me all night. They could tell I was an instigator, and blamed me. In truth, we men sort of avoided looking at the other couple and hoped to god a fight didn't break out—I didn't need the memory of Laura standing over me, defending my honor, while I bled and whined. I have enough of those sorts of memories.

I'm a lover, not a fighter.

The reception was pretty typical, and except for an hallucinogenic moment in the middle when the band played hard-rock versions of "Play that Funky Music" and "Devil Went Down to Georgia" back to back (20 minutes of my life I'd certainly like to have back) the only thing which marked the evening was the fact that Laura's brother's girlfriend kept disappearing for long stretches of time. She would just wander off and leave the poor guy sitting at the table alone, staring into space. In-between daring her stomach virus to attack, Laura and I noticed the girlfriend talking to various men during the evening, and I wondered if tragedy was rearing its ugly head. The thought brought joy to my heart, and I gladly prepared for drama and angst. Little did I know the only drama and angst I was going to get was courtesy of Laura's wayward gastrointestinal system.

At one point, Laura and I snuck out to have a cadged cigarette or two, standing by the bathrooms in the lobby and gossiping about her brother. It was nice; I don't see Laura much, and it occurred to me that maybe the ultimate purpose of weddings in my life is simply to get together with people I don't normally see. Standing in the lobby with Laura, this seemed likely, and I wondered, privately, if I would ever figure out a way to make money off of my skills as a rent-a-date. I didn't mention this to Laura, knowing how easily I am misinterpreted these days.

By the time the Venetian room was opened up, I could smell disaster in the air but Laura couldn't resist, and an hour later we were leaving, a slightly green Laura bravely staying awake for the whole ride to make sure I didn't wander in the wrong direction entirely, which I almost managed despite her efforts. Driving for me, especially when I'm wearing tight, uncomfortable shoes, is a very Zen experience. I just sort of pick a car and follow it, and hope it knows where it's going. This works better than you might imagine. As I dropped Laura off at home and sped away, I thought that if nothing else I learned that sometimes you just have to lay off the seafood.

THE END

American Wedding Confidential #7

Will The Real Best Man Please Stand Up?

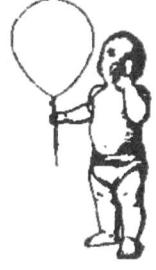

IN WHICH I LEARN THE EXPLOSIVE FORCE OF LOVE: About a year ago this Thursday my old friend Emil got married and asked me to be his best man. Emil's a good friend of *The Inner Swine* Inner Circle (TISIC) in general, and there was some resentment, jealousy, and harsh words concerning my elevation to Best Man status. There were also isolated incidents of violence. Eventually, Emil managed to cool tempers and remind the rest of TISIC that they were, above all else, contractually obligated to me in perpetuity. After that impassioned speech, the members of TISIC retreated to their various abodes to scan the fine print of their contracts, only to return in remarkably more manageable moods.

The Best Man has a lot of duties in the modern wedding. Whereas in the good old days he was merely a responsible member of the groom's clan who vouched for the groom's sanity, financial solvency, and lack of venereal diseases, these days the Best Man has lots to do: organize a bachelor party (I'm told it was a humdinger; personally I don't remember much after that fifth body shot off of Lola the stripper's washboard stomach), deliver the viciously hungover groom to the actual wedding the next day (Emil still had his emergency room ID bracelet on), manage not to vomit during the ceremony, and then, finally, and most importantly, make a speech at the reception.

The Best Man's speech is supposed to accomplish a few minor but cherished conventions: It's supposed to compliment the groom, his choice of bride, and form a verbal bridge between the carefree days of the groom's

Appeared in Volume 4, Issue 4, December 1998

prior friendships and the more complex but equally rewarding years of mature friendship to come. In other words, the Best Man's job is to reassure the groom's buddies that they will indeed see him from time to time despite the nag he's chaining himself to, and to reassure the groom that his buddies will always be there to say mean things about his wife in private if he needs them to.

I worked very hard on my speech in the ambulance, riding with Emil to the ER after the bachelor party had taken a dramatic turn. The transcript that follows is taken from the wedding video, and more accurately reflects what was actually said than the scrawled speech written on cocktail napkins in the ambulance. I think I accomplished the goals of the Best Man's speech admirably:

Ladies and Gentlemen, friends and family, I've known Emil for sixteen years. When we met back in prison we didn't like each other very much; he always wanted to pitch and I never let him. Being cell mates gave us time to get to know each other and by the time our parole hearing came up I was proud to stand next to him, hold his hand, and testify that we had each found Jesus and would dedicate our lives to upholding the laws of the land if we were released.

In short, I've known Emil long and well. And in many ways, most of which I don't wish to discuss here.

Over the years Emil and I have gone through a great many things and we've always supported each other: When my dog Skippy died, Emil was there to help me through it, tenderly digging a grave for poor Skippy and getting me drunk later that night before we traced the plate number of the car that hit Skippy and set it on fire, in revenge.

When I became addicted to Internet porn a few years ago, alienating my friends and family, losing my job and at one point getting busted for public lewdness in The @ Café in New York City, Emil was the one who came to my apartment one July evening, knocked me cold, and kidnapped me. Emil kept me in a damp, dark basement for six months, de-programming me. To this day whenever I see a computer keyboard I shake and vomit helplessly. While this has caused me difficulty and unpopularity at work, it saved me: If not for Emil and the vicious torture he put me through in that basement, I would be in some asylum somewhere, trying to log onto the Internet from a pay phone.

Emil has always been there for me, and I am pleased to be here for him today, the day he marries Petra.

In the four and a half days I've had the pleasure of knowing Petra, I've realized that Emil's prior life was but an empty and meaningless melange of sex, drugs, and progressive jazz music. In less than a week, she has become not only a dear friend of mine, but a dear friend of all the members of The Inner Swine *Inner Circle,* The Inner Swine *being the magazine I publish, which I really think you all ought to read and* purchase subscriptions to, because you see that large black guy in the back standing with several dozen men in fatigues? That's Ken West and he's going to be waiting for you after the reception, and all I can say is that he's much nicer to people who have subscriptions than to anyone else, and I can also say that I have less and less influence over him everyday.

What? All right, all right, Emil, Jesus, calm the fuck down, okay?

Anyway, as I was saying, Petra has not only redeemed Emil from his obvious descent into damnation and syphilitic degeneration, but she has entered and improved the lives of all of us. She's a rare and delicate flower of womanhood, she's a compassionate and beautiful creature whose. . .energy and. . .emotion. . .and. . .and. . .ladies and gentlemen, I love her. Petra, I love you.

I cannot stand here and pretend that everything is okay, while I am dying inside! Petra, I've been dying inside all these past few days! Ever since Tuesday night I've been tortured by my love for you, while you marry this troll, this monster, this syphilitic mistake masquerading as a man! Oh, the stories I could tell you! Emil, the whoremonger! Emil the petty thief! The man he killed in Mexico! The drugs he dealt to little kids while on work release! The kiddie porn! Oh, Petra, you're making a mistake!

Ladies and gentlemen, keep that madman away from me! Excuse me. . .pardon me. . .Ken! Help! Ladies and gentlemen, I beseech you! Petra! Petra!

(At this point the audio becomes garbled as many voices intrude and the action on-screen gets a little hectic. Occasionally you can hear me shouting "Not the face!", but I don't think technically that's part of the speech. At this point I felt the explosive power of love, and it certainly beat the shit out of me.)

I often wonder what became of Emil and Petra. I suspect he still communicates with other members of TISIC, but none of the bastards will admit it, and the court order prevents me from finding out for myself. If anyone has heard of Emil and Petra's whereabouts, please contact me. There's money in it for you.

THE END

American Wedding Confidential #8

Gabba Gabba Hey: "One of Us!"

It's always vaguely troubling when one of my intimates decides to chuck the glories and wonders of single life and get hitched. Not only is there a subtle hint that single life isn't as glorious and wonderful as I'd like to believe, but there is also the strong possibility that the wedding ceremony will be closely followed by children, Tupperware parties, and stony silence when I next call them at 3 AM drunkenly demanding that they come out and get pancakes with me. In short, when a member of *The Inner Swine* Inner Circle announces plans to get married, I smile, congratulate them, excuse myself, and spend an hour in the bathroom weeping and beating my head against the wall, crying "Why!? WHY?!" Don't get me wrong; I'm not anti-relationship. I'm anti-marriage. I could go on and on about why I think it's an outdated convention, but I'll spare you, gentle reader. Just accept it as part of the TIS canon and let's move on, shall we?

So, when Cassie Moore, TIS Publisher and dues-paying member of TISIC for the past six years announced she was getting married, I spent my hour in the bathroom moaning and then did the only sensible thing one can do: I went out and bought a new suit to wear to the wedding, because the number one rule of being **Jeff Somers, Superstar,** is that you must always look incredible. My whole reputation is based on looking **disco-hot** all the time, you know. Of course, I did not go out and purchase this suit by myself. You don't get to look **disco-hot** when you're cursed with my fashion sense; you have to get chicks to shop for you. Luckily, women in general are always happy to shop for men—it's genetically programmed into them, you see—and TIS Legal Counsel Danette Knopp was more than happy to shop specifically for me. We went to the mall, and I don't remember anything in-between parking the car and waking up in the trunk along with several bags

Appeared in Volume 6, Issue 4, December 2000

from Macy's about three hours later. Danette's ways are mysterious ways, but she had procured for me the specified **disco-hot** suit, so all was well.

The wedding itself was being held in Staten Island, which is a vague place filled with fear and foreboding, or it was all of us who were filled with fear and foreboding and Staten Island is just a borough of New York. In any event, the intrepid members of TISIC had rented a pair of rooms so we'd have someplace to pass out later, and the bride and groom had thoughtfully rented a bus to take guests from the hotel to the church to the reception and back to the hotel, saving countless lives. We carefully sized up the pros and cons of starting the alcohol consumption right there at the hotel, but eventually decided (after some harsh words and implied violence) that Satan was already working through us far too easily, and being sober in church was the least we owed Cassie, who had already made several verbal threats concerning our behavior at her wedding.

The ceremony is lost to the mists of time, of course; my instinctual defense mechanisms cause me to pass out cold the moment I enter any type of holy ground. Misty Quinn and Danette propped me gently against one of the confessionals, or so I'm told, keeping me well out of harm's way, except for a minor speaking-in-tongues incident and one attempted exorcism, prevented by Security Chief Ken West, apparently by using a handy crucifix as a club and shouting "The Power of Christ Compels You!"

I came to on the bus as we arrived at the reception hall; mysteriously, I already had a beer in one hand and someone had removed my undergarments. We descended on the cocktail hour like a well-oiled machine, spreading out to cover all the wet bars and commandeering a large table in the back, where I sat with the ubiquitous Tim Reynolds and critiqued the fashion sense of our fellow invitees, who were not at all **disco-hot**. Two drinks later and we were called into the dining room, where we descended upon the place like the aforementioned well-oiled machine, spreading out to cover the wet bars. Buckets of beer bottles were procured, shots were ordered up, and by the time the reception ended several transformations had taken place:

1. **Karen Accavallo had relinquished her title as "Dancing Queen"**. Some years ago I attended a wedding as Karen's 'date', which inspired the original American Wedding Confidential[1]. In that watershed TIS article, I dubbed her the **Dancing Queen** because, after several rum-and-cokes served up in large plastic cups, Karen twisted the night away, often regardless of my presence on the dance floor with her. This evening, however, the lovely and formidable Danette Knopp took the title away from Karen after she took me to the dance floor several times, often using brutal force. Fearing for my safety, I danced as I have never danced before. Oh, the horror.

2. **TISIC had changed from "The Odd-Looking Strangers at**

---

[1]*Karen was named "Carla" in the article to protect her dignity. Now she has none left, so it's okay to use her name.*

Table Six" to "Cassie's Frightening Friends Who Set That Mutha Off". Indeed, despite Cassie's desperate attempts to distance herself from us all evening, by the time we were forcibly removed from the reception hall (Jeof Vita having been pried away from the beer taps in an embarrassing episode of weeping and begging) everyone in the place knew who we were and rightly feared us, mostly due to the many times Misty Quinn grabbed the microphone from the DJ to introduce us and sing torch songs in a low, smoky voice. By the time the priest took off his collar and began whipping one of the Best Men mercilessly with it[1], we were all at the point where that didn't bother us at all.

3. **Several Gallons of Alcohol Had Become Several Terrific Hangovers.** From Jeof Vita's first screams of "The Sun! It Burns Us!" to the last-minute search of the hotel for a missing Ken West (found sobbing softly in a linen closet on the fifth floor, an empty bottle of schnapps clutched to his chest), the morning-after was not a pretty sight at all.

And so TISIC gathered to send one of its own off into the frightening world of adult relationships. Cassie may not ever speak to us again, but that's okay. We've got dirt on her to last a lifetime.

Congrats to Cassie and Mex Carey, who got married in spite of my best advice.

THE END

---

[1] This actually happened. I swear.

American Wedding Confidential #9

Return of The Gigolo

THE IRRESISTIBLE PULL OF COCKTAIL HOURS: Despite domestic happiness in Hoboken, Your Humble Editor has not retired his Wedding Man status, and when old friend Carla (a.k.a. Karen Accavallo, from the original American Wedding Confidential) asked me to be her date-for-hire at a friend's wedding, I was ecstatic to break out one of my two suits and cut a rug or two with her.

"Uh," she said carefully, "just so you know, it's not going to be a normal wedding."

"What the hell does that mean?" I asked, picturing circus performers and possibly animal sacrifice.

"Well, my friend doesn't want any of the usual bullshit. No hokey-pokey, no chicken dance, no garters and bouquets."

"Oh," I said, disappointed. "No circus performers?"

Having secured my enthusiastic participation, Carla began the delicate process of negotiating for my services with Legal Counsel Danette Knopp. After an undisclosed sum of cash changed hands, Danette's permission was granted and I took my suit to the cleaners to have several mysterious stains removed. I then began my rigorous pre-wedding training program, which involves drinking fluids until the pale-yellow color fades from my skin, the dark bags under my eyes retreat, and the constant shaking ceases. By the time the date arrived I was looking fairly normal, as long as you define "normal" as "aged way beyond his years".

Carla arrived and collected me from Danette, and we drove approximately six hours to the church, which was located in what can only be described as the hinterlands of New Jersey, the land of cows and asphalt.

Appeared in Volume 7, Issue 2, June 2001

On the way, Carla instructed me in the rules and regulations of my wedding attendance:

"Rule the first: You will not speak to anyone unless I invite you to. For example: *Jeff, tell her about your recent bout of scabies.* Unless I preface a statement with the words "Jeff, tell him/her," you will assume that silence is preferable."

"Uh -"

"Silence! Rule the second: If anyone assumes that we are a couple of any sort, you will disabuse them of that notion immediately, you frotcher."

"How can I do that without speak -"

"Silence! Rule the third: Your pants must remain on at all times."

"Aw, that's just mean."

"Silence! Finally, rule the fourth: You cannot write about this in your lame publication."

I nodded solemnly. "I wouldn't dream of it." And made a note on my hand in black ink: *mention rules in piece on wedding.*

The wedding itself was a sadly typical Catholic ceremony, filled with endless chanting and prayers, and, of course, a full two minutes of "Ave Maria". The minister launched into a hippie-ish little speech about midway through, talking some rubbish about how life was a song and god was the bassline, and we all bring our own melodies into it. I swear if you'd simply inserted the word "man!" after each sentence, you would have had a stoner's monologue, a typical college-evening conversation, instead of a priestly homily:

"The Universe is like a piece of wonderful music, man! And god is like the bassline, man! And these two wonderful people bring their own melodies to it, man!"

After this spirited outburst I dozed quietly until the wedding was over, was prodded awake in time to join the line and shake hands with the perplexed bridal party, none of whom had any clear idea of who I was. Carla hustled me back into the car and we drove approximately four feet to the reception hall, where, thank goodness, booze was waiting.

By this time, word had circulated that news of my retirement from rent-a-date events had been greatly exaggerated, and the whole reception hall began buzzing with whispers. The liquor was removed to a secure location and all booze orders had to be conveyed via radio. I acquired a permanent shadow, a waiter assigned to follow me around and prevent, I assumed, property damage. He seemed a little afraid of me. I called him Rico. His name was something else, but I called him Rico.

Carla and I were seated at your usual Motley Crew table of loose ends, people whom no one knew exactly what to do with. Carla made the introductions and we managed some painfully awkward conversation for a while, until I managed to worm my way into the lager supply and began ignoring everyone rudely. It shortly became apparent that I was more of a non-entity to Carla than usual, as she was obsessed with the bride's brother,

American Wedding Confidential #9

a gorgeous young man who rendered Carla simultaneously speechless and unable to look away.

"Why don't you just go over there and say hello?" I suggested.

"Oh, no." She sputtered, tracking his movement across the room. "I couldn't do that." Her eyes flicked to me briefly. "By the way, I told everyone we were married."

I took this in stride. The reception was proving to be a sedate affair: no dancing (although a belligerently middle-aged couple went through a series of forbidden dances in spite of this Amish attitude) and none of the typical wedding embarrassments. As a result, Carla was not able to continue her traditional wedding behavior of double-fisting rum and cokes and dancing the Twist to every song. This was fine, because she replaced that behavior with grim, silent stalking of the bride's brother.

Dinner was tasty, although one of our tablemates ate two portions of the fish before thinking to inquire about its crabmeat content, then promptly swelled to twice his size and turned a bright shade of red. The rest of us crowded away from him. Carla suddenly grabbed me fiercely.

"Go move him." she hissed. "He's blocking my view of my future husband."

"I wouldn't touch me," the crab-beast advised from puffy lips. "There may be some scaling."

We crowded closer together. At this point we were saved by the arrival of the wedding cake, each individual slice wrapped in wax paper, the words THANK YOU FOR COMING NOW GET OUT written on it. We were all strongly urged to just leave and not make a fuss. Carla and I made our way to her car wearily.

THE END?

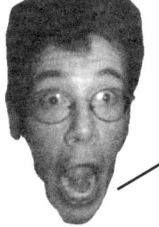

JEFF SEZ: I still enjoy attending other people's weddings, as it is the only time I get to practice painting an amusing face on my stomach and dancing around shirtless with a giant top-hat on the upper portion of my abdomen. It's always seemed to me that life can be boiled down to weddings and funerals: ceremonies in which we essentially commemorate the beginnings and endings of life, respectively. You're always either gearing up to attend a wedding or a funeral, if you think about it.

If I live long enough, and if I continue to have nothing better to do than publish this magazine, I'm sure eventually there will be a series of Funeral Confidentials as well.

Freaks and Forums: I Am Here to Educate and Make the World a Better Place

THE FREAKS ARE WINNING. How do I know? Because I am a freak-magnet. I can't walk in public without attracting every weirdo and oddity the cosmos has lovingly gifted the earth with. Their numbers are legion, and one day they're going to realize that there are more of them than there are of us, and we'll be lost.

All kidding aside, I spend a great deal of my daily life abjectly fleeing Freaks. Flight is the only viable option, you know, because if you let them start talking, all is lost.

*In the following section, I impart my anti-freak wisdom, explaining how to **identify** and **deal with** all manner of Freaks. Plus, there are some forums, where I attempt to plumb the depths of life's great mysteries. Or something. Ignore this advice at your own peril.*

Lonely and I'm Cold

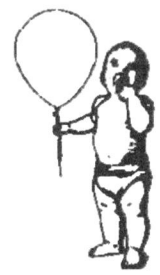

Your Gentle Editor's Hang-ups

Fans, I know I spend an awful lot of time in this zine (the key word there being 'awful') pissing about the "freaks" I meet. I'm obviously a very intolerant bastard with a lot of issues. I'm generally an unfriendly backstabbing pain in the ass, that's clear, but my tirades against the Freaks inspire some people to mutter about throwing the first stones and pots calling other people freaks and stuff like that. *The Inner Swine* is all about openness and honesty, as long as that openness and honesty is a) carefully vetted by Legal Counsel Danette Knopp before being released to the general public and b) easily refuted in a court of law.

With that in mind, I'd like to waste a few pages in my arrogant little personal publication to clear the air concerning my prejudice against the Freaks. Certainly, if you take that sort of thinking too far, *everyone* becomes a freak, and before long you've got Freak Death Camps set up processing anyone I don't like into Soylent Green. No one wants this! At least no one wants this badly enough to put in the kind of work and effort (not to mention expense) that this sort of societal change would require, you dig? Besides, I am fully aware that under such an intolerant and violent system, I would be a prime example of freakdom, and probably would end up burned to ash in one of my own ovens.

So, let's let my Freak Flag Fly for a little bit, shall we? Just to prove that while I hate almost everyone and fear daily contact with the balance of the human race, I certainly don't think I'm any better than the rest of you. Smarter, definitely, better-looking in tastefully flared bellbottom velvet trousers, almost certainly, but *better*? No. To show my good faith, I'm devoting these couple of pages to a discussion of:

Appeared in Volume 5, Issue 3, September 1999

Your Editor's Personal Hang-Ups

HANG-UP #1: *WAITERS AND WAITRESSES MAKE ME NERVOUS.* Anyone who's been conned into buying me dinner has witnessed my pathetic display of discomfort whenever the waiter/waitress approaches the table. I get ultra-fawningly polite. I wring my hands. I tense up and start to sweat. It has ruined more than one otherwise pleasant evening. Why is this? I'm not sure. Certainly I cannot recall any bad experiences with homicidal and drugged-up waitresses when I was a youngster, and as far as I know no one has ever spat in my food out of spite (note: *as far as I know*; if anyone has information to the contrary please contact me immediately). I think it might have to do with the fact that we Somers' are simple folk, and the idea of having someone serve us is pretty weird. Deep down, I kind of feel like I should take my table's order, serve the food, and bus the table. I mean, what am I, some sort of *royalty*, that I need a servant? I buy my clothes at Bradlees, for Christ's sake.

HANG-UP #2: *I CANNOT EAT AT RESTAURANTS OR ATTEND MOVIES BY MYSELF.* Once, during a fit of suicidal depression some years ago (brought on by an overdose of roach poison) I went to see *Thelma and Louise* in the theater by myself. This was the first and last time this has ever happened, and it was only because I was already sucking the pipe in the back of my mind. Now that I've regained my mental health, I can't possibly do it. These two activities are so ingrained in my mind as *social* activities the idea of doing them alone is the same as admitting I'm an irritating loser who has no friends. Which is what I think everyone else in the restaurant or theater is saying about me when they run into each other in the lobby or the bathroom: "*Hey, didja see that guy by himself out there?*" "*Yeah, he must be that irritating friendless loser I keep hearing about, Jeff Somers. Writes that stupid zine,* The Inner Banana *or something.*"

HANG-UP #3: *I WILL ENDURE ANY WEATHER CONDITIONS OR OTHER DEPRIVATIONS TO AVOID PUBLIC TRANSPORTATION.* The New York City Subway System scares the living shit out of me, and I have walked miles in blizzard conditions to avoid having to figure out the trains. I would rather walk my legs down to bloody stumps than get lost in Queens, which is what I am sure would happen if I chanced the subway. I could take the #7 bus in Jersey City and end up lost in Queens. Trust me.

Freaks and Forums: Lonely and I'm Cold

HANG-UP #4: *THE MOMENT SOME WOMAN SHOWS MORE THAN NOMINAL INTEREST IN ME, I EXPERIENCE A DETAILED AND LENGTHY HALLUCINATION INVOLVING OUR MESSY AND VIOLENT DIVORCE PROCEEDINGS DURING WHICH I AM CHARGED WITH CONTEMPT OF COURT SEVERAL TIMES FOR SCREECHING "YOU BOWLEGGED BITCH YOU'VE RUINED MY LIFE I'LL KILL YOU!" AND DIVING AT HER, RESTRAINED BY COURT OFFICERS AND MY ATTORNEYS WHO ALL SUSTAIN PAINFUL BRUISES IN THE PROCESS, AND THE COURT OFFICERS BEAT THE SHIT OUT OF ME LATER ON IN THE HOLDING CELLS IN REVENGE, AND BECAUSE THE BOWLEGGED BITCH PAID THEM EACH $25.* Uh, I'm sorry, I blacked out there for a moment. . .that definitely sums up my inclination to remain single. Sure, marriage is a sham of ancient pagan superstition and just obviously doesn't work, but the honest reason your gentle Editor here remains single despite his obvious charms is pure, blinding, feral *fear*.

HANG-UP #5: *I SUFFER FROM "THE GEORGE COSTANZA EVERYONE MUST LIKE ME" SYNDROME".* In brief, while I feel smugly justified in hating everyone and loathing humanity in general, I demand that I be regarded with respect and affection by everyone. This means that I am, generally speaking, a yellow-bellied wanker who will smile and make polite conversation to your face and then shudder and write terrible things about you in this zine that I will then never show you. HAHAHAHAHAHAHAHA!

HANG-UP #6: *I REFUSE TO ENGAGE IN CONVERSATION IN PUBLIC RESTROOMS.* Well, I don't *refuse*, because of the aforementioned Hang-Up #5, but I dread it and avoid it whenever possible. I'd rather drink urine than speak to people while we're taking a piss. Men who speak to me in bathrooms are instantly disliked and avoided by me in the future. I can't help it. Something inside me just feels like it's within centimeters of having sex with this guy: we're partially undressed, in a private area, touching ourselves. I'd rather avoid anything, like speaking, which potentially leads to *intimacy*.

There are, of course, hundreds more. I won't even mention the fact that I am terrified of clowns; I mean, who isn't? But there's so much more. However, I think this sampling covers the basics and demonstrates my point, which is that I'm a deeply fucked-up individual who leads a sad lonely life inside his little box, and that I deserve all the pity sex I can get.

My Friends are Cranky, Mean-Spirited Bastards

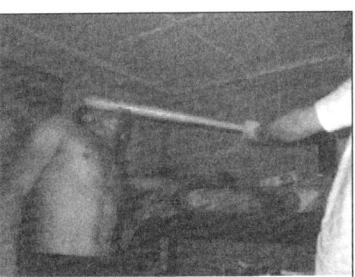

This is how we here at The Inner Swine *get along: We beat the shit out of each other with baseball bats, and the last man or woman standing chooses what bar we go to.*

I used to write articles for my company's newsletter, back before my company merged with 17 other publishing houses to form Whothefuckareyou, Inc., with 7,000 employees and more money than they can keep track of (we're constantly finding big garbage bags of cash in back rooms, bathroom stalls, and empty offices). When we were a small company and everyone knew everyone it was fun to do the newsletter thing. As the company grew it got less fun as the acceptable level of goofiness plummeted in reverse proportion to the expected level of "professionalism", and by the end of it I was exclusively writing those dumb "meet your fellow employee" pieces that corporate newsletters include in order to pretend that the company cares about its employees. I would meet with the person for about half an hour, ask them about their lives and their role in the company, and write 700 words about them for the newsletter. Not inspiring, but it took very little time and energy, so I didn't mind.

One of the last ones I wrote focussed on a lady who had worked at the company for about 40 years. Whothefuckareyou had just bought her company and they thought it would be nice to focus on one of the new members of "the family" in the newsletter, so off I went. This woman—let's call her Larry—had a slightly skewed concept of the nature of these articles, however; when I arrived she seemed to be under the impression that this was going to be a human interest documentary or something. She had brought in photo albums, articles, clippings, notes—the whole shebang. Three hours she kept me there, filling me in on the dull details of her life. I had about 700 words worth of Larry within five minutes. By the end of that excruciating morning I could have written a book about Larry, had I cared to. I didn't. My mild apathy towards her had grown into full-fledged dislike, and it underscored what I think is wrong with 99% of the people in this world: the immense arrogance masquerading as friendliness. These are the most evil Freaks in the world, of whom Larry may have been Queen. Combined with the more populous species of Freak we'll call *Random-Best-Friend Generators (RBFG)*, they make up about 90% of the population, and I not only want nothing to do with them, I actively flee them.

Let me state for the record: I don't trust friendly people. My friends are cranky, mean-spirited bastards, and that's why I love 'em.

Groucho Marx once said that he didn't want to join any club that would have him as a member. I say, I don't want to be friends with anyone who wants to *be* my friend. When I meet someone, the less excited they seem to be about getting to know me, the more attracted to them I am. Is this some dark psychological scar that prevents me from seeking happiness? Nope, it is intelligence, our great burden here at *The Inner Swine*. Our huge and unwieldy brains force us to recognize that people who love people are the stupidest fucks in the world.

I expect normal, healthy people to satisfy two important criteria before I slap the terms *normal* and *healthy* on their dossiers: 1. They have enough going on in their lives (interests, projects, events, etc.) that they don't have any time or energy left over for random relationship-forging with strangers on mass transit or in malls or whatever, and 2. They have enough friends and associates that forcing someone into *simple human contact* is not exactly a priority for them. If you start a conversation with me out of nowhere, I assume you are missing one or both of these important attributes, and therefore I begin inching away from you because I *do* satisfy these requirements—you are, in other words, a RBFG. After all, if you're so pathetic/sad/strange/violent/disease-ridden that you can't maintain a relationship and thus must troll the streets of the city looking for polite suckers you can trick into conversation, explain to me why I should be happy to speak with you?

There is, of course, simple politeness. A stranger stopping me to ask where Varick Street is and then thanking me for my help, maybe making a humorous comment or two or complimenting me on my obvious fashion sense is okay. It *makes sense*. Turning to me on the PATH train platform and saying, "Hi, my name is Marvin and I like ferrets, do you like ferrets?" is not. And never will be.

People who act as if they are already overburdened with amazing people and couldn't possibly make time for one more acquaintance, however, are obviously people with something going on in their lives. If you happen to *by chance* enter into a situation where you meet them and converse a little, well, you might both grudgingly admit you enjoyed each other's company and then over a period of time, through a process of cautious advances and numerous retreats, become friends. This is the normal mode, to my mind. With all the insane people in this world you have to take the process of "getting to know" someone slowly and carefully. This is one of the most intimate and potentially dangerous things you as a human being can do; you're opening yourself up to someone else's inspection and learning things about someone that few others know. This is not something that is supposed to be done easily, quickly, or with anyone who just comes along.

Christ, if you don't *screen*, why should I feel so fucking special having been chosen? In other words, if you're talking to any stranger on the fucking PATH train platform, why in the world am I supposed to be thrilled that you chose me?

On the other hand, my friends and loved ones are so bitter, so mean, so outwardly hostile to anyone or anything that tries to breach their protective shells, I get a warm feeling in my toes when I think about the fact that these miserable shits embrace me—because they embrace so few. I'm fucking *special*, dammit.

So, I wrote a touchy-feely article about Larry. I somehow squeezed three hours of numbing lecture into 700 words of trite corporate-suck writing. I often wonder if she was offended or disappointed that we had not published a special edition of the company newsletter dedicated to her amazing life. Larry is not a RBFG; she is a personable person who obviously had a lot going on, had friends and family, and yet still qualifies on my "too-friendly" scale: Larry was actively recruiting friends—not to fill some awesome loneliness stemming from her freakishness but to fill us with her wonderful personality. To people like Larry, the evil shadows of the other weirdos, we are all just vessels to fill with their anecdotes, wisdom, and experiences.

As a result, it is impossible for these people to actually perceive you as a person. You exist only to be filled with their wonderfulness. Why would anyone who wasn't one of the aforementioned desperate-for-contact freaks want this sort of vampire in their lives? I left Larry that day with the grim understanding that I had been in the presence of a soul-sucking terror, and had survived just barely. When I see her around the office now, I usually try to inconspicuously run away. And I feel no shame.

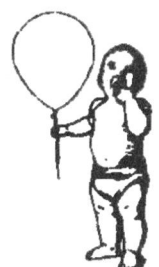 LIKE MA BELL, I GOT THE ILL COMMUNICATION

The Weirdness of Communication Today

There are a lot of strange people out there, folks, and I know a disproportionate number of them. *Weird* is, of course, a diffuse term difficult to really define; it means different things to different people, and we all tend to define it based on our own backgrounds and needs. Fairness and evenhandedness has never been one of *The Inner Swine*'s priorities, however; we tend to concentrate on *Revenge Against Our Enemies* and *Shitloads of Money*. Freed from smallminded concerns about objectivity and justice, we're glad to define *weird* for you: just about everyone we talk to on a regular basis.

These freaks we otherwise call our friends and neighbors fall into one of two weirdness categories: **Phone Freaks** or **E-Mail Cretins**. During some period in their childhoods these people must have been locked in basements or closets for long periods of time, because their grasp of the conventions and demands of a civilized society is tenuous at best. I don't understand why such a primal and instinctive urge as *communication* gets so confused and convoluted.

PHONE FREAKS A-GO-GO

The most common offenses occur on the phone, which is still the primary device of communication in my backwater social circle. Most people understand the concept of conversing on the phone, but some of my associates, I am convinced, only recently encountered the device. Among the offenders are:

Appeared in Volume 4, Issue 4, December 1998

WORK TALKERS. These are the people who only call you while they are at work. How far out of their general train of thought you have to be to be relegated to this mental ghetto I'm not sure, but it ain't far from spiritual Siberia. The implication in a consistent and on-purpose work-talking cycle is that you do not rank high enough on their list to justify making you a part of their private life, but you are not yet unimportant enough for them to ignore completely. Many people regard work as the time and place during which they must perform a load of unwanted tasks anyway, and they might as well call you while they're at it. Not to mention the plethora of easy excuses when the conversation drags on too long. A call now and again from someone while they are at work is no reason to panic. Three or four in a row and you should re-evaluate your relationship.

MACHINE TALKERS. These are the people who ludicrously phone you at home and leave messages on your answering machine during times when the entire universe, including complete strangers halfway across the world, know you are not home. Machine Talkers do not want to even speak to you, you are so low a priority with them. They either merely need to impart information to you or have not yet crossed the line of not returning your calls; in other words, they are cowards. In fairness, some Machine Talkers are not trying to scrape you from the shoe of their social life, but rather actually *prefer* speaking to your machine. These people aren't cowards, they're just *strange*.

NON-MESSAGE LEAVERS. The phone rings at 11:15 PM on a Wednesday night. You figure it could be any number of good friends, or it could be that girl you said you'd call three days ago, tracking you down. So, you decide to screen calls. The phone rings again. Twice more. And then—nothing. The machine doesn't pick up, the phone stops ringing, *the bastard hung up on you*. You get up and pad slowly towards the phone, wondering if it will start ringing again. You stare at it, pick it up, and verify that there's a dial tone. Then you dial *69 and find out it was your good friend. They just didn't leave a message. Why? No one will ever know. Even the Non-Message Leavers have no idea why they don't leave messages. They just turn purple and sputter when you ask them.

CAR PHONERS. One of the lower castes of the Hellbound, the Car Phoners are a close relative of the Work Talkers. These are the people who consistently call you from their car or cell phone. The conversations are generally brief and confusing: a mix of garbled phrases, fade outs, tunnels, and the distractions of high-speed traffic. A typical conversation with a Car Phoner goes something like this:

YOU: Hello?
CAR PHONER: Hi! It's <garbled>y!
YOU: Mary? Is that you?
CP: Yes! I'm <garbled> on the <garbled>.

YOU: What?
CP: Listen! I've been <garbled> you, I need a <garbled> favor!
YOU: Favor? Sure. What?
CP: <garbled>
YOU: What?
CP: <garbled>fuck you, asshole!
YOU: WHAT?
CP: Not you! There was this <garbled> who tried to <garbled> in my <garbled> so I stuck my <garbled> up his <garbled>!
YOU: Oh. . .what can I do for you?
CP: I need you to <garbled> when they <garbled> Wait, a tunnel's <garbled>
YOU: Hello? Hello?
CP: <disconnect><dial tone>

Why do they do this? Like the Work Talkers, they give the impression that the only time they can bother with your onerous friendship is when they can do nothing else anyway. There is also the possibility that they feel safer knowing someone will know the instant they get smacked by a truck.

NO TIME NOWERS. This amazing sect of Ayn Rand achievers are the ones who never have any time to talk to you or anyone. No matter when you choose to phone them, they will bark "I have no time now!" and hang up on you. These people clearly suffer from an immense ego and inflated sense of self-importance; I have never once been so busy that I couldn't spend five minutes talking with someone. Most days I am sitting by the phone using my Obi-Wan powers to make it ring, for god's sake. Maybe if you're trapped in a burning elevator with your hand clamped over someone's spurting carotid artery, maybe *then* you don't have time. Otherwise, I think it is one of the main tenets of civilization that you at least ask "How are you?" before moving into Talk To You Later Mode. Once in a while, I can see it—but every time? The key word in "I have no time to talk to you now" is **YOU**. It implies there are plenty of people they have time for, you're just not one of them.

E-MAIL CRETINS ON THE HALF SHELL

Then there are those who like to communicate via the faux-letter device of e-mail, the invention of which will either save or doom us. The things that infuriate me about e-mail are not the same things that infuriate the two-decade veteran of e-mail; people who were e-mailing back in the day yearn for the apparently utopian society that existed on the Usenet back then, and have all sorts of complex rules of politeness and etiquette, which have been ignored by the unwashed masses on AOL. Nuts to them, I say. They're also the bastards who invented the smiley face :) so they deserve it all.

EXCLUSIVE SPAMMERS. The biggest freaks in the world of e-mail, my fine readers, are those who never actually send you a personal note at all, but who communicate with you via jokes, spams, bitmaps, and chain letters. They don't send you a note saying "Hey Jeff, how are you? Gotten rid of that infection yet?". They send you Lewinsky limericks, blonde jokes, cookie recipes, and other such chaff. The really creepy part is, they don't even bother with a "Hey, thought you'd like this" tag that would at least let you know they consciously mailed it to you, that you weren't buried in the middle of some 105-name grouping they can't even remember the members of anymore. It's just the joke/spam by itself, hollow and abandoned, as if an auto-mailer had you on a list. I get chills.

COMPULSIVE CC'ERS. These friendly folks believe in free speech and work overtime to make it even more free than it already is. Every scrap of correspondence they generate is carbon copied to everyone they know. If you respond to a joke, they cc their reply to you. If you ask them a question, it comes back with 55 names attached to the **TO** line. You start getting e-mails about subjects you've never heard of, people you've never met, social events you weren't invited to. You start getting cc'd replies to e-mails *you* didn't even get yet, causing mass confusion. Why do these people do it? There are only two possible explanations: a) They believe so fiercely in full exposure and free speech that they open up their every communication to scrutiny to prove they have nothing to hide; or b) They do not quite comprehend the mechanism of e-mail and don't even realize what they're doing, nor could they disable it if they did.

KAREN ACCAVALLO. Ah, dear, sweetly mad Karen warrants her own section in this article for the affliction that only she generates: One Word E-mails. While some people can be refreshingly brief in their mail, sending a simple "Good morning!" or "Thanks!", Karen takes this minimalist urge one step further and often sends me one syllable words which are not, upon closer inspection, actually words at all. E-mails that read BLAG or YURNF are not uncommon. Sometimes these e-mails are uninvited arrivals, shocking me out of my otherwise enjoyable day, sometimes they are actually in response to a question or invitation. I am not sure, but I strongly suspect that Karen believes these words have meaning, since she is always surprised when I complain. I think that when Karen writes BLAG she thinks she is writing "Why yes, I'd love to consume a beer with you this evening in some appropriately public place; it must be public as I fear you will grope me if I don't have witnesses to protect me."

Oh well. I am not guiltless in this department, after all; I am an Answering Machine Obsessor and annoy everyone I know by making 12-minute mini-arias as outgoing messages, and I check my answering machine about 17 times an evening, on average. But, as the saying goes, this is my zine and you can start your own if you want to complain about me.

It takes different strokes to move the world, after all, and *The Inner Swine* is all about tolerance. . .at least until we can get ourselves a better class of friend.

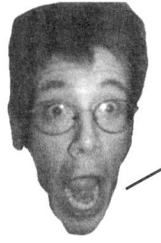

JEFF SEZ: I'm pretty famous for my obsession with telephone messages and e-mails. There was a time when I could not be out with friends without checking my messages at home three or four times a night. Nowadays I know that no one ever calls me, so I don't bother. But I do check my email about 300 times a day, stabbing spastically at the keyboard like one of them there cocaine-addicted monkeys.

It Takes a Nation of Freaks to Hold Me Back

If I told you that the piece of technology you or anyone needs most in today's beguilingly complex world was the *Freak-O-Meter 2000*, you would probably tell me to: A) get more sleep, B) quit writing this endless stream of annoying articles no one reads anyway, or, in Mom's case, tell me to C) quit spending all my Sunday mornings drinking and start going to church to apologize. It's true, however: we are all in need of functioning *Freak-O-Meters* hardwired into our heads. What, you ask before passing out from complete disinterest, is a *Freak-O-Meter*? These amazing examples of organic technology allow us to quickly scan every individual we meet in life and determine to our own satisfaction whether or not that person is a Freak. My Webster's New World Dictionary defines **freak** as follows:

> **freak** (frek) n. **1.** An odd notion; whim **2.** An unusual happening **3.** Any abnormal animal, person, or plant **4.** [Slang] a) a drug user b) a devotee [a rock **freak**] adj. queer; abnormal freak (out) [Slang] **1.** To experience extreme reactions as from a psychedelic drug **2.** To become a hippie –freakish adj.

The last definition caused me to flip to the copyright page of my dictionary and, sure enough, the damned thing was published in 1972. Here's *The Inner Swine* definition of **freak**:

> **freak** (frek) n. **1.** Anyone who intrudes on your existence without invitation, purpose, or consideration, under the delusion that their sad

Appeared in Volume 5, Issue 1, March 1999

lives are interesting to you or that they deserve attention and interest simply because they take the time, trouble, and mental energy to breathe; **2.** Everyone else in the universe except maybe three or four people, and I'm not so sure about them.

It's funny how everyone in the universe believes they are beset by freaks. Obviously this cannot be true, since if everyone was beset by freaks there would, logically, be no freaks to beset us. Using the exciting new technology of the *Freak-O-Meter*, I have personally identified 2,567 freaks active in my everyday life, so I know some of these people are either lying or extremely deluded. My *Freak-O-Meter* goes off so often I have a constant buzzing in my head, much like a soft chorus of voices.

Everyone has that instinct that makes you note some aspect of a person, compare it with your own experience and sensibility, and conclude with a wrinkled nose and an intolerant snort that the person is a freak, an abnormal animal, person, or plant (see definition above). But sometimes we distrust our instincts in this modern world, so we need to rely on technology to guide us. That's right, the *Freak-O-Meter*, once installed in your head, tells you whether the people you meet are abnormal animals, humans, or plants. It's difficult to determine this without the use of your *Freak-O-Meter*. I often do not realize that people I've been conversing/flirting/living with are abnormal plants until my *Freak-O-Meter* starts that buzzing in my head. I pause, cock my head, and listen to the buzzing, and it's usually whispering *freakfreakfreakfreakfreakfreak*.

Using this exciting new technology, *The Inner Swine* has been able to study, classify, and catalogue the main species of freaks in the world, so that people without access to the *Freak-O-Meter* can examine the people in their lives and determine which ones are freaks and which are normal folk, like me[1]. If you cannot afford a *Freak-O-Meter 2000* on your own, I strongly suggest that you use this guide in your everyday interaction, so you can tell the freaks from the merely annoying.

TYPE OF FREAK: *Dressed-in-Black-and-Waiting-to-Die Artiste.*
IDENTIFYING TRAITS: Pale skin, wardrobe exclusively black, combat boots, disorganized notebooks filled with suicide notes in poem form, walkman playing endless songs by The Cure, complete lack of enthusiasm for any activity due to belief that life is one big existential joke on them, because secretly they think they're the center of the universe.
HOW TO DISCOURAGE: When introduced, smile broadly and ask them if they saw "FRIENDS" last week. They'll never speak to you again.

---

[1] *Karen Accavallo counts me as a freak, due to my "boyish demeanor, girlish laugh, lack of social skills, inability to appreciate me as the goddess I clearly am, and bad taste in clothes." Karen's opinion is hers and does not represent* The Inner Swine *Inner Circle—or at least not very much of it.*

TYPE OF FREAK: *Creepily Friendly Cheerleader-Type.*
IDENTIFYING TRAITS: Bubbly, chatty, always looking to converse, feigns interest easily, capable of discussing anything, even the most bone-chillingly boring subjects, such as their cat's love life, their collection of unusually shaped toenail clippings, or their opinions on just about anything.
HOW TO DISCOURAGE: Try physical violence; it's usually the only way.

TYPE OF FREAK: *The Lovers of Inappropriate Intimacy.*
IDENTIFYING TRAITS: The shuddering need to share every unnecessary intimate detail of their lives with whomever they meet, such as their sad love lives, their precarious health, or their faulty finances, usually encouraging any residual sympathetic urges left in the listener.
HOW TO DISCOURAGE: Insulting them outright sometimes works, but can cause larger problems. Your only solution? *The Telecommunications Shield*: Arrange to have a friend phone you whenever these freaks are seen speaking to you, so you can excuse yourself, and then gossip about them.

TYPE OF FREAK: *Religious True-Believer.*
IDENTIFYING TRAITS: The calm certainty that everyone but them will burn in Hell, on-purpose ignorance of many subjects smacking of **evil**, eagerness to bring up god, faith, and religion at inappropriate and unwelcome times, argumentative and sanctimonious.
HOW TO DISCOURAGE: This isn't as simple as you might think. Devil worship only attracts them and causes their discussion to attain sermon-levels, and overt verbal abuse simply convinces them that they are martyrs to their cause. It's best to resort to physical violence. No one can argue with a busted lip, not even Jesus.

TYPE OF FREAK: *Inveterate Complainer.*
IDENTIFYING TRAITS: Entrenched pessimism, rare ability to breed unhappiness where there was none, inability to see any bright sides or silver linings, compulsion to take their complaints to whatever poor soul is nearby and spend hours detailing the excruciating and pathetic misery of their lives despite having a good job, nice apartment, running car, and plenty of vacation time. Can often be found at 9 PM as the only morons still at work, because they are convinced their jobs are more difficult, demanding, and suffocating than anyone else's. But at least we're at the bar by that point.
HOW TO DISCOURAGE: It is important to never get involved in a bitch contest with these people: *You cannot convince them that you are more miserable than they are.* Nothing trumps them. If you say your mother died this morning, they will tell you the story of *their* mother's death, and trust me, you will lose. Your only choice is complete apathy towards their problems. This will seem cruel to them and you will be marked down as a complete asshole for the chill wind coming off you, but it will save you hours

of hearing how much their life stinks.

TYPE OF FREAK: *Zine Editor.*
IDENTIFYING TRAITS: Immense ego, martyr complex, ink-smudged hands, constantly giggling under breath. Will usually beg people to write for him and then summarily despise anything that is submitted to him. Delusions of Grandeur.
HOW TO DISCOURAGE: You can't.

My little mantra these past few years has been *The Freaks Are Winning*, and it's true. Being able to identify these wretched souls is the only way to avoid them. The saddest part is, we're doomed to lose eventually, because only the stupid people are breeding.

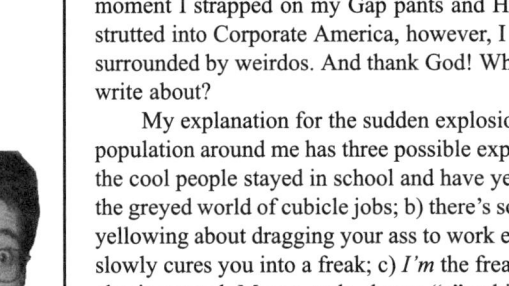

JEFF SEZ: The concept of the Freaks was a slow-evolving one for me, and one which stemmed almost completely from working for a living. I don't know why, but in my school days everyone seemed to be moderately normal. The moment I strapped on my Gap pants and Hush Puppies and strutted into Corporate America, however, I found myself surrounded by weirdos. And thank God! What else would I write about?

My explanation for the sudden explosion of the freak population around me has three possible explanations: a) all the cool people stayed in school and have yet to emerge into the greyed world of cubicle jobs; b) there's something yellowing about dragging your ass to work every day which slowly cures you into a freak; c) *I'm* the freak, and everyone else is normal. Most people choose "c", which is why I think most people are freaks.

The Inner Swine Forums

Misconnected Dimensions Resulting in Rippling Distortions in the Subatomic Connections of our Visible Universe Causing the Sun to Douse, Planets to Explode, Destruction, Despair, and Eventual. . .Death

Or: **The Inner Swine** *on Relationships*

Hosted by Jeff Somers

If I could somehow bottle the tension and hostility present in your average romantic relationship—just one—I'd be able to focus it through a lense and destroy entire planets with a flash of light so intense that people on nearby moons would be blinded, their palsied eyes useless for eternity. Of course, to harness this power we would first have to define it. In most relationships this bubbling hostility is a diffuse and formless presence looming between the principals, unnamed, denied, ill-defined.

Oh, but it's there. Scorching innocent bystanders with static discharge, enveloping lovers in fear and loathing—it's there all right. Most of us, however, are so trained to fear being alone, so conditioned to desire a partner, that we'd rather put ourselves through hell than find peace in solitude. In short: so afraid of the single life are we that we gladly embrace the soul erosion, time-suckage, and misery that most relationships—if only we were men and women enough to admit it—represent.

This, of course, begs the question: *Why do we then spend so much time pursuing relationships, if they suck so much?* The answer to that depends on many factors. I am but one mildly bitter young man, however. So I decided to turn this dilemma over to a qualified panel of experts, forming a sort of round-table discussion group of celebrities. As all of us who watch *Entertainment Tonight* know full well, celebrities can answer any dilemma, because *they are the best people in the world.*

The Entertainment Division of Oinking Sow—*The Inner Swine*'s parent company—has a long reach in Hollywood, and it was easy to gather a strong team of well-known stars at my small Jersey City apartment one sweltering July evening. With no air conditioning and eight people—one of whom was quite aromatic (those kooky stars!)—things were a little sticky, but the erudite and serious subject matter at hand kept everyone in a contemplative and calm mood throughout the evening.

THE DISCUSSION GROUP CELEBRITIES:

Jean-Luc Picard, *Captain of the Starship Enterprise*
Frank Sinatra, *recently deceased lounge singer*
Jenny McCarthy, *amazing animatronic doll, as seen on TV!*
MacLean Stevenson, *of "Hello Larry!" fame*
"Rowdy" Roddy Piper, *former wrestler in the WWF*
Bea Arthur, *formerly known as our beloved "Maude"*
Jimmy "Dyn-o-Mite!" Walker, *from "Good Times"*
Dana Plato, *the lovable moppet turned slutty criminal from "Diff'rent Strokes"*

I acted as moderator and host. My main duty would be to keep the discussion going if it ever lagged, and to make sure that the various riders on their appearance contracts were fulfilled. This was not always easy. Captain Picard's contract, for instance, insisted that I refer to him as "Patrick Stewart". I figured this odd request had something to do with a covert operation involving the Klingon spies in my apartment building, but was afraid I'd forget and slip up. Jenny McCarthy's contract demanded a separate dressing room and two bottles of iced champagne, so I was forced to convert my bathroom into a "dressing room", which I accomplished by cutting her name out of construction paper and taping it to the bathroom door. I didn't have any champagne, so I filled the sink with ice and put two bottles of Olympia Beer in it. I hoped she wouldn't notice.

Mr. Sinatra's arrival was a little more complex. I had to pay Ken West 2,000 Japanese yen to fetch the Chairman. Only two minutes before we were scheduled to begin, a light tapping at my bedroom window turned out to be Ken, dangling from a hovering helicopter and dressed in his "Cat Burglar" outfit, which is a pair of pitch-black fatigues and infrared goggles.

"Where you want it?" he shouted over the roar of the copter blades.

"Right through here!" I shouted, indicating the door leading to the living room. After several minutes we had Frank leaned up against the wall. Frank had no contractual obligations, per se, but he ended up requiring several dozen Glade air fresheners.

Dana Plato and Jimmy Walker had each been promised $200 for making the appearance, but upon arrival I had to sheepishly admit I had spent all my liquid assets on acquiring Frank Sinatra, so I offered them each $10 worth of McDonald's gift certificates. Dana was elated, but Mr. Walker became ill-tempered and verbally abusive. Eventually he settled down. Dana offered to have sex with me for another coupon book, but I reminded her that we had work to do.

MacLean Stevenson, who had once been Colonel Blake on the hit show M*A*S*H, seemed happy to be involved and smiled politely at everything I said. He had no contract. He sadly explained to me that he'd lost his agent and any chance of ever working again shortly after *Fantasy Island* went off the air, and that he'd recently died. I gave him a book of gift certificates because I felt sorry for him, and he seemed pleased. Dana Plato was upset at this.

Bea Arthur showed up just long enough to serve me with some court papers having to do with the previous issue of *The Inner Swine (*refer to "I Found This Fake Nude Photo of Bea Arthur on the Internet and Christ Am I Disturbed"), and then attempted to leave. Ken West was still cleaning mud off his fatigues in Jenny's dressing room, so I asked him to subdue Ms. Arthur, which he accomplished with duct tape and a hard-backed chair. He charged me another fifty bucks though.

"Rowdy" Roddy Piper showed up pretty drunk and offered to stay only if I could supply him with booze to "fortify" him. I only had a half-full bottle of Jagermeister, which he accepted cheerfully.

Now that we were all present and accounted for (Captain Picard looking almost normal in his 20th-century costume, which didn't strike me odd because it's standard Starfleet procedure when traveling backwards in time to change history, which is pretty obviously what was happening here) I moved everyone into the living room. I didn't have enough seats. Captain Picard, Jenny McCarthy, and Roddy Piper sat on the couch (Picard seemed unduly interested in Ms. McCarthy, and I made a mental note to discourage this; love and the Prime Directive do not mix!), Dana Plato sat in the recliner, Jimmy Walker took up position in the chair next to Frank, and I brought in chairs from the kitchen for MacLean Stevenson and Bea Arthur, who was already conveniently tied to one. I sat on my desk with an official-looking clipboard, and began the discussion.

JS: *On behalf of* The Inner Swine *I'd like to thank you all for coming—*
JW: *Hey, man, you got anything to eat around here?*
JS: *Um. . .the discussion has started, Mr. Walker.*
JW: *Aw, man—I'm starving! They usually cater these things.*
RRP: *Yeah, pig-boy! I'm hungry too!*
(At this point Roddy Piper made an obscene and threatening gesture towards me with the bottle of *Jagermeister*)
JS: *Uh. . .all right. I think I've got some Doritos in the kitchen. . .*

JS: *Okay, let's start this again. I'd like to thank you all for coming. As you must all be aware, love and relationships are two subjects we all have to deal with on a daily basis; the pursuit of love is one of our primary obsessions and yet it seems to bring us more misery and violence than satisfaction and joy. Tonight our goal is to serve our fellow man by plumbing the depths of this dilemma and—*
COTSSE: *Excuse me?*
JS: *One moment, Captain. As I was saying, we're going to solve this dilemma as a service to our fellow man. As celebrities, you have access to experience and wisdom denied us scuttling rejects known as your public. Would anyone like to start us off with a personal anecdote? Mr. Sinatra—Frank, if I may—you have been a national symbol for romance and style for four decades. Any overall thoughts on the nature of love?*
FS:
JM: *Eeeew! Is that a freakin' body?*
JS: *Well, Frank, feel free to dive into the discussion at any time. Captain Picard, you had something you wanted to say?*
COTSSE: *Ahhh, if you would please, my name is Patrick—Mr. Stewart.*
JS: *Oh! Of course. I understand, "Mr. Stewart"!*
JM: *Eeeew! What is that?*
COTSSE: *My goodness, son, what's wrong with your face? Are you smiling?*
JS: *Yes. Why?*
RRP: *My god, man, yer givin us the stinkeye!*
(At this point Mr. Piper threw his bottle at me, barely missing my face. I would have asked him to leave, but he immediately slumped down and

passed out noisily.)

JS: *If we could stay on the subject—*

DP: *Did that Scottish guy have any gift certificates? Could I have his, if he isn't going to use 'em?*

JS: *No! Now, please, does anyone have anything to say about love and the misery it inflicts upon us?*

JW: *I do, my man. Love is DYN-O-MITE!*

(At this point an eerie silence settled on the room. Ken West poked his head in from the kitchen to make sure no one had been killed).

COTSSE: *Son, please do not do that again.*

JS: *Thank you, Cap—er, "Mr. Stewart".*

COTSSE: *Did you just wink at me?*

JS: *No. Moving on—Ms. McCarthy, you're a current sex symbol in our culture. You've been in a committed relationship yet you must have had plenty of opportunities to cheat. Any thoughts on why love never seems to bring us joy?*

JM: *Are you hitting on me?*

JS: *Ummm. . .why would you ask that?*

JM: *You're staring at my breasts.*

JS: *They dominate my field of vision.*

COTSSE: *Young man, you had better start being polite.*

JS: *Uh—I am sorry. I'll look over there. Mr. Sinatra! Someone has to be on my side! What would you say about a broad like Jenny over here?*

FS:

MS: *Am I allowed to say something? Is that okay?*

JS: *Of course! Please, what's on your mind?*

MS: *It's really freaking me out when you talk to the dead guy.*

JS: *You're dead too, smartass.*

MS: *But no one knows it. You've got to have faith for that to work.*

JS: *Is that all you wanted to say?*

MS: *Yes.*

JS: *Duly noted. Bea? You seem suddenly excited over there. Do you have something to say on this subject? If I remove the gag will you promise not to scream? Yes? Was that a yes? Okay, here it comes. Remember your promise!*

BA: *Watch out! He's going to puke!*

JS: *Who is a—OH MY GOD!*

(On the tape here there is a lot of confusion as Mr. Piper contributed the prodigious contents of his stomach to our discussion. I had to have Ken West escort him from the apartment by force. During the scuffle, Captain Picard and Jenny McCarthy somehow disappeared (beamed up, no doubt by the ever faithful Number One), and Bea Arthur somehow escaped, taking with her one of my better kitchen chairs. This left me with a dwindling star panel in my living room. In order to make them stay I was forced to give Mr.

Walker and Ms. Plato each one of the Olympias I had been saving for Ms. McCarthy.)

JS: *Wow! That was exciting! Thank you for sticking it out. Now, Frank, I know you have a reputation to protect, but please no more outbursts! Okay, where were we?*

JW: *Man, you are whacked.*

(I silently marked Mr. Walker down for elimination via *The Inner Swine Black Ops Department*, run by Ken West, naturally, because he's black.)

JS: *My sanity is not the issue here. Ms. Plato, you've posed nude in magazines, how do you think pornography impacts our ability to discern a "normal" relationship from irrational media-fed fantasies?*

DP: *Uh. . .May I go to the bathroom?*

JS: *Well. . .technically that's Jenny McCarthy's dressing room. . .all right. Just be careful. Jimmy, would you like to field that last question?*

JW: *Naw, man. I think I gots to get going. OTB is closing soon.*

JS: *You've got to have something to say about love in the modern world! Please!*

JW: *Love is DYN-O-MITE baby!*

JS: *. . .Get out.*

And so ended our attempt at bringing the healing powers of celebrity to bear on the problem of why love makes so many of us so unhappy. Ms. Plato never returned; I later discovered my microwave and all the money in my sugar jar on the fridge missing. I cleaned up and went to sleep, and the next day I found MacLean Stevenson sleeping in the same kitchen chair; I'd completely forgotten about him. Frank had sprouted mushrooms.

I shook Mr. Stevenson gently and shooed him out; he seemed strangely eager to stay.

"For god's sake," he whimpered, "I've been dead for two years and no one's noticed. . ."

I pushed him out of the apartment and pondered how once again the universe had failed to live up to the high standards of *The Inner Swine*.

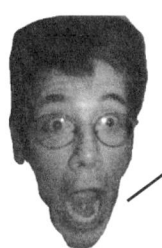

JEFF SEZ: If I win the Nobel Peace Prize for anything, it will likely be for inventing *The Inner Swine* Forums, where celebrities bend their awesome power to the world's problems. This remains one of my absolute favorite things to write. The trick, of course, is to come up with that one celebrity who brings the whole thing across the border from merely weird to inspired insanity. I didn't think I could top the dead, grimly silent Frank Sinatra...but I did.

The Inner Swine *Forums*

ANGER: WHY RESIST?

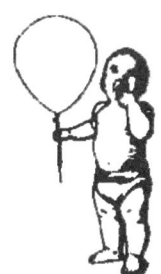

Discussing Anger Management and the Universal Can of Whoopass

Hosted by Jeff Somers

Recently, The Inner Swine's *humble Editor, Jeff Somers, sent out an interoffice memo demanding that TIS staff plan, organize, and host a series of Community Forums designed to educate and empower our community. Ever the leader by example, Mr. Somers then developed this* Inner Swine *Forum, presented here for your growth as a human being.*

ANGER: Why Resist?
Hosted by: Jeff Somers, Editor, *The Inner Swine*
Forum Participants:

KAREN ACCAVALLO: TIS Staff Proofreader/Writer
RUSSELL CROWE: Monosyllabic Actor
JEOF VITA: TIS Staff Artist
JOHN McENROE: Former Tennis Pro
and

MUMM-RA: The Ever Living

JS: Welcome to *The Inner Swine* Forums! Today we've gathered a

Appeared in Volume 6, Issue 3, September 2000

panel of celebrity experts to discuss the most primitive of human emotions: anger. Specifically, we're going to probe the usefulness of anger, its pros and cons, and ultimately answer the nagging question: *Is the fact that I am a bubbling cauldron of rage all the time really a bad thing?* Let's take a moment to introduce our celebrity panel. First off, we have our very own Jeof Vita, TIS Staff Artist who creates our wonderful cover art for every issue!

JV: Fuck you!

JS: Indeed. Then we have John McEnroe, sadly faded former tennis champion who has struggled mightily to gain meaning in his life since his career ended some time ago.

JM: Uh...good to be here. I think. Is there a phone? I need to call my agent; I'm not sure this is where I'm supposed to be...

JS: Sorry, no phones here. Think of this as a "zen" moment: By virtue of being here, this is where you were supposed to be all along. To your right, uh, um, well, while not strictly-speaking a "celebrity"—

KA: Bite me, pencil-dick.

JS: We have the lovely and talented Karen Accavallo, proofreader and occasional writer for *The Inner Swine*. And next—

KA: I have an announcement to make.

JS: Uh, we don't really—

KA: Don't make me twist your head off like a bottlecap! I would just like to tell the world that you're not very funny, and they should stop reading or listening to this immediately, before they waste more of their precious lives on your swill. Thank you.

JS: Yes...I see. Ahem, to Karen's right we have film actor Russell Crowe.

RC: What the hell's her problem, then?

KA: Back off, pretty boy! I could snap you like old brittle newsprint!

RC: ...I believe you, sister.

JS: Uh, Mr. Crowe, I'm sorry, but there's no smoking in here.

RC:

JS: Okay! As long as that's settled. Will someone please get Mr. Crowe an ashtray! And finally, our final panel member is former television character Mumm-Ra, the Ever Living.

MR: Pleased to be here, Jeff.

KA: Is that smell *you*, corpse-boy?

MR: I am afraid so, miss. I have been decomposing for thousands of years, kept alive by black magic and a careful hoarding of my life-essence. It can't be helped.

KA: Stay upwind then.

JS: So, this is how we're going to work things today. The basic question before us is whether anger is something that needs to be managed or controlled, or if perhaps it is a useful and natural component to our interactions. In other words, should we even bother trying to resist our tendency towards rage? Towards that end I'll give the group situations and you'll discuss for the benefit of our audience whether anger is an appropriate and healthy response or not. Are we ready to begin?

JV: Fuck you.

KA: Is lunch being served?

RC: Or cocktails, mate?

JS: All right then! Let's get started. Here's our first hypothetical situation—

KA: How's this for a hypothetical situation—

JS: Uh, now, Ms. Accavallo, I'm running this—

KA: Shush, monkey-boy. Here's a situation: I agree to be the proofreader of a dinky little zine. My name gets pasted on the masthead. But I never get to proofread any issues because the dingbat Editor has his head buried too far up his ass. So every issue is crammed full of mistakes and grammar atrocities, and because my name is there on the masthead everyone thinks I'm an idiot. Question: Should I be angry about that? Follow-up question: If so, am I justified in setting the Editor's car on fire?

JS: That was you?

RC: I think that's justified. He's makin you look like a proper moron, isn't 'e? I were you, dearie, e'd be lucky if I didn't pop 'im one in the nose.

JS: Justified? She's prevented from proofing *The Inner Swine* so she's justified in blowing up my car?

RC: I don't much care for your tone, mate.

JM: Yeah, it seems extreme, but you are hurting her reputation. You can buy a new car. She might never get her rep back.

JS: Jeof! Someone's got to be on my side!

JV: Fuck you!

MR: Gentlemen! I believe you have missed the point of this exercise! This scrawny mortal has asked not if her anger is justifiable, but rather does it serve a purpose? Does it accomplish anything? She has destroyed his vehicle, but does that remove the stain from her reputation? Has it improved or worsened the situation, or left it unaffected?

RC: For a corpse you're gettin' kinda uppity, ask me.

MR: Speak in that tone to me again and I will turn you into a fine powder.

JS: Uh, Mr. Ra is correct, though. Let's stick with this unfortunate example now that we're so far into it: Does anger further our purposes, or is it a waste of energy? Think of it this way...

KA: Oh, lord. Wake me when he's done.

JS: ...Our emotions are instinctual, we're born with them. Even little babies display anger, sadness, fear. They must have served a purpose in our evolution, in our survival. Fear, for example: We feel fear when we're threatened. Our adrenaline levels rise, we focus, our senses become finer. Fear is a very useful reaction to threats. Anger, then, must serve a similar purpose.

RC: Sure, sure, I see where the little git is goin' wit' this! When someone fucks wit' ya, you get pissed. Without it, you'd just slink along. So yeah, anger serves a frick'in' purpose, eh? It keeps you from getting pissed on. Where the hell's the bar in this place?

JS: Okay, so anger helps us defend our interests. Gives us an immediate reaction to conflict that maybe gets us through dangerous situations we might otherwise run from. But does it *still* serve a purpose? In this day and age, is anger something that serves us, or is it a primitive residue of our animalistic selves that is as much an impediment as it is a boon?

RC: Boon? You talk like a queer, y'know that?

MR: I think I can speak on this subject, Jeff. You see, for millennia I have relied on my simmering, ever-present rage to keep me alive. Why, if I ever lost my ability to hate every living thing around me, I'd most likely just get really really tired and die.

KA: You know, maybe you're not so useless, Mr. Corpse. I too can feel the ancient rage of millennia coursing through my veins. How can I become immortal?

JS: Karen, I can't really condone using a TIS event to seek Eternal Servitude to the Dark Forces.

KA: Yeah yeah, button it, small fry. I'm doing business.

MR: Yes, that's good. I can feel your rage from here, like a small sun.

JS: Uh, since I seem to have lost control over this side of the room, I'll ask you, Mr. McEnroe: Do you think your angry outbursts during tennis games advanced your cause? Or was it a primitive remnant that served no purpose?

JM: Well, Jeff, the way I see it, if it scared some of those fucking assholes into calling one thing my way that normally they would have called against me, then it was all worth it, the bad press, the death threats, the migraines.

JS: Interesting. If I may indulge in a bit of translation, I think you're saying that even primitive drives and emotions, if channeled intelligently, can be used to attain civilized goals. Like winning a tennis match.

RC: Sure, mate, that what I been sayin', y'know?

JS: You didn't say anything. You've been quite obviously peering down Karen's blouse.

KA: It's okay. I asked him to.

RC: Oy, she's a goer, that one! But any rate, I was sayin', it's like when you're makin' a business deal, in there to sign the contracts. If you makes 'em a little afraid of you, flashes a temper, see, you get a better deal. There's a difference between bein' ruled by rage and rulin' *by* rage, get it?

JS: You sure talk funny, Russ, but it underscores what I've always said: Celebrities are the best people in the world, and know everything. If we could just get you and Mel Gibson working on the cancer problem, it'd be solved in a few days.

RC: Amen, brother. I guess you ain't such a bad sort, huh?

JV: Oh yes he is. And fuck you.

RC: Friend, I know you didn't say that to me.

JV: Yeah, *mate*? (*jumps to feet, tears off shirt*) LET'S GET IT ON!

JS: Oh! Watch the furniture! This set cost money! Well, I'll move over to this side of the stage, where Karen and Mr. Ra seem to be praying. John, do you have anything else to add to our forum?

JM: Nah. I think the subject's been covered. I'm gonna get home before the two beefcake boys here decide they want to tear off *my* shirt and grunt and sweat with *me*.

RC: That sounded like an un-savry accusation, mate.

JV: (*whispering*) I think he called you a *fag*.

RC: Right. Come on, ball-boy!

JM: NOT THE FACE!

JS: Karen, will you salvage this with a pithy closing comment?

KA: Sure sure. You're right: Anger might be a primitive, blind emotion in the dark cave of our subconscious, but it still serves a purpose if managed intelligently. Not that you would know. Now go away, I'm selling my soul for immortality. I think I shall call myself K-Ra, the Ever Shopping.

MR: Not bad, my child. Now concentrate! Feel the evil! Can you smell it?

KA: I thought that was Somers.

MR: No, that's evil. Well. . .now that you mention it, evil isn't usually that *strong*.

JS: Well, there you go folks. I'll just step off the stage here and put some distance between me and the fracas going on up there. We all get angry, and we've been getting angry since the race was young, as opposed to new emotions only recently developed, like Happiness and Freakiness. The primitive emotion of anger can still be useful to us in the modern world if we filter it through our intellects, which is the difference between self-destructive rage and constructive use of verbal threats. So use your anger, folks, don't get used by it.

Until next time, I'm Jeff Somers, and this has been an *Inner Swine* Forum. Holy—

[*sound of metal folding chair hitting Mr. Somers in back of head*]

JEFF SEZ: I sure hope the people who made those groovy *Thundercats* cartoons don't sue me for using Mumm-Ra's image here. I will blame it all on clint johns.

BASTARDS: Specious Argument and Unsupported Opinions

SINCE WE GENERALLY DON'T START writing each issue of TIS until about a week before it's due at the distributor, we don't have time to do any research, request reprint permissions, or spellcheck anything effectively. This does not stop us from expressing our opinions, however. As a matter of fact, it grants us the freedom to just invent an opinion on the spot (in the unlikely absence of a preexisting one). In fact, I have built a complex machine out of spare pinball machine parts. This machine will print out a random opinion for me in the event that I find myself without one.

Although most of the writing in each issue is delivered, hot and steaming, more or less for entertainment value, there are always actual opinions underpinning the jokes. That these opinions are not the most informed in the world does not, we don't think, detract much from their value, since opinions in general are worthless, especially other people's.

In this section, we have selected some of the more lucid essays expressing the millions of opinions endorsed by The Inner Swine. *No actual lucidity, however, is guaranteed.*

How I Conquered the Country, Grew Fat on the Blood of my Subjects, Tired of Absolute Power, Abdicated the Throne, and Returned to my Ancestral Home

(Or, South Dakota and Back in a Few Short Days)

The cross-country trip is an icon of the American experience, a dream that has lost none of its attraction with the aging of our culture. The United States' interstate highway system never fails to fascinate; the concept of going *anywhere* boggles the mind. You could fit Europe inside the U.S., and *we can drive from one end to another, anytime we want*. I know it made *me* giddy. I suppose I had the same romantic vision most people have: just me and Jack Kerouac motoring down empty roads bathed in pure sunshine, eating local food and making new friends, laying the local girls and somehow burning my name into this cold land of ours. At some point, I thought, MTV would be secretly filming me for use in one of their shows.

If not that, then I would have the sort of intense experience that brings about books, that brings about movie rights for the complex, moving tale of a young man finding himself in the heartland of America. I could entitle it *Wild Country* or *Dark Roads* or something like that and be hailed as the brooding new artist of the shadows, writing biting commentary about our fellow Americans while still managing an epiphany or wisdom, of sorts. I would come back a changed man, I thought: How could I not?

I'll tell you how. Because there are more Bob's Big Boys out there than local diners, because no one living out there gives a shit that you're driving cross-country and finding yourself, because the cops are all pricks when your license plates aren't local, because gas is too fucking expensive, and the local girls don't fuck the drifters prowling through like thinned wolves looking for a fire to lay down next to. Because the closest things to friends I made were two drunk guys named Todd and Marty who owned a Chevy Malibu with a rusted tailpipe and a trunk full of beer, because the closest thing to an epiphany or wisdom I managed was the realization that *there is absolutely no reason to ever, ever enter Nebraska.*

So, I suppose in a way I learned a great deal by attempting to drive cross-country, since I now know better than to ever do it again.

That's right, *attempting*. You see, I tried to do the USA on $20 a day deal, I tried to drive cross-country when I was unemployed and broke, and after staring at Mount Rushmore for a few hours I realized that if I drove all the way out to California I'd be walking home. But let's not get to that, yet, let's not get to the dark foray into a pit called Nebraska, let's not talk about terror and motor oil at 3 AM. Let's begin at the beginning and we'll get to the end eventually.

THE TRIP: I owned, by chance and luck, a perfect vehicle for this amazing adventure: a 1978 Chevy Nova, rusty, four doors, and a parking brake that was basically theoretical, a leak in the oil line you could push a small rodent through, and a leak in the back windshield that loomed over the coming weeks with a leering, demonic grin. For supplies, I bought Pop-Tarts. *Seventy-two Pop-Tarts,* because I am a strong believer in the Catholic splinter group I founded: The Eternal Power of Pop-Tarts. With a shelf life just slightly less than forever, and with a million uses—some of which no one has encountered yet—there is no situation you cannot solve or in some way placate with Pop-Tarts. If I got hungry, I knew I could eat them. With 72 of them, I knew I could eat Pop-Tarts from one side of the country to the other and still have one left over when I got home. If I needed to I could use them as effective insulation against the cold. If I let them harden in the air I could use them as weapons against attackers. If I ate enough of them I would see visions. If I stuffed some into my gas tank I knew that my tired and wheezy 1978 Chevy Nova would roar into life, belching multi-colored and fruit-flavored exhaust. When people ask me how I did it, I invariably reply: *Pop-Tarts.*

I roared out of Jersey City one hot afternoon with $400 and a full tank of gas, the aforementioned 72 Pop-Tarts and, I suppose, a few changes of clothes for my mother's peace of mind. In fact, I remained relatively clean over my trip mainly because I grew fearless about getting naked in front of strangers. There is simply no way you can wash up in a rest-stop bathroom without getting naked in front of strangers, who will mostly pretend that there isn't a naked guy washing his hair in the sink next to them. Rest stops are my new salvation, my temples. They are like little parks along the highways, with art exhibits and free coffee, literature, and conversation. There are people there to greet you, to answer questions, give directions. There are vending machines, shining beacons filled to bursting with overpriced Pepsi and Snapple. A man could live a fine life flitting from rest area to rest area, and never stop in a regular town again.

This country is big and beautiful, with gorgeous little roads that meander through hills and farmland. Hills and farmland is what you mostly see when you're tooling about the country, and hills and farmland are fine when you're 12 and on the field trip bus and don't give a rat's ass where you're headed, only that it's: a) away from school and b) nice scenery. After a day of staring at hills and farmland you can only wish that you never see another hill or another farm as long as you live, you can only vow to gouge both eyes out in self-defense if you wake up the next day and find more hills and farmland. This is, I think, a normal enough response to the overweening beauty of our unspoiled (or at least only moderately spoiled) country and leaves you with only one difficulty: The nature of the interstate highway system brings you past more hills and farmland than anything else, except perhaps cows. The only mental defense against this is to speed and sit, hunched over the steering wheel with a bloody grin on your face and no intention of stopping until you reach Chicago.

In New York State, all I met were lonely convenience store workers who thought you'd come into their mini-mart because you could hear the tender keening of their tortured, bereft souls. I'd drive all day, stopping here and there, eat shitty food (trying to conserve my Pop-Tarts until they're *really* needed) and end up low on gas on some county road that doesn't even lead anywhere, and when I pull into a Gulf station to gas up I *don't* want to make friends. This is precisely the atmosphere in which that species of human I will dub *The Talkers* thrives.

The Talkers are normal-looking but horribly mutated humanoids who lurk in lonely, dark areas of the country. They cannot tolerate large crowds. They cannot accept criticism. What they can, and will, do is talk to you. They will pick the least convenient time, the least interesting subject, the least appropriate place to speak to you, and once you look up and grin that polite grin, they burrow their pointy little heads into your skin and begin to suck.

Now, maybe some of us drive cross-country to talk to new and exciting people. I didn't. If I'd wanted to *talk* all the way, I would have gone with one of my crummy friends. *The Talkers*, though, don't care what you want. Their existence is primarily focussed on them, their crummy opinions, and their crummy jokes. They will sneak up on you in the Gas N' Sip, right by the microwave in the back, and catch your attention with a slight smile, or a nod. You nod back, and it happens. *The Talker* begins to talk. He begins to tell you how he's worked in that Gas N' Sip for 13 years. You smile slightly and say, "Wow". He shakes his head and says he's seen it all, a lot of weird things. Uh-huh, you say, searching for beef burritos. He says he could tell you a tale or two and before you know it you're standing at the register and he's just *talking* to you, on and on, and because mom raised you right you just keep nodding and grunting. Time goes by, and you can feel yourself getting weaker and weaker, your will to go on beginning to wilt. Or maybe you're ringing up gas and snacks, and the girl behind the register begins to complain. *Complainers* are just a subspecies of *The Talkers*. She will tell you she's been working since 6 in the morning, which, in case you were interested, is an 18-hour shift, that she has to drive down to Albany in the morning and then be back there at noon to work another 10-hour shift. All this while she holds your Doritos hostage, all this while you just want to scream and smack her, hard, across the face.

The Talkers will talk, I have found, until you are rude. You will simply have to swallow air and belch forth attitude until they get angry and pissily hustle you out of their domain. It might seem unduly mean-spirited, but only until you find yourself in the same situation, believe me. When you glance at your watch and it says 1:07 AM and you pulled in for a Big Gulp 27 minutes ago and have been hearing about all the times Ernie there behind the counter's been robbed in his tenure as night manager of the 7-11, you get rude quick.

Between New York and Illinois, I don't remember too much, really. Just more rolling fields of green and hallucinatory levels of heat as I trundled down the highways under the heartless sun. I can recall Todd and Marty, who may have been a hallucination or perhaps ghosts, haunting Route 20. Perhaps it is no secret that the interstate highway system in this country *is not quite finished yet*. There are roads on the maps that aren't there yet; there are roads on the maps that end before they're supposed to. And every road in this land of ours is under repair, and has been for decades.

I met Marty and Todd while cruising the peaceful side of Ohio, just emptiness and Amish country, and the only nuclear reactor I've ever seen up close. This one had big bellowing clouds of black smoke pouring from it; I'm not sure if it was supposed to be doing that. If I bear X-men for children, you alone will know why. Suddenly, at a point where Route 20 turns into a two-lane dust bowl, traffic stopped, and about 10 cars or so found themselves waiting for work crews to move an uncooperative bulldozer off the road. I was behind a gray Malibu, badly painted (just like my Nova!) and in need of serious bodywork (just like my Nova!). After idling for a few minutes, it was obvious to all of us that we weren't going anywhere, not really, and we all cut our engines and got out. If we had been parked in molten lava it would have been cooler outside than in our cars. Todd and Marty were gangly, cheerful tokers in jeans and tie-dyes, and greeted me with more than polite good cheer, walked determinedly to their trunk, and popped it open to reveal a literal trunkload of Coors. There are several types of people in the world, and I have narrowed it down to three. One type of person debates the wisdom of keeping your beer in the veritable oven your car trunk becomes on the highways. A second type of person wonders what kind of moron drinks and drives *that much*. The third type is simply disgusted the moment they read the word *Coors*, thinking that if you're going to buy that much beer, at least buy beer you can *drink*.

At any rate, Marty and Todd were friendly and offered beer to the half dozen or so stranded drivers, and we passed the half hour we were stuck in high spirits, drinking warm beer under the harsh Ohio sun, listening to Marty and Todd convince each other that there would be some sort of wisdom in moving out to California with only a trunkload of beer to their name. The road cleared, we all got back into our cars, and I for one have yet to see or hear of Marty and Todd again.

From this point on I entered what I call the *Great Zone of Nothing* in Ohio. It is a dark era in my trip's history, a painful memory. It is the point where I almost starved to death right there in my car, right there on Route 20. Of course, that's melodrama. I had my Pop-Tarts. I couldn't starve.

The Great Zone of Nothing was a stretch of about four hours of absolutely nothing but dazzling scenery and empty horizons. I have photos of this expanse, pictures I took while driving (believe me, you could drive like you had nothing to lose in the *Zone* and nothing would happen—the likelihood of seeing another car was somewhere between doubtful and laughable), photos which, when I show them to my crummy friends, inevitably get the reaction, "Hey—I don't see anything in this picture". I just nod my head heavily. "Exactly." I say. *"Exactly!"*

I drove through the *Zone* from 10 in the morning until 2 in the afternoon one hot day and by the end of it I was feverish and desperate for a place to pull over. But there was nothing. No restaurants, no gas stations, no *people*. I screamed and grunted, I exceeded speed limits and cursed. And by 2 in the afternoon I was starving for a bite of lunch. Even a 7-Eleven burrito would have been a godsend, at that point. I became afraid that I had been swallowed up by the *Zone*, that I had become just another part of the *Nothing*, unseen by traveling eyes, ignored by the waking world. And then I finally saw a sign for I-90.

Now, let's not confuse *The Great Zone of Nothing* with *Nebraska*, though the similarity is strong. The *Zone* is merely that, a section of emptiness in Ohio that I happened to get lost in for a while during my ill-advised tour of that state. ("Want to see different Amish people than the ones in your home state? Come to Ohio!") *Nebraska* is an entire state. It

147

has a large population, and, supposedly, several large cities. Somehow, in my nightmarish ride through Nebraska, I failed to find any of them. If Ohio houses a *Great Zone of Nothing*, then Nebraska must be a *Black Hole*, so empty there's just no *room* for anything. That only makes sense to me, I think, but then I'm the one who's been to this shadowy Ur-Nebraska, so whatever I say goes.

I guess the circumstances of my arrival in the *Black Hole* colored my perception of it somewhat. I had arrived at Mount Rushmore with the fresh realization that I was broke much, much sooner than I had ever expected to be, and that left me with two choices: turn around or get a job in California. So, I spurned California. I hung around Mount Rushmore to see the lighting ceremony and then I hopped in my car and drove, literally, into the wilderness. I saw an interesting looking turn, and I took it in the full spirit of my trip. *This* was what I'd intended to do, *this* was the whole idea: getting lost on purpose. I was tattered and weary and close to broke, but I was hurtling into the Black Hills without a clue as to where I was going. It was fun for about an hour. Then I started to get sleepy; I started to wonder where I was going to sleep that night; I started to wonder if those "Cow-Crossing" signs were meant to be taken seriously. I decided they were after a cow loomed up in front of my car so quickly as to give me mental whiplash, so that every time I turned a curve from then on I had nightmare visions of cow chewing cud, sleeping in the middle of the highway.

By the time I realized how badly lost I was, I had already entered the *Black Hole* without realizing it. Instead of the dense forests of the Black Hills, there was: corn. And only corn. Corn as far as the eye could see, which admittedly wasn't too far in the near-total darkness. All through this, I played a tape a friend of mine had made for my trip, and the ghostly voice of Steve Miller took on an hypnotic rhythm, a terrifyingly chant-like tone:

> My Grandpa he's 95,
> He keeps on dancin', he's still alive;
> My Grandma, she's 92,
> She still dances, and sings some too,
> I don't know, but I been told
> If you keep on dancing you'll never grow old

If this is not freaky enough for you, then I have a trump card. You may recall a mention of my car's amazing ability to leak stupendous amounts of oil on a steady basis: This is the payoff. While travelling the *Black Hole* in desperation, near madness from the dark and the corn and the velvet tones of Steve Miller, my oil light comes on and stares at me, angry red, pulsing with quiet insistence and it was saying just one thing, over and over again: *Pull over and put oil in the car, monkeyboy, or you'll have a whole new definition of "black hole" when this engine seizes up and turns into one.* I pulled over, I killed the engine, and then I sat there, for a moment, listening.

Nothing. Nothing but corn, swaying in the strong wind. Nothing but that.

What followed were perhaps the most intensely irrational moments of my life, a time when I was thoroughly convinced that I was about to be murdered by the several hundred ghoulies and boogies I thought had been left behind years ago. I performed what may be the fastest oil operation in the known history of old cars, dashing into the forsaken night to rip open my hood, pour two quarts of 10W-30 into the engine, and then dive back into the car with my heart pounding and a chill slime of sweat all over my body. I can't say that I envisioned wolves, prowling the back roads, or that I had a *Children of the Corn* flash (especially since I've never seen the movie) but I was definitely terrified. Sounds bad, huh? Sounds like no fun at all, you think? Now, imagine that it's not just a small area, not just a "zone" of terror, *but an entire state.* A *Black Hole*, a sinkhole of fear and silence and swaying corn, an endless expanse of emptiness called *Nebraska.*

I have never driven so far so fast, all in the name of getting the hell out of Nebraska. By light of day it wasn't terrifying, it was just empty. So empty you wonder that Nebraska has any Representatives in Congress at all. I can recall sitting in my car just outside of Lincoln, reading my Fodor's Guide to the USA, and reading that there are over a million people in Nebraska. And I thought: Well, they must all be in Lincoln enjoying cable TV, because there ain't a one of them back in the *Hole* with the corn.

Now, I am back in the lap of luxury on the East Coast, where we have invented streetlights and no highway strays far from an industrial park. We don't have any cornfields, and nobody drives cross-country to get *here*. What have I learned from this experience? I've learned that you can't eat Pop-Tarts everyday and keep your good humor. I've learned that you can't bring enough albums to keep yourself from the blues. You can't sleep in your car and expect to feel good. You can't make it across the country with $400. I learned that Des Moines, Iowa is the nicest city in the world, even though its citizens are going mad with boredom. But most of all, I learned the one thing I gladly traded my summer away for, the one bit of wisdom I will doubtless cherish for years to come, that will doubtless inspire me in dark times: *There is absolutely no reason to ever, ever enter Nebraska.*

CHEERIOS, TATERS, AND A BIG BOWL OF ICE

The Single Woman's Guide to Economic Food Shopping

By Karen Accavallo, *authority*

You know, it's amazing. Yesterday I was chatting with a friend of mine, and he mentioned he wanted to come over and see my apartment. Now I've known Jeff too long, I know what he means by "see your apartment." Obviously he wanted sex. I decided to play along.

"OK," I said, "But don't expect me to offer you anything to eat or drink."

"Huh," Jeff answered, which is normal for him anyway, but I knew he was really confused this time.

"Yeah, don't expect anything to eat or drink, because I ain't got nothing," I said. (*Actually you've probably guessed this is a lie. Everyone knows that a grammar nazi like myself would probably have said something like, "I cannot provide for your sustenance within my living quarters, young friend." But you get the idea.*)

Before I moved out of my parents' house, I sat down with my mother and tried to figure out a budget for myself. I could divvy up my paltry publishing paycheck (!) between rent, the phone bill, the electric bill, therapy, "medicine" from High Spirits Discount Liquors, and 1,200 clams a year for a car that is six years old and has been recalled twice by Ford. That left me with about $10 a month for "miscellaneous."

"And what do you expect to do about food?" my mother asked. "You have no money left for food. I think you need to rethink this. You don't make enough money to live on your own."

I thought for a moment— pondering, sweating, clenching. "I'll steal food," I told her. She laughed. I didn't.

I'm totally paranoid that my roommate from college is going to ask me to be in her wedding. Now it would probably be fun and all, but all I can picture is some apologetic bridal shop clerk who in a very polite manner basically tells me that there is not enough material on this earth that will go around my wide ass. I figure a lot of women have this problem, so I've gone and done something so groundbreaking, I'm considering quitting my job and touring with:

THE SINGLE WOMAN'S COOKBOOK

Staying Alive on $10 a Month

It's ridiculous and unnecessary to spend a lot of money on food. All you need is some creative planning and a good imagination. Here's a typical day's menu:

> **BREAKFAST**
>
> Big Glass of Tap Water: If you concentrate hard enough, you can convince yourself it's orange juice.
> 1 Slice of Bread: After the first week, you'll believe that you're munching on a big, sloppy egg, bacon and cheese sandwich.
>
> **LUNCH**
>
> You don't need lunch, because you should be concentrating on your job. If you must indulge, Skittles only cost 65 cents a bag and they are most filling. But don't make it a habit.
>
> **DINNER**
>
> Here's the fun part!
> Big Glass of Tap Water (or is that champagne!!!!!)
> Rice
> Cheez-Its
>
> **DESSERT**
>
> Mmmm! If you're feeling particularly naughty that day, a big bowl of ice usually hits the spot.

Let's add up our food expense for today:

Tap Water: FREE
Bread Slice: about 5 cents
Skittles: 65 cents
Rice: Convince your mother to buy you a 10 lb. bag, and that's free too!
Cheez-Its: about 1 cent a piece. You are allowed three.

See there! We've spent under $1 on food today. What's that, you say? Even $1 a day adds up to 30 DOLLARS a month! Not if you only eat Tuesday through Thursday like I do!!!

The key here is prioritizing your life. Now, with a little discipline you can convince yourself that you're chowing down on filet mignon instead of one lone Pop-Tart. You can either fritter your money away on food, or you can save that money for shoes. Gotta have shoes to walk around in, but ya ain't gotta fill your belly just to ward off temporary dizziness. It's all about control.

I know what you're thinking. You want to eat healthy. OK, here's another day's menu:

BREAKFAST

Two Big Glasses of Tap Water
Banana (25 cents from the guy on the street; cheaper if you buy a bunch from Grand Union)

LUNCH

Now what did I tell you about lunch?

DINNER

Big Bowl of Corn
Three Enormous Glasses of Free Delicious Tap Water

Grand Union frozen corn costs oh. . .I don't know. . .say, $2 a bag. Do you know how many meals you can make of this? I don't know why the world hasn't caught on sooner.

If frozen corn isn't your scene, a bag of microwave popcorn also makes a hearty meal.

Another fantastic value is Cheerios. When you do need to shop, be sure only to shop in bulk. But don't be silly enough to buy your own membership to BJ's, or Price Club, or what have you; leech onto a friend that has one. I bought a massive box of Cheerios in January, and I'm still enjoying them.

Potatoes are another great choice. A bag of Idahos can last weeks. Just thinking about a potato and a gallon of tap water waiting for me when I get home is enough to get me through a hard day at work.

Woo. . .I can feel the oxygen leaving my brain. What was I talking about? Oh yes, it's all about control. Get a hold of yourself. Soon your body's coma-like state will make you forget all about shelling out some $15 a week or some crazy figure like that. Start saving!!

Editor's Note: *Karen is obviously under a great deal of stress.*

JEFF SEZ: Careful readers may have noticed that this piece by sweetly mad Karen Accavallo is the only piece in this book that was not written by Your Humble Editor. Certainly *The Inner Swine* is as per a perzine as you get: Hardly a page goes by which is not thoroughly devoted to "the Joy of Jeffhood", so why would you expect otherwise from this book?

This does beg the question, then, of why bother having any non-Jeff material at all. The short answer is that there was no conscious decision to exclude non-Jeff material, this was simply the only piece that I didn't write that still made me laugh when I read it. The long answer involves an ancient prophecy and the battle between good and evil for all your souls. I don't have time for that here.

I wish Karen would write a new article for every issue of *The Inner Swine*. When I suggest this, however, she gets very angry and accuses me of using her to "fill your sorry little rag up because you're not man enough to do it by yourself".

THE STINK OF WASTED BACHELORHOOD

I Have Seen the Future and It Is Larry from "Three's Company"

WITH the ruins of my youth behind me, I have noted amongst my friends a dangerous proclivity towards *couplehood*. In the immediate, this only changes my social life in that I find myself pretending to like people I don't really like much more often, pretty much every time an until-that-moment sane friend of mine introduces his/her new beau, and I find myself staring down the dark maw of *The Weird*. But aside from these mundane annoyances, I can't say that this creeping coupling is really affecting my life in the adverse right now. The hardest part is probably tracking people down; men and women who used to spend all their free time sitting on their couches are now out all the time, or, apparently, having sex, which usually means they don't answer the phone.

Ah, but there is the future to contemplate. I'd like to wallow in the present and live free or die, but time stops for no man and my ever-expanding waistline compels me to consider my fate. And my fate is, very simply, to be *Everybody's Weird Bachelor Friend*.

The thin line between being a simple wasted bachelor and being a weird old man whom no one ever wanted is a blurry one, and comes upon you with a blinding sort of speed—you go to sleep swinging bachelor number one, you wake up potential homosexual/pedophile/weird bachelor friend no one knows how to invite to weddings. Or if they even want to. I'm hurtling towards this transformation with every passing moment, because everyone I know is moving inexorably towards couplehood and the trappings thereof. Gone are late nights out at bars, in are late night feedings. Out are drunken flirtations up against the jukebox, in are cynical matchmaking discussions about your aging bachelor friend. Gone are late shows at clubs, in are holidays spent with the family. And before I know it I'm the only one getting a ticket for public urination—and no one's impressed anymore. Ah, the sweet, fleeting bird of youth.

What it boils down to is, I've lost my cover. All wild animals require camouflage at certain moments in their lives, to ensure our survival. Wasted bachelors thrive when surrounded by others of their ilk, but in a pinch any group of singles, happy or otherwise, will do. We need to blend in. Take away our cover and we shrivel and wilt, much like the buffalo of our great nation's midwest. We either waste away or are hunted down by the one great predator we fear: spinsters. Wasting away, while by far the preferable fate, has a dark side; in fact, it is pretty much *all* dark side. Consider these awful side effects of being an aging wasted bachelor:

1. *VICTIMIZATION BY FASHION.* The problem with men is they have no concept of clothing. If they do, they're usually homosexual. I have nothing bad to say about being homosexual, but being single at age 50 because you're gay is a little different than being a Wasted Bachelor, you know? When we're young we either make anything look good or we're tuned into the culture just enough to know that plaid bellbottoms were a government conspiracy. As we age, however, we lose touch with the cultural barometers that have kept us on the sane path to khakis and we definitely lose the ability to make tie-dye look cool. Set adrift on the pret-a-porter sea of torment, we suffer.

Most men, by this time, have by way of self-defense taken on a wife or, at the very least, one of those eternally-suffering long-term girlfriends for the sole and noble purpose of making sure they're dressed appropriately. One of the reasons married men are so attractive to other women, I'm convinced, is the simple fact that there's someone at home dressing them. The rest of us wander around looking unkempt and vaguely out of date. We've got no chance. As we bachelors age it gets worse, until our increasingly desperate attempts to clothe ourselves eventually result in terminal clashing, unrestrained use of polyester, and eventual. . .death.

2. *EXTINCTION OF RENT-A-DATES.* I personally believe that at least 75% of anyone's decision to "settle down" with one significant other has to do with the natural human aversion to having to attend social functions alone. At the heart of romance, I think, is the concept of the *permanent date*.

Wasted Bachelors abuse this system of freewheeling socializing. We like to go to big events like weddings, funerals, or the Superbowl, dragging along some platonic (or otherwise) friend. We have someone to talk to all night, someone to dance with, someone to make unwanted sexual overtures to, and in the end we don't have to call them the next day or worry about remembering their name. In other words, we don't have to *live* with them after their usefulness as a social companion is over.

And hell, if those unwanted sexual overtures turn out to be wanted, after a mixture of romantic 80's tunes, tequila Fanny-Bangers, and your own well-worn but nonetheless effective charm—it's okay. The rent-a-date is usually a friend and that guarantees the uncomfortable *Jesus I've never been quite so drunk* conversation the next morning, wherein the Wasted Bachelor is absolved of guilt, free to go dig into future buffets with other unsuspecting rent-a-dates.

As everyone scrambles for the safety of couplehood, however, rent-a-date possibilities dry up, leaving the Wasted Bachelor dangerously exposed. Any women he might actually consider stimulating conversation are snapped up at an early age, leaving behind dangerously uninteresting and unattractive alternatives. Many Wasted Bachelors willingly become hermits when faced with this cruel turn of nature.

3. *MATCHMAKING.* Nothing can make a species wither and run for the cool comfort of extinction like women looking to bring the world the happiness they have found in couplehood. Everyone claims to dislike the practice, no one will openly admit to it, but the subtle tendrils of matchmaking can be traced back to *someone* in your social group. The real masters of the art, the *Queen Mothers* of matchmaking, can do it with a series of long-range subtle suggestions you likely wouldn't even recognize as such. They create longing with a phrase, desire with an observation, and flee the scene before anyone can trace the machinations back to them.

Of course, any matchmaking you experience as a young and swinging member of your little group is nothing compared to the torrent of romance-peddling the aging Wasted Bachelor will endure in his brief, agonizing existence. After all, they're *Wasted* Bachelors: wasted time, wasted energy, wasted money. Time, energy, and money that could be going to a deserving spinster—and as you get older, time is running out to take advantage of your natural resources. Every time you step out into the sunlight, you'll be bombarded with friends, cousins, sisters, twice-divorced black widows, and various unattached women. Eventually, all Wasted Bachelors are taught to fear the outside world, and end up hiding out in the darkened gloom of their apartments, waiting to die.

As Colonel Ripper said in *Dr. Strangelove*, "I don't avoid women. . .but I do deny them my essence."

Now, I know that the many women friends I count myself lucky to have are even now measuring out rope to lynch me, because they all think I'm referring to them when I use the word *spinster*. But Wasted Bachelors are much worse off than Aging Spinsters, since spinsters can at least begin purchasing cats for companionship and seem to slip effortlessly into a grandmotherly middle age of peace, calmly finding new life after sex. Wasted Bachelors, however, are never quite left alone. Even as dotards we're valuable, as long as we can stand up without assistance long enough to mumble something that can be interpreted as "I do." Until we *die*, we're marriage fodder, bwana.

4. *HAVING ANONYMOUS SEX WITH MULTIPLE PARTNERS FOR THE REST OF YOUR LIFE*. Oops—sorry, this isn't a drawback.

Remaining a bachelor becomes more risky as the years go by. Not only are we forced to run the gauntlet of matchmaking everyday, but we also have to risk the possibility that settling down isn't so bad and that maybe we are going to end up like Grandpa Simpson, alone in The Retirement Home, ignored by everyone, simply because we never spawned. The concept of a legacy is a seductive one to us humans, who are terrified by our own mortality and seek to live forever through our progeny. That's all well and good if your legacy is *Microsoft* or some other incredible body of work. It doesn't work so well if your legacy is a unique talent at unhooking bra straps and the legendary ability to look dignified in leopard-skin Speedos, or perhaps being able to proudly say that "it takes more than a fifth of *Early Times* to make me pass out, baby!" In short, men who pursue the rocky road of Wasted Bachelorhood maybe ought to remain childless, for the good of the future, which promises to be a lot less fun, and thus less tolerant of us.

So, it occurs to me that we men who pursue Wasted Bachelorhood are really heroes for our times, eh? We do not scurry for the warm refuge of couplehood; we do not cower under the umbrella of a healthy and supportive relationship. We do not flee from the forces of darkness—we *are* the forces of darkness, and after all what could be more modern than the forces of darkness? I'm proud to be one of the lieutenants in the dark army, marching across the dance floors of the world with a stiff drink in one hand and a dog-eared copy of *1001 Great Pickup Lines* in the other. If you think about it, we're the great anarchists of our times, since one of the main engines of society has always been the drive towards the nuclear family. Resisting that drive is embracing the dark side of freedom, baby, and planting your flag firmly in the pungent topsoil of revolution.

Don't believe that grown men exercising the libidos of 13-year-olds can be heroes? Obviously you've never had to scramble for a wedding date or endure the pitying stares of friends and coworkers, especially on those days when you show up at work hungover on a Monday wearing the same clothes you had on *before* the weekend started, or when you get tossed out of a wedding for propositioning the bride in the mistaken belief that your lifelong desire to write an original *Forum* letter is a noble one, a goal that any American would want to help out with. That, in my opinion, is the definition of an honest mistake, and I wish my family would stop bringing it up whenever I attend family functions.

Screw it. Heroes aren't always recognized in their lifetimes (look at Dean Martin, whose tremendous contribution to this cause is only now slowly being revealed), and I'm content to know that when Armageddon comes our way I'll be in Satan's Singles Bar, juggling cocktails and chasing skirts. Or, possibly, kneeling at god's feet begging for salvation, depending on how things go.

BIG-HATTED WOMAN, WHERE HAVE YOU BEEN ALL MY LIFE?

A Day in the Life of your Editor: The Saint Patrick's Day Parade in Hoboken, New Jersey

Mandy Cuervo succumbs to my obvious charms.

Back in March I was invited to the hometown of two of my lovely assistants (known here as Mandy Cuervo and Carolyn Millivanilli in order to protect their reputations, though their real names are Misty S. Quinn, Esq. and Cassie Carey) to watch a lame parade and then drink all day. What follows is a report on our activities. It is my hope that this will help others who are victims of the "Big Hats" at these parades; my therapy is ongoing.

TIME LINE OF THE BIG HATS

11:30 AM: I arrive. Mandy is frying bacon naked in the kitchen. Carolyn has already consumed a whole bottle of champagne and is passed out on the floor. I step over her gently.

12:00 PM: The sound of the Clancy Brothers on the stereo awakens Carolyn, who immediately begins a painful, off-key wailing I quickly identify as singing. Mandy has put on overalls. I sneak into Carolyn's room to desperately phone Ken West, promising him $50 if he will join us.

12:30 PM: After consuming six pounds of bacon and two Mimosas, I am experiencing heart palpitations. Carolyn is once again unconscious and Mandy threatens to disrobe again to attend the parade "alfresco". I bundle the women out the door and we march up to Washington Street, which shows absolutely no signs of a parade occurring there this day.

1:00 PM: We meet friends and friends-of-friends at Sullivan's bar for a drink. The friends-of-friends are snooty, and Mandy tearfully threatens everyone in the bar with serial nudity unless they are nice to her. Carolyn quickly attracts a crowd of men and dances for them.

1:05 PM: Having been politely asked to leave by the bar's management, we boldly strike out to find a good viewing place for the parade.

1:06 PM: Distracted by a bar called The Mile Square, we enter to bolster our resolve with a pint and the women don attractive, humongous, bright green hats, which are just slightly larger than the women themselves. Carolyn gathers a crowd of drunken men around her and allows them to place things in her hat. Mandy pretends she has "lost" her socks, a foreboding warning of things to come.

1:30 PM: While the women hoot and flash the bagpipers marching by, I notice police forming a line around us and closing in, so I begin backing away slowly. Ken West arrives and attacks us with Silly String. Mandy is delighted and claims his silly string has "ruined" her T-shirt, and happily removes it. We decide to move on and have to extricate Carolyn from a large crowd of police, who are clapping their hands and hollering as she dances for them.

2:00 PM: We arrive at a bar called Hennesey's, where Carolyn immediately finds a group of men to surround herself with. Ken, Mandy, and I have drinks at the bar. Mandy's hat keeps overbalancing her, and she eventually finishes our visit sitting on the floor, drinking anything handed to her. When we leave to get pizza, she has mysteriously lost her brassiere.

3:00 PM: At a bar called Willie McBrides, a large crowd of men are waiting for us, applauding Carolyn and holding banners that read "CAROLYN MILLIVANILLI WE LOVE YOU". We enter the bar with great difficulty due to dangerous crowding. Carolyn holds court by the bar in the back while Mandy and I are nauseated by a "dirty" dancing couple next to us. Ken arrives in the nick of time to demand we leave immediately. We must resort to force to remove Carolyn from her admirers, and in the scuffle, Mandy loses her overalls.

5:00 PM: We are at The Quiet Woman after several other bars, aware of the disturbances the women have been causing, have refused to admit us. At The Quiet Woman, Carolyn quickly assembles a small group of men to entertain her. Ken and I talk baseball in a quiet corner. Mandy is now wearing her large hat around herself, as clothing. She keeps bugging Ken and I to dance with her, but we refuse, knowing that this is just a ruse so she can "lose" her underwear as well.

5:10 PM: Mandy has "lost" her underwear anyway, and Ken boogies with her, defeated.

10:00 PM: I find myself walking along Park Avenue towards Moran's; I have no idea where the past five hours have gone. Mandy is nude except for the huge hat she is wearing on her head. Ken has the grim look of a concentration-camp survivor. I smell like minestrone and vaguely remember the women dancing on the bar to the tune of "Mexican Radio". A large mob of men follows us at a safe distance, watching to see where Carolyn goes next.

10:15 PM: At Moran's Tavern, Carolyn's arrival causes a riot. We drink Baileys and Ken and I get separated from the women as a huge wave of men enters to surround Carolyn. I claim to be Mandy's brother.

2:00 AM: We leave Moran's to have pizza and leftovers at the chicks' house. Mandy reveals that she has been hiding her clothing in her hat. Ken wisely leaves, but I am too weak and am wrestled to the ground and robbed by the women, who taunt me, calling me "little man". I am cast out into the street and my pants are removed.

JEFF SEZ: The St. Patrick's Day Parade in Hoboken is usually a beer-soaked event filled with tragedy and suffering, but I go every year anyway, and usually drag a few friends along with me to share the pain. Legal Counsel Danette Knopp, as one of her main responsibilities, has to attend this fiasco with me every year, and does so with stoic aplomb. While this account is somewhat fictionalized, the spirit is pretty much accurate, and at least one detail is true: I often do lose my pants by evening's end.

LIES BRANDON TARTIKOFF TOLD ME

The Subtle Manipulation of TV Sitcoms

LET'S CONSIDER YOUR UNHAPPINESS: Most Americans today will not only admit to being unhappy, they will single you out at parties and talk to you endlessly about being unhappy. They will practically shove their misery down your throat. If you generate enough sympathy and interest to ask them why they are so unsatisfied (we here at *The Inner Swine* usually feign a stroke whenever this happens to us at parties[1]), urban citizens will usually give you the following three main reasons: a) They have no money; b) they have no love life; c) their apartment is too small.

This unhappiness is purely the fault of television situation comedies.

Consider the following, undeniable truth: *Television programs must accomplish two things in order to attract an audience large enough to generate ad revenues: a) They must cause people to identify with and connect with the characters and situations presented in the show, and b) they must carefully present these characters and their situations as slightly above and beyond the normal life, because, let's face it, watching yourself belly-crawl through your own dull life is not very interesting.*

This results in a mostly white, 18 to 35-year-old cast of characters getting into situations that generally involve their jobs, their friends, and their romantic lives—universals that most of us white folk (who, sorry to say, still pretty much dominate the country's population[2]) can easily identify with. But the characters are usually just slightly better-looking than you, their friends

---

[1] *Actually, after six or seven strong Tequila Fanny-Bangers, the stroke is often not feigned.*

[2] *Unless you live in the Northeast or Miami, which are pretty much becoming separate countries within the U.S., from a demographic and lifestyle point of view.*

Appeared in Volume 4, Issue 4, December 1998

say slightly wittier things than your slow buddies, their apartments are generally bigger and funkier than yours, their romantic interests are guest stars and yours are psychopaths. Situation comedies present you your life, only better—not so much better than yours that you hate the pampered bastards who inhabit it with a white-hot jealous rage that leaves you shaking and sweaty hours after you've destroyed the television, but better enough that you *watch*. They try to present you with people and situations more interesting enough than yours to keep you enviously fascinated, but not so grandiose that you turn away in disgust.

When they do it right, it's almost imperceptible. Look at *Friends*, that NBC study in adult immaturity wherein six pals of an under-30 persuasion get to act like children and get away with it. Consider: The apartments shown are lived in by people who are either chronically unemployed or working low-rent, entry-level positions. If you don't live in New York City I have a hint for you: The sheer size of the apartments shown on that show would beggar a small third-world country. Consider: No one on the show really seriously worries about money, or venereal disease, or unwanted pregnancy, or getting fired. Not *seriously*. Consider how no one is ever alone on that show. Not one of those fuckers is ever alone on a Saturday night, drinking Scotch by themselves, feeling low. They're always with their fucking friends, laughing. Laughing at *us*.

Okay, okay, it's a *comedy*, after all. Aside from the Very Special Episodes ("Tonight, Monica deals with a recipe she's never had to before: *rock cocaine*") it isn't supposed to be a downer. But you see, once we as an audience connect and identify with the cast, once we have the slightest inkling that we wish our lives were that bright, cheerful, and filled with chicks like Jennifer Aniston who can get away with not wearing a bra[3], once that happens, pigs, we're fucked. Because deep down, in places we don't like to talk about at parties, we're gonna be disappointed every time we open our eyes in the morning and find ourselves somewhere other than our favorite sitcom.

That's how they fuck us, kids.

To illustrate the point, *The Inner Swine* is proud to present *The Jeff Somers Show*. First: A true story that happened to me not too long ago, in all its boring and slightly embarrassing detail. Second: The same story, told in sitcom form[4].

---

[3]*Not that we're complaining.*
[4]*And, as a special bonus, here's how that same true story eventually appears in the hallowed pages of* The Inner Swine, *so you can see what kind of filters your Editor puts on reality around here:*

The Day I Accidentally Killed Misty's Cat
By Jeff Somers

Back in September Misty and Jeof had booked a walking tour of south Jersey's Dirt Farms, from the Brown Loam Valley to the Salted Earth Badlands just south of Cherry Hill. This was their big romantic getaway for the year, since they both love dirt. Since I am a close intimate friend of both World Famous Cartoonist Jeof Vita

How I Took Care of Misty's Cat Over Labor Day Weekend

We were on our way to Ted and Jo's to have a cocktail when Misty asked me to take care of her cat while she and Jeof were away romancing in the country. Ignoring the implication that I could not possibly have any plans for the holiday weekend, I said sure, mostly because this would give me an opportunity to go through Jeof's private stuff.

The first two days went pretty smoothly; I showed up at Jeof's dank and dark apartment, which often looks like thieves have rampaged through it, fed the cat, and then played with the poor lonely thing for a half an hour or so, then went home. At the end of the second day, however, I went to the bathroom and left the toilet seat up. When I came back on the third day I found that the cat had had a grand old time skinny dipping in the toilet and then tracking kitty litter all over itself, the apartment, and, in a tragic twist of events, me.

Later on that morning I tried to air out the place since the cat appeared to be suffering from oxygen deprivation, and in my clumsy attempt to open up the bedroom window I almost killed myself (and the cat) when the frame practically came apart in my hands. I patched it together with spit and duct tape and quickly got the hell out of there.

When the happy couple returned I was sad to give the cat's welfare back into their able hands, but got over it, especially since I am still finding kitty litter in my clothes.

Well, that was exciting, eh? Now, the sitcom version of the above story, embellished and stylized to match the typical television version of real life:

---

and National Streaking Champ Misty Quinn, they asked me to look after their little cat, Mangy. Feed it twice a day, play with it a little, make sure nothing heavy had fallen on him.

The first day went smoothly. I fed Mangy Mexican Jumping Beans and styrofoam pellets, which he enjoyed once I'd dipped them in barbecue sauce.

The second day began with tragedy: Mangy had died overnight of unknowable causes (unknowable once I'd cleaned up the various piles of styrofoam-flecked puke). Jeof's apartment had also somehow been burned to the ground, apparently by a carelessly discarded match I'd tossed to the carpet as I'd left the day before, which can hardly be blamed on me, since Jeof doesn't have any ashtrays out, like the insensitive little *artiste* he is.

Since there was obviously nothing I could do, I went out for an early brunch of Mimosas and Bloody Marys.

When Jeof and Misty returned, I expressed amazement and sympathy, and offered to help them clean up the place a little. I helped them drape a tarp over the rubble (one corner of the living room wall was still standing) and create a rough shelter for the young couple. Then I helped them build a fire and skin and clean Mangy, 'cause cats is good eatin.

THE JEFF SOMERS SHOW

Starring

Jeff Somers

Sandra Bernhard as **Lauren Strutzel**

Bea Arthur as **Misty Quinn**

James Earl Jones as **Ken West**

Jackie Chan as **Jeof Vita**

and **Ernest Borgnine** as **"Benny"**

ACT ONE

EXT. A CLEAR AND BREEZY EVENING ON A HOBOKEN STREET. **JEFF** (an incredibly handsome and charming young man), **MISTY** (a cute-as-a-button young woman wearing no bra), **JEOF** (an incredibly handsome and charming young man), **KEN** (an incredibly handsome and charming young man), **LAUREN** (a cute-as-a-button young woman wearing no bra), and others are walking along the street, chatting amiably.

JEFF: And then I said "Don't make me break my foot off in your ass!"

(laughter)

JEOF: There's the ATM.

Everyone lines up to get cash from the machine.

KEN: So, where are you two going over the weekend?

JEOF: We're staying at a bed and breakfast, and there's a lot to do down there.

JEFF: Do you only get breakfast at a B&B? No lunch? No dinner?

JEOF: Just breakfast.

JEFF: No brunch?

JEOF: No brunch.

JEFF: What about snacks?

JEOF: (grim) Just breakfast, you moron. Hence the term "bed and *breakfast.*"

JEFF: (beat) So, is there other furniture involved?

JEOF: (simmering stare)

LAUREN: What are you doing over the holiday weekend, Jeff?

JEFF: (darkly) Sitting in my room, making lists of all my enemies.

KEN: In other words, nothing.

(laughter)

MISTY: Hey! Could you take care of my Muff while we're gone?

JEFF: (beat) Uh, won't that be a little difficult with you—

LAUREN: It's her cat, stupid.

JEFF: (darkly) Remember that list of enemies?

MISTY: Can you?

JEFF: Well, since I have nothing better to do anyway. . .

MISTY: Great! Thank goodness you're such a loser, Jeff. I don't know what we'd do without you!

(laughter)

CUT TO:

CREDITS

(Theme song: "Nobody Told Me" by John Lennon, as performed by NOFX; cast cavorts cheerfully)

DISSOLVE TO:

ACT TWO:

INT. **JEOF'S APARTMENT.**

A spacious five-room apartment with new furniture, high windows, and more square footage than Giants Stadium. **JEFF** sits huddled beneath a coffee table with a telephone to his ear and a terrified look on his face. He has a deep scratch on one cheek. In the background, running water and a wailing cat can be heard.

JEFF: (whispering) Ken! You gotta get over here! I need help!

(pause)

JEFF: (louder) No, now! Dammit, Ken, this cat is some sort of creature of hell! It came flying at me the moment I opened the door, and every time it meows I swear I can hear the word "redrum"! I stumbled into the bathroom and beat it off me with the plunger, and in the ensuing melee I got it wedged into the toilet!

(pause)

JEFF: That's right, the toilet! Now get your black ass over here with some baby oil and a drain snake and make it snappy or I'm gonna be cat chow! Are you—

(The cat's wailing gains volume, and there is a wet sounding sploink in the background.)

JEFF: (Getting to his knees and hitting his head on the table.) Ken! In the name of all that's holy! Get over here!

CUT TO:

INT. **KEN'S APARTMENT.**

A spacious five-room apartment with new furniture, high windows, and more square footage than Giants Stadium. **KEN** and **LAUREN** are sitting in matching easy chairs, watching a huge television.

LAUREN: (Not looking away from the TV) What's going on?

KEN: Jeff jammed Muff the cat in the toilet or something.

LAUREN: You going over there?

KEN: (Turning slightly to look at her in shock) What? And miss "Gilligan"?

CUT TO:

ACT THREE:

INT. **JEOF**'S APARTMENT.

    JEFF stands in the center of the living room, staring at the front door from under his eyebrows. He is dripping wet, as is the rest of the room. He has many more scratches and several tears in his clothing. He is breathing heavily. There is a knock on the door.

    JEFF: (darkly) Come in.

    ENTER **KEN**. He is wearing a black wetsuit with the words THE FIXER stenciled on the back, and is carrying a big economy-sized tub of mayonnaise and a duffel bag.

    KEN: Wow. What happened?

    JEFF: It was horrible. He got free of the toilet and came for me. I held him off with some couch cushions and tried to make a break for it, but. . .he was too quick for me. I feinted for the bedroom, but he cut me off and backed me towards the bathroom again. The toilet was spurting water. . .the cat was screeching REDRUM REDRUM! And I grabbed up the plunger again and fought for my life!

    KEN: (beat) What happened?!? Where's the cat?

    JEFF: (swallowing) Flushed.

    KEN: Flushed?

    JEFF: (smiling evilly) Like a goldfish.

CUT TO:

EPILOGUE

INT. HALLWAY OUTSIDE **JEOF**'S APARTMENT.

    JEFF, **JEOF**, and **MISTY** walk up to the front door, where **JEFF** turns to face them.

JEFF: All right, listen. I wasn't completely honest with you about the cat. I can't lie to you guys. You're my friends.

MISTY: (horrified) You mean Muffy's not in Hollywood making cat food commercials?!

JEOF: (horrified) You mean we're not going to get thousands of dollars in commercial residuals?!

JEFF: (glum) No, I'm afraid that Muff is (beat) no longer with us.

MISTY: (confused) Where is he?

JEFF: (looking off into the distance) Oh, the Atlantic Ocean by now, I should think.

CUT TO:
END CREDITS

And there you have it, kids, two versions of reality: The way it really happened, and the way NBC would have presented it to you[5]. Don't ever doubt that every single thing shown to you on television has been filtered somewhat with the explicit purpose of manipulating your reaction to it. Is this mind control? Of course not. But it's as close as they've been able to get, and they don't think twice before using it to its full potential.

This of course doesn't have to be harmful. Getting you to pay attention to a sitcom is not exactly the Devil's work (some may disagree with that). If they didn't play with reality a little no one *would* watch, so it's really just part of the entertainment experience—Shakespeare did it, why not NBC? Ah, but at least people pay close attention when they read Shakespeare.

---

[5]*Just let me note for the record that no cats were ever harmed by your Editor here. Muff is a purely fictional creation. While I have murdered and consumed countless other mammals in my bizarre desire to keep on living in the style I am accustomed to, never have I done so to a cat. At least not that I know of. There are a few drunkenly hazy moments.*

You Can Live on Ramen Noodles for $200 a Year

Surviving the Coming Economic Crash

I don't understand anything more complicated than *Celebrity Jeopardy*, really. I put on airs sometimes that I'm an intellectual, much to the annoyance (and irritation) of my long-suffering close family and friends, but the truth is I'm the sort of guy who can easily become confused trying to keep the relationships on *Friends* straight. As a matter of fact, the dangerously skyrocketing number of references to that white underbellied little sitcom in this filthy rag is one reason I question not only if I've lost my youthful edge, but whether I ever had one at all. That has nothing to do with my intellect or capability to understand complex subjects, but it sure explains a whole lot of other things, if you ask me.

So, being slightly dim to begin with, I find it difficult to stay awake whenever the talking heads on my television screen or the icons writing for the major periodicals start going on and on about economics and national policy and the World Bank blah blah blah. I don't understand how people like Imelda Marcos can bleed a third-string backup country like the Phillippines for *billions of dollars*, and yet we in this country might actually have to go through some hard times despite the fact that we shit a billion dollars accidentally on a daily basis. What can I say? I'm a simple lad. I like to live in a simple world, and anything that complicates my puddle gets ignored rather viciously.

So, a few months ago *Esquire* put out an interesting article about how experts agree the USA is headed for a major economic dustup, likening it to the Great Depression. At least, I assume it was an interesting article; I didn't actually read it (heavens no! I barely have enough time for finding porno on the net as it is!) I just scanned the cover, which featured a disturbing graphic of a man's head smashed into pieces with the headline *What Did You Do Aafter the Crash, Daddy?* emblazoned across the top. Using my immense intellect, I got the gist of the article without reading it, trust me. As I said, I'm a simple lad. Aside from the fact that major magazines (and TV shows and any other media-conglomerate that treats information as a commodity) are faced with the daunting task of finding something interesting to write about on a monthly basis, it should be obvious to anyone who pays any sort of attention that media sources, talking heads, and generally every single person in the world is pretty much wrong half the time anyway. The universe thwarts all attempts to predict its next move. So I sort of don't see the point in paying much attention to magazines like *Esquire*, especially since *Esquire* isn't even bright enough to put a naked woman on its cover like all the other magazines. How do you expect to sell me a magazine without boobs on the cover? I mean, come on.

Such a breathtakingly provincial attitude is all well and good when there's plenty of gravy floating around this swollen nation, and even marginally talented yokels such as your Editor here can get paid by a major corporation for services rendered, if only just barely. But even I have to pull my head from my fascinating ass and wonder: what happens if there really is a crash? What happens if I can't even manage to earn the pitiable little salary I've managed to scratch out for myself? Perhaps a little deprivation and poverty would teach my bloated generation a little character, a little humility. Maybe a few years of desperation would remind us that we're not owed anything by life and that we have to work hard for everything. Maybe it would teach us something.

Not if you follow these simple rules, pigs.

The Inner Swine is not about improving your soul or deepening your character or making you grow as a person, so herein we'll explore how you can maintain the life of a useless slacker even in the face of catastrophic financial collapse. As long as the USA doesn't completely collapse, leaving us with no choice but to join up with insane warlords in some *Thunderdome* scenario, you ought to be able to keep on contributing nothing to history, culture, or anything else for that matter and still keep your *Baywatch* rerun viewing at a maximum.

1. Cut Expenses. You don't need to eat every day.

In the event that the American economy turns into pudding, your first object is to ensure daily survival. You can't spend your days fondling the remote control and yourself if you don't have scratch, friend, and during *Grapes of Wrath*-like turmoil your previously touchable friends will become a little more miserly, trust me. But don't despair! Even assuming the Republican assholes (who will no doubt overrun Congress just before their dangerous fiscal policies (amounting to fairy dust and Masonic rituals, IMHO) cause the aforementioned crash) deny you and your ilk government assistance, you can still manage to live. First and foremost, though, you'll have to adjust your spending to reflect the new situation.

What are your essential needs? Here's a quick guide to the only things you really need: **food, television, candy, and liquor.**

What can you eliminate? Easy. Anything that will not cause you immediate and sudden death. New clothes? You can survive without for a while. A car? Walking is healthy. Shelter? If you can't find a friend or relative surviving the disaster with condo intact, there are plenty of alternatives as long as you can *look* respectable (see next section). Everything you truly need is listed above. Let's see how we can acquire them on a regular basis without spending much money.

FOOD. As the title of this article suggests, you can live off of Ramen Noodles for about 50¢ a day. All you need is boiling water. Water is free. Scratch up 50¢ a day my friend and you'll be eating Beef Ramen until you'd rather you were dead. I've determined through painful personal experimentation that you reach that *I'd-rather-be-dead-than-eat-one-more-bowl-of-Ramen-Noodles* stage after 34 straight days of Ramen consumption.

TELEVISION. Now, television is free, but you'll have to somehow manage to not sell your TV for one of the other items on the list. Of course, you could always stand in front of store windows and watch TV there, assuming the aforementioned warlord situation isn't in effect, because then there would probably be no television anyway.

CANDY. Your best bet for candy would probably be those newsstands in Manhattan where they put the candy out on display while the proprietor of the stand sits inside, collecting monies. It isn't too hard to snatch a Clark Bar and run. By the time the poor sap extricates himself from within the stand, you're two blocks away, licking chocolate off your fingers.

LIQUOR. Obviously the most difficult item on our list to acquire, and yet the most necessary. I can survive anything as long as I'm armed with a snootful of cheap booze. My best suggestion is to steal liquor from your friends and family. Even after they kick you out and tell you not to come back, you'll be able to use your intimate knowledge of their homes to break in and rob them blind.

Total costs: 50¢ a day.

2. GET CREATIVE. IT'S ALL ABOUT APPEARANCES.

Some of you might be reading this and wondering why shelter isn't on the list above. You simpering snobs think having a decent place to live is essential and I must echo Yoda when I reply: *that is why you'll fail*. While you're desperately trying to hang onto your apartment, smarter people like me will be hoarding our booze and exploring less expensive lodgings, which is to say *free*.

The key is your appearance. You'd be amazed what you can get away with in this sad world as long as you look nice. People who complain about there being no public bathrooms in New York City obviously look like bums, because you can take a crap just about anywhere in this town if you just look respectable. If you put on a nice suit and tie you can waltz over to the Waldorf and use their bathrooms. Just looking nice will get you in.

So, if you manage to keep yourself fairly groomed you'll be able to worm your way into all sorts of public buildings, which will give you access to the most important ingredient in grooming: running water. Once you're in a gas station restroom or public library bathroom, you can wash up (assuming getting partially naked in public places doesn't bother you) shave, even rinse out your underwear. It's a bum's paradise. The key is, you have to look presentable to get through the doors, so you have to begin your grooming program the moment the crash hits and you get evicted for non-payment of rent. Be ready.

Of course, maybe you've got a family member or friend who's surviving the crash easily, in style, and you can live with them and leave it at that. If not, aside from running water you'll need a place to sleep, and no matter how presentable you look no place will let you sleep there that night. So, chances are you ain't far from some big city, and big cities always have large selections of abandoned buildings, some even in pretty decent neighborhoods. While the local haunted house or condemned building won't have much by way of heat or electricity, it will keep you out of the rain and give you someplace to sleep. Sometimes the power company even leaves the power on in these places, since it often costs more to send someone out there to disconnect than it does to just leave things be.

Not an ideal life, perhaps, but much better than being a migrant worker, getting paid pennies to pick beans somewhere, better than living in some pathetic tent city in a park where TV news correspondents come by every week to do human interest stories on you. The easiest way to stay unemployed during the coming Depression, friends, is to too closely resemble Henry Fonda from *The Grapes of Wrath*. Not only do you look dirty, disheveled, and criminal, you also look ready to bust some heads at a moment's notice. Stay relatively clean and you might just get a job, or at least be able to steal some stuff.

Total costs: Just your dignity, and what's that worth? Nothin'.

3. Lie, Cheat, and Steal. It'll be a disaster, after all

If the Depression hits, one thing is for sure: There will be no jobs. That's my working definition of a Depression anyway. I can't comprehend corporate politics as it is, so the trials and tribulations of our overpaid CEOs won't concern me much beyond cheering every time one of these overfed assholes takes a swandive off the Empire State Building, so you can talk at me about World Economic Forces or Domestic Fiscal Actions, and it won't mean anything. Thirty million able-bodied people out of work, now *there's* a situation I can wrap my head around. So there's only one solution to your situation if the big whammy puts us all out on the street: Toss those traditional morals over the side and start cutting purses.

In the event of a major Depression, *The Inner Swine* fully endorses crime and thuggery as a personal short-term solution. You won't be able to get a job, after all; even if you do spend your days standing around a parking lot hoping to be chosen by fat cats looking for cheap hard labor, you'll get paid shit for 18 hours of back-breaking work. I don't know about you, but the staff here at TIS long ago decided that death would be preferable to back-breaking labor, and we meant it. The cyanide capsules were handed out, and we all know in our hearts of hearts that if we ever found ourselves wearing work gloves it wouldn't be long before we were found foam-mouthed, twitching on the ground. If you were going to get paid well and solve all your financial difficulties with labor, I suppose it could be excused. But let's face it, in a major economic crisis you're going to be working to *eat*. All we can say about that is: See the first sentence of this paragraph.

So, consider a life of crime. Not murderous, *evil* crime, but simple thievery and con-artistry. For a few hours of light running everyday, you could be eating well and kicking back while the other suckers drag themselves through the killing fields. A major economic crash like this would be a national disaster, after all, and if we've learned anything from movies we've learned that disasters require drastic measures. It isn't your fault that the bottom fell out of the world's economy, is it? Nope. It's the morons running this world and the idiots who've been playing with imaginary money too long, so stick it to them. Here are some easy-to-plan and relatively danger-free scams you can inflict on the innocent rubes who still have some cash:

1. THE OLE' PUSH AND RUN: A classic street crime, this one has small returns (usually) and a bit of danger, and it involves a great deal of running. Basically you pick out a slow-looking victim with a purse, give 'em a good shove, and run with purse in hand. If you're careful to stay out of neighborhoods you're known in and run pretty fast, you have a shot at making a few bucks every few hours. If you get caught, it's usually only a petty larceny rap. On the plus side, you'll stay in shape, and this crime requires absolutely no skill whatsoever. On the down side, the money is small potatoes and getting caught is pretty embarrassing, especially if the old biddy you tried to rob is beating you senseless with a purse that feels like it's full of rocks.

2. THE DEVIL-MAY-CARE CHURCH ROBBERY: Just wait at the back of the congregation politely, and when the collection plate is handed to you, turn and run like the wind. Chances are no one will chase you. If they do, remind them that they're supposed to be good god-fearing folk.

3. THE CORPORATE RANSACK: Security in all those midtown office buildings is handled by slack-jawed morons in the best of times; during economic crises it might get slightly better because of the flood of able-bodied applicants but it's doubtful. Wait until about 5:10 PM on a Friday and saunter into an elevator. Pick a floor at random and try to get into the space (you can usually just get past the receptionist with a breezy lie; if you have those neato jumpsuits that custodial workers worldwide wear you won't even get questioned) and then steal steal steal. There's all sorts of good stuff in corporate space: foodstuffs, milk money funds, fenceable equipment. Clothing. Hell, if you're careful you might even have a place to live! These buildings are always crawling with contractors, messengers, and the like, so getting in is usually easy and walking around is usually safe. Even the most secure offices get robbed now and then in this manner, and if you encounter some stormtrooper security you can just shrug, get back on the elevator, and try another floor.

Of course, if you get caught, getting out can be difficult, but looking the part helps avoid this (almost no one questions you if you're in the right uniform) and hell, if you do get busted, that brings us right to our next section!

Total costs: None, assuming you can lay your hands on some work clothes.

4. PRISON. IT WON'T BE JUST FOR CRIMINALS ANYMORE

During an economic disaster, is there any sweeter deal than a few months in a state pen? We here at TIS doubt it. Free food and lodging, plenty of company, and access to all sorts of amenities, like a library, television, gym equipment, and games. You might be forced to perform labor, but it won't be nearly as back-breaking as the "free" freelancers on the outside, because the prison system is government-regulated. Even if you're breaking rocks on the highways, you're getting a pretty good deal. And if you happen to get beaten to a pulp every night and anally raped every Thursday by a guy named Tiny, well, without risk there is no glory, right?

If you plan well, you can ride out the entire crisis in the comfort of your heated cell and emerge 10 years later into the economic recovery, a more cheerful world with plenty of job opportunities. You'll have learned a lot, not only from the libraries but from your fellow inmates, who no doubt have plenty of lessons to teach, and no hesitation in teaching them. Most importantly, you will not have spent a dime during your stay in the big house! Hell, if you spent your time making license plates or such, you might even emerge with *more* money than when you entered!

Costs: physical wear and tear from beatings and rapes. Otherwise, free!

Hopefully the wizards and Masons who secretly run this world will figure out how to avoid this predicted crash, and I won't have to learn to say those magical words, *do you want fries with that,* or to run really fast while clutching ladies' handbags to my chest (a skill, to my shame, I think I've already mastered). If not, you will have this little pocket guide to help you through the rough spots, said rough spots being pretty much all there is.

If not, don't call me. I certainly don't want to hear it, and the rest of the TIS staff will only jeer you heartlessly.

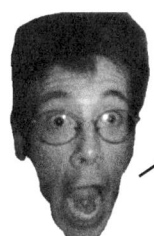

JEFF SEZ: If any of the wizards and Masons who run this world are reading this, please induct me into your secret society of Implementors immediately. I can pay the dues, and I'm tired of living in squalor like a sucker.

THE ICE WEASELS ARE LIVING IN MY PANTS

How to Be an Expert at First Glance

"Love is like racing across the frozen tundra on a snowmobile which flips over, trapping you underneath. At night, the ice-weasels come."
- Nietzsche[1]

Ken West and Jeof Vita prove that reality is mutable....verrrry mutable, baby. Please ignore obvious tape.

THE INNER SWINE has never been about "truth" or "honesty" or "accuracy in reporting". In these modern days, truth is a hollow concept co-opted by TV shows and advertising, honesty will more than likely get you vilification and blame, and that last part just makes us sleepy. As far as *The Inner Swine* is concerned, it ain't what you know, it's what you *seem* to know; appearance is everything. An easily proven fact is that I don't know anything of any consequence; my head is filled with earned run averages and pornography. Yet I have cultivated a reputation as a minor savant. This isn't any kind of major achievement, kids; it's the result of an easily mastered technique we will term *The Inner Swine* Faux Knowledge Generator (FKG).

People respect knowledge, even in these dangerously lowbrow times where Jewel is a poetess and David Cassidy is writing screenplays.

---

[1] *This quote has nothing to do with the rest of the article. Nor can I really say for sure that Nietzsche said this. If he didn't, someone should have.*

Appeared in Volume 4, Issue 4, December 1998

Unfortunately, actual knowledge isn't easy to accumulate: It requires time, energy, and (ugh) research. We live in increasingly fractured, fast-paced, and specialized times, though. The age of the Renaissance Man is over. It takes too long to become an expert in something for us to be experts in more than one or two things, if that. Most of us aren't experts in anything, except perhaps our jobs, which can't be that difficult or we wouldn't be doing them in the first place. There are thousands of subcultures, disciplines, and minorities out there, each with its own jargon, hardware, and traditions. To know it all would take several lifetimes.

Too many of us, however, swoon in defeat at the sight of this breadth of knowledge and resign ourselves to a lifetime of being dullards, of standing quietly at parties, at having nothing to say. We here at *The Inner Swine* refuse to give in to our own ignorance! Our time is too divided up between *BayWatch* reruns and *JenniCam* viewings for actual learning, but we have invented the Faux Knowledge Generator for those of you who, like us, enjoy *appearing* to be smart without actually knowing anything.

The FKG can be summed up in three words: keyword, sources, and attitude. Using this simple system you will find that you can win any argument, dominate any discussion, and generally appear to be an insufferable know-it-all—as long as no actual experts on the subject at hand are within earshot.

The Faux Knowledge Generator

KEYWORDS. Actual knowledge could be defined as having an understanding of the definitions, processes, and reasonings behind something. You have a knowledge of chess openings if you can identify them by name and understand how the moves are made and why they're made at certain times. It is absurdly simple, however, to simulate knowledge by the smart use of keywords or jargon. Technical jargon exists for just about any body of knowledge because, as pointed out succinctly in The Jargon File (www.tuxedo.org/~ESR/jargon/), "All human cultures use slang in [a] threefold way -- as a tool of communication, and of inclusion, and of exclusion." In other words, it's a way for the members of a subculture or discipline to identify each other and keep the rubes out. As a result, jargon becomes a powerful tool, and using it in a confident way can convince anyone not intimately familiar with it that you know what you're talking about.

This requires a small amount of research. Every discipline or subculture has a book somewhere, or a web page, or FTP site, or *something* that will list and explain most of the jargon. Just picking up a few keywords and having a working knowledge of what they mean and refer to is immeasurably valuable in convincing people that you're an expert. If your audience has only a small familiarity with your chosen subject, or perhaps no familiarity at all, throwing around a few words authoritatively will go a long way towards establishing yourself as an expert in the field.

The key is in the presentation. The jargon should roll off your tongue as if you've been using it so long to communicate with your fellow experts you've forgotten that most people don't understand the meaning. You shouldn't be self-conscious about using the jargon, and you should never stoop to explaining what a keyword means unless asked to. In other words, the strength of jargon is its opaqueness: The words form a protective wall between your actual ignorance and the crowd's interest. As long as they don't know what it all really means, you can babble it all night and they'll never figure out you're as dumb as they are.

Note of caution: Never make up words and try to pass them off as jargon. You never know who in your audience might just know a thing or two about your chosen area of bullshit, and there's one truth about words you should never forget: Made-up words have an odd habit of sounding made-up, despite the fact that all words were, at one time, made-up.

SOURCES. Just parroting jargon or accepted wisdom may not be enough; depending on your charisma factor and ability to bullshit, your audience may not be willing to accept your pronouncements at face value. The second most powerful trick to faking knowledge is the quotation of qualified sources. By attributing a quotation or fact to a legitimate repository of specific knowledge you assemble a whole roomful of experts behind you. Sources are divided into two distinct categories: *Renowned* and *Underground*. You should utilize examples from both in your quest to appear smarter and more knowledgeable than you really are.

I would stress here that you should not feel the need to have actual quotes from these sources; make them up by all means. The trick is in attributing the fake stats, quotes, or data to a source. Much more powerful than simply claiming you "happen to know" or that you "heard somewhere". By invoking some sources, you're cutting off any dissent before it begins.

Renowned sources (such as *The New York Times*) are famous general publications which boast a wide range of interests. They are well known to just about everyone and have some sort of good reputation, so I wouldn't go quoting *The Fortrean Times* in this instance. While you may like TFT and read it seriously, many people do not. Don't ever associate yourself with a Renowned source that has a bad rep, like *Brill's Content*. Pick bland, conservative publications that seem like they've been around since the beginning of time.

Underground sources (for example *Acta Gynecolgica Scandinavia*) are very narrow-focussed publications that usually target a small, specific audience instead of a general market; all disciplines and many subcultures have journals, FAQs, and magazines dedicated to their sphere of interest. They may be well-known within their circle, but are probably not on your local newsstand. Pick carefully, a lot of Underground sources have very bad reps, since the standards and practices of Underground publications are generally lower and more mutable than Renowned sources, which is, sadly, one reason why paranoids dislike Renowned sources. The Underground source should be chosen for a careful combination of narrow focus (making it unlikely anyone in your audience might have heard of it) and good rep (just in case someone has).

Note of caution: Never make up an Underground source; you'd be amazed how often this is sniffed out by the dullest audience.

ATTITUDE. Perhaps most important, depending on your skill with the other aspects of the FKG, is the manner in which you present your Faux Knowledge. This will be most sorely tested when you encounter a Doubter, who suspects you are bullshitting and decides to test you. How you react will decide whether you walk away a genius or a moron. Remember: You chose to present yourself as an expert. If you get caught, it will be difficult to keep your dignity, eh?

Be confident. Admit no doubt. If someone presents contradictory information after your stunningly ill-informed soliloquy, admit nothing, stay calm, and lie your ass off. It is an undeniable fact that most arguments are won by force of personality, not by facts. Once you establish yourself as an expert, you can wither any opponents with a dexterous stream of jargonbabble, complex statistical proofs, and searing disdain. The searing disdain, I might add, is the most important aspect of the defense.

Don't be afraid to lie. No one is going to go home after a night spent drinking with you and change the course of their lives because you were very convincing explaining Einstein's Theory of Relativity to them ("As most everyone knows today, Einstein overvalued the Time/Space variable by as much as 6%, irreversibly compromising his data and probably warping the continuum for years to come."). You won't be responsible for career changes and suicides; you'll merely have built a reputation as a smart person when in reality you have trouble remembering phone numbers. So, when challenged, lie your ass off. Bullshitting is like building a castle in the swamp: If you keep piling enough on, eventually it'll reach critical mass and stabilize in spite of its nature. In other words, keep lying and eventually no one will be able to parse it enough to tell you *are* lying. And if you're not lying you must be telling the truth.

If you do get zapped by someone who actually possesses knowledge on a subject, retreat. *The Inner Swine* applauds those who wisely run away rather than get slain in battle; better to be blown out of the water early and regarded as someone who had one misconception than to doggedly pursue brilliance and bury yourself beneath debunkings. Pull back in the face of actual knowledge, lick your wounds, and live to lie another day!

Utilizing this easy system, any schmo without any valued training or expertise whatsoever can dominate arguments and appear much more brilliant than they actually are. It's certainly worked for us here at *The Inner Swine*. After all, reality is what you believe it to be, and most of us have a tenuous hold on our beliefs as it is—easy enough to make the deep magic and fold the lies around you like a royal robe, affect history, alter society irrevocably.

Or to get chicks, which is what we use it for, mostly.

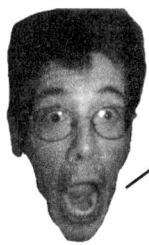

JEFF SEZ: TIS Legal Counsel Danette Knopp wants me to point out that I am no longer using this, or any other, technique to 'get chicks' since it worked to perfection with her and now has no further purpose in my life. Thank you.

Baby Levon Rocks On at the DOT

I can't keep this damned car on the street.

LIKE the seasons coming, my car has to get towed by some municipality at least once a year or the universe would be unbalanced. Some might suggest the frequency with which you find me running down streets waving my hands wildly and screaming after a tow truck is a direct result of my own moron-level IQ—but that's just Jeff-bashing, if you ask me, and I thought we'd advanced as a civilization to the point where I could live free from anti-Jeff prejudice. Whatever the reason, the fact is that my car getting towed must be some sort of holiday event for Department of Transportation employees the world over—a challenge, perhaps. Maybe after bagging my car they rush to their offices to e-mail DOT people the world over, posting to alt.towers.municipal that they got Somers again! It's really the only explanation for the sheer number of times I have parked my car, turned to scan the horizon, and turned back to find it being carted off by grinning, burly men in DOT uniforms.

The worst is when it gets towed in Manhattan. The Manhattan impound lot is on 12th avenue and 33rd street, which means it might as well be in the Hudson River. It costs $150 to get your car out of stir, and *then* there's a summons on your windshield, just in case you thought $150 was getting off easy. But the worst of the Manhattan experience is actually while you're at the impound lot trying to get your car back. I explained some of this in issue 4(1) of *The Inner Swine* in the article "Ten Short Stories About *The Inner Swine*" (p. 13) when my car last got towed in New York City, and now I'm

Appeared in Volume 7, Issue 2, June 2001

back to explain it again, because I feel the need to, and because I have 60 goddamn pages to fill in this issue and it ain't easy. I make it look easy, but it ain't.

Having been through the mill a few times, I knew the moment I discovered empty space where my car had been that I'd been towed, so I walked to the nearest ATM machine, took $150 out of my weary checking account, and hailed a cab. I made it to the impound yard before my car had actually been towed in, which I thought was a new record.

The secret to any transaction with government employees, I am convinced, is whiteboy politeness. No matter what your race or religion, you should reach in for your internal whiteboy and push it up onto your face as far as it will go. The people who work for city, state, or federal agencies don't give a shit about your situation, don't forget; they neither put you there nor care much how you got there, and the worst thing you can do is try to make them empathize with you in any way. Now, I *am* a whiteboy, and I was raised polite, so I am something of a force of nature when I walk into grim government offices. People who have come to enjoy crushing the hopes of their fellow humans are often reduced to giggles by a simple *thank you* from me.

So, I got on line with all the other poor souls who came in with the red hot DOT poker rammed up their asses. We all waddled in, smoke still drifting up from our cauterized wounds, and stand in line, waiting for someone to notice us. I went to the window, gave them my information, and then waddled off to stand in a corner and wait, which is my advised course of action under these circumstances. I found some old friends who'd also been towed, and we stood around trading war stories and politely ignoring the steaming hot poker protruding from our asses, which is also strongly advised. Call attention to someone else's screwing and it'll just boomerang back at you, badly.

We settled back to watch the rubes come in and make a fuss. It's always amusing.

First came in a woman I will refer to as *Charlize Theron Put Away Wet* and her husband. I call her that because she resembled the actress Charlize Theron except with a yellowed, alcoholic cast to her features and a chubby, sheets-to-the-wind look in her eyes. She was also wearing leather pants, which anyone will tell you just pisses me off. Not because of some animal-rights senility, but because they look ridiculous on everyone, and people ought to just realize that.

Charlize was outraged that anyone would dare tow her car, and seemed incapable of going more than five minutes without letting us all know it. She also couldn't seem to utter a sentence without reminding everyone that her car was a BMW. Her husband just followed her around grimacing apologetically at everyone, and we all felt sorry for him, but not sorry enough to smack his wife around for him, which was obviously what he wanted. You could literally see this couple's chances of getting their car back before the next invasion by Martians get dimmer and dimmer each time Charlize strutted to the window and hissed, "I DON'T UNDERSTAND WHY IT'S TAKING SO LONG TO GET MY *BMW* BACK!!!" I could have sworn I saw DOT workers shredding her paperwork, grinning happily.

After a few more moments of frustration, Charlize took to quizzing everyone waiting about where they'd been towed from. Discovering two others who received their hot pokers in the same area, she became convinced a conspiracy was afoot. This added a nice whiff of coke-addled paranoia to her outbursts at the window, and even the suffering workers seemed to warm up to her a little, as a figure of fun.

In the midst of Charlize's display of poor judgement, a second rube strolled in convinced that somehow his importance to the universe would sway the bored employees of the DOT. My fellow seasoned DOTers and I dubbed this guy *Dr. Dumb*, since he was some sort of professor and he had the good sense of a chihuahua. Dr. Dumb marched to the window and we observed the following exchange:

Dr. Dumb: I have a plane to catch!
DOT Worker:
Dr. Dumb: I cannot miss my plane!
DOT Worker:
Dr. Dumb: Hello?
DOT Worker: License and registration. Wait for your name to be called.
Dr. Dumb: How long will this take? I have a plane to catch!
DOT Worker:

Charlize then corralled Dr. Dumb and began quizzing him, researching her conspiracy theory. Dr. Dumb seemed quite alarmed by Charlize, which made us upgrade his IQ rating a little. At least the obvious didn't escape him.

Our pokers having cooled to the point where we could safely remove them, my fellow veterans relaxed in the dark orange chairs bolted to the walls of the DOT waiting room and began singing *Leavin' on a Jet Plane* in harmony. Dr. Dumb worked the phones, apparently calling everyone he knew simply to announce that his car had been towed and that he could not miss his plane, although what the people on the other end of the line (assuming there actually were people, and not dial tones) were supposed to do with this information was not immediately clear to us.

Around this time a new aspect of the DOT conspiracy theory entered into Charlize's brain, and she began quizzing everyone as to how long they had been waiting. Charlize, who was shrewd but obviously illiterate, had observed several people who had come in after her receive passes to get their cars, but did not seem to be able to read the sign posted in the middle of the wall, on which was written **ALL TOWED VEHICLES ARE HANDLED IN DUE PROCESS, NOT NECESSARILY THE ORDER YOU CAME IN** in large, black print letters. A common mistake rookies at the DOT impound make is to assume that time has meaning to people who are trapped inside the impound yard eight hours a day. The last time your typical DOT worker saw sunlight was 1953, and one hour is the same as one day to them. The veterans and I chuckled at Charlize. Her husband seemed to be trying to kill himself via Jedi mind tricks.

Just before my own name was called, a final rube strolled in to amuse us. This guy under the impression that Member's Only jackets were still acceptable fashion, at least for men over 50. He was smart enough to wait on line quietly, and smart enough to be polite to the workers, but just when we were about to suggest he join us in serenading Charlize with *Drive My Car* he tumbled over a rookie ledge and landed, broken and beaten, on the rocks below. In other words, he began disputing his summons with the DOT workers.

If there's one thing DOT workers care less about than the inconvenience your towed car is causing you, it's whether or not your car deserved to be towed. Now, most people who get the lucky chance of coming to the DOT impound know they're screwed: I, for example, know I parked in a crosswalk. However, some people have apparently studied the parking laws of New York City and can't keep quiet until the trial. This new rube, who we'll call Member's Only for obvious reasons, was one of these. He asked the DOT worker why his car got towed. In a moment of awe-inspiring shock for us veterans, the DOT worker stared at Member's Only for a moment, and then *actually informed him.* Apparently Member's Only had been towed because he'd parked the car in a no-standing zone.

"But the car has commercial plates." He protested. "That's why we *pay* for commercial plates, so we can park the car in commercial zones."

Our sense of awe dissolved into glee as we realized that Member's Only, who'd had a chance to be a DOT legend after actually inspiring information from the good employees of the impound yard, had overstepped his abilities and gone crashing into DOT hell. The DOT employees gave him the standard blank stare. Rule number one, even if you recklessly ignore the other rules, is *never ever argue the summons*. Nothing irritates DOT workers more. They didn't ticket your car, they can't do anything about it, why do they have to hear it? People who imagine that the man or woman filling out the paperwork to release your car from the impound have the legal authority to dismiss tickets and tow fees on the spot have a childlike view of the legal system in this country, and get nothing but contempt from us DOT veterans.

Member's Only persisted, however, explaining in detail how the commercial license plates worked. The DOT workers stared at him and then decided to have some fun, and told Member's Only to go to his car in the impound and retrieve the ticket so they could look at it. As Member's Only huffed out to do so, I joined hands with my fellow vets and we sang *I Fought the Law* in honor of the valiant but foolish man. Sure enough, when he returned with the orange ticket in hand, the DOT workers, amused, looked it over, decided they could do nothing about it, and told Member's Only he would have to wait for his name to be called.

    Finally, my own name was called, and I went to the window, paid my tow fee, and got my car back. I waved at my fellow veterans a little sadly, and rode the little golf cart to my car, which sagged in its slot, ashamed and dejected. Lovingly, I started her up and drove her home. I knew I'd be back soon enough.

In the Event of Disaster
I Would Eat My Cat

We're civilized, right? That's what the brochure says, anyway. *Welcome to the Human Race, civilized since 2000 B.C.* Since we're civilized, we ignore a lot of the fight-or-flight responses that normally come up and refine our thinking and decision-making to a sharp point, meaning that the primitive instinct to *seek shelter* has mutated into the gross acquisitiveness of *seek-five-bedroom-duplex-with-ocean-view*. So many of our instinctive needs and compulsions are satisfied on a daily basis, we're free as a race to wallow in the muddy darkness of our ids and superegos, making life more and more complicated because. . .well, because we *can*. Complicating your life is a way of celebrating your complexity. *See*, your complexity gloats, *I'm so fucking complex a creature, simply securing sustenance for myself isn't enough, it has to be cholesterol-free vegan tofu Thai food and a Diet Slice.*

We're pigs after all, every one of us. Satisfying our egos is pretty fucking important.

All this complexity, however, all these little rules we develop over time to display how special we are, how advanced and, most importantly, *how in control we are*, is just an illusion. We're not special, pigs, we're not very advanced, and we are most certainly absolutely not in control of anything, ourselves or the events unfolding around us. The proof of this statement is found in what scientists and historians have termed the Somers Principle of Dead Cats, which states the following: *After a nuclear holocaust if a vegan cat owner is trapped in their basement with their beloved pet and slowly realizes that there is no food and they will quickly starve to death, it will take them about five minutes after this realization to strangle their beloved cat to death and begin preparing the carcass for consumption.*

    It's a simple concept, really: All the rules we come up with for life are only possible because we've managed, through the strangulation of the Third World and our brutal exploitation of the Earth's natural resources, to make the satisfaction of our basic need pretty automatic. We no longer have to search for clean, potable water: It's piped into our homes. This leaves us free to demand more and more complex beverages, like herbal teas with a twist of lemon. We no longer have to cautiously hunt the fearsome Crocostimpy in a quest for food; it's shipped, butchered and trimmed into steaks, to our local supermarket, leaving us free to demand tofu and any other complicated dietary system. Clothing is plentiful and cheap, leaving us free to decide that fur is murder and to go around throwing red paint on people (leaving your Editor to ponder who is the greater idiot: fashion designers or the PETA people; so far, a tie). Shelter, heat, clothing—it's all simple, these days, unless you're poor and homeless, of course. Even then there are free shelters, free clothing, and free food. Not enough, of course, but that's mostly because the rest of us are too busy procuring faux fur and sending back the Taco Burger at Joe's Diner for being too rare. With no work left for our survival instincts to do, we come up with all these bizarre schools of thought: veganism, low-salt diets, fur is murder, whatever. The point is, only our current prosperity and ease of survival gives us the elbow room to exercise this sort of individualistic idiocy. When the bomb drops, our bullshit lifestyle choices will drop even faster.

    I love my cat. I'd also club her head in with a crowbar and skin her in preparation for cat stew if I was trapped in my basement after the apocalypse. I'd whistle "Memories" from *Cats* while I did so, too. And I'll tell you one more disturbing thing: Since your cat doesn't have the sort of civilized bullshit that we do, if you did starve yourself in order to spare your cat and passed out on day seven post apocalypse, your cat would not hesitate a second to start eating *you*. Hell, it would purr the *tune* of "Memories" from *Cats* while it did so.

    The Somers Principle of Dead Cats has been a main tenet of *Inner Swine* philosophy for years now, and it never fails to get groans and protests from your Editor's intimates. That's mostly because we're fat and happy enough as a race to embrace artificial codes and belief systems. There's nothing wrong with that. As long as we remain this fat and lazy, I'm fine with thinking of dogs and cats and canaries and such as sacred house animals that are inappropriate to consume. Why not? Kidding yourself and wasting your time on meaningless beliefs hurts no one as long as civilization continues. What bothers me, mostly, is the dumb, blind belief that our civilization is a guaranteed force, and that therefore these belief systems will continue forever and ever. Ha! Civilization is precarious, always will be, and thus these beliefs are always in jeopardy. The statement *humans must consume proteins and other materials to live* will never be untrue, pigs. The statement *Fluffy the cat is part of the family and thus we can't eat her* could become a funny joke in the span of 20 minutes, which is about how long the TISIC science labs have calculated it would take civilization to collapse under the right circumstances.

For now, I urge everyone to enjoy whatever system of life they've developed to cope with the yawning fears of death, meaninglessness, and futility we all have inside us. Think being carnivorous is evil? Eat plants, what do I care. Think buying clothing made out of polyester is a scandal? Drape yourself in velvet, no one here gives a shit. Just remember that when (not if) the world starts to crumble and a Thunderdome-like society sprouts up, all your bullshit will dry up like stagnant water in the desert: so much miserable illusion. And remember, next time you invite me over to your house and I'm petting your cat with a glazed look on my face, I'm probably estimating how much white meat is on it.

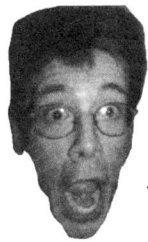

JEFF SEZ: Opinions don't get any more specious than that. Thanks to homemade liquor and a high lead content in my tapwater, I haven't had a coherent thought in years.

Everybody's Talkin' at Me: Reviews, Letters, Legal Threats

BEING AN INTERNATIONALLY FAMOUS zine publisher means I get lots and lots of mail, most of it crude threats. Sometimes, however, people decide to review the magazine, or to simply communicate their sad and lonely thoughts to me. I don't mind; if I can bring a moment of joy to their otherwise gray and joyless lives, I'm happy.

The Inner Swine, however, has never reviewed other publications in its hallowed pages. We do, however, reprint every review about us that comes to our attention. Actually, it doesn't even have to be a review: It just has to have my name in it. J-E-F-F S-O-M-E-R-S. That's the magic recipe for publication in TIS. Whenever I see my own name in print I get this sort of sappy look on my face and stare at it in a dreamy sort of way for a long time, humming happily.

Because I imagine that you all enjoy seeing my name in print as much as I do, I have included here the best and worst reviews we've ever gotten (along with my mega-super funny comments on them) and some of the stranger things people have sent us in the mail.

EVERYBODY'S TALKIN' AT ME
Reviews, Letters, Legal Threats

Send me a letter with my name in it and I guarantee publication.

THE INNER SWINE published its first issue in May, 1995. For a very long time after that, nothing happened. No one seemed to know we even existed. Glancing through old issues in my hurried preparation for this book[1] I discovered that we didn't receive our first real review until 1996, when *HiJinx* #1 gave us a favorable write-up I can no longer locate. As a matter of fact, in the first five or six issues of TIS my "Letters to the Editor" section was most often filled with bitter rants concerning the lack of such letters. I started publishing my own zine for the same reason everyone does: I wanted gushing letters from young women asking to meet me in secluded restaurants so they could bask in my brilliance. Discovering that this might never happen was a bitter pill to swallow.

Still, by late 1997 I *was* getting mail. That was good! Unfortunately, all the mail was from Freaks. That was bad! But most of the Freak Letters were entertaining, and filled up plenty of space in each issue, freeing me from the yoke of actually creating content. That was good!

I also began to get some notice and some reviews, many of which were

---

[1] *What happened was, clint johns called me and, as usual, I immediately began daydreaming that he was calling me to tell me that Tower Magazines was going to stop paying me in American money and start paying me in bottles of liquor. When I came out of my reverie all I heard was clint saying, "Well, great, we'll expect all that in a few months!" leaving me to wonder what, exactly, I'd promised to do. It turned out I'd promised to create this book. By the time this dawned on me I had about 36 hours left to work with. I called clint to beg for more time and he threatened to burn my house down and hit me in the face repeatedly.*

surprisingly positive. Where other, lesser zine publishers might have been tempted into weak-kneed reciprocation, *The Inner Swine* decided its own selfish interest would be best served by exclusively reprinting reviews *about* itself. What could be more Swine-like? As we discovered, not everyone gets this joke.

REVIEWS

The first review we reprinted in TIS for the strict purpose of tooting our own glorious horn appeared in Volume 3, Issue 2, in September 1997: "*The innards of this swollen sixty paged pig are stuffed with witty, creative and opinionated slop. Its neatly typed characters and smart lay out are an ironic twist to the slimy snouted fiction and commentaries it contains. According to zinester Jeff Somers. . .this zine is not designed to shock but to 'get you to think, a little.' Well Jeff, [it] sits rather nicely in my tummy after a midnight meal of skewered tofu and veggies dipped in tomato sauce and cheese. Bon appetite!*" This review appeared on a web site called *Disquieting Muses*, where it resides still, and was penned by someone called Venus Zarcas. I have never heard from Venus again. This was typical: People would appear, send me wonderful reviews, and then fade away. I wonder sometimes if maybe they aren't all figments of my imagination.

By December of that year, I knew we had finally arrived, because we received the following brief review from **Factsheet Five** shortly before that fine publication disappeared for years, apparently with the publisher flying off into the sunset with several overstuffed bags marked with dollar signs: "Inner Swine*: A conglomerate of essays and short fiction that bats around .500 for entertainment. Jeof tells you how to sneak personal work into the office while Jeff explains how to tell real friends from passing acquaintances and why vegetarians are assholes.*" I figured after getting listed in F5 we'd be on easy street, with Hollywood knocking, but no such luck.

From then on, I started finding a few reviews of TIS every month or so, and the business of printing other people's reviews of TIS in my own zine took off and became a distinctive feature. I don't review other people's zines because: a) There are already too many people who think the world needs their input on that front, and b) I don't enjoy reading other people's writing enough to do it sincerely. Why do I insist on printing other people's reviews of TIS? Even the bad ones tickle me, because it's my fucking name in print, because it's someone taking notice—yahoo! And it occurred to me early that nothing was more swinish than printing my own reviews, giving the reviews a mirror-against-mirror aspect I like a lot. My policy generally is that I'll print any correspondence that comes my way, unless obviously private or obviously impersonal. I wonder if a spinoff zine is in there somewhere? A *Reader's Digest* of TIS reviews. It's got potential, and you people will buy anything.

Uh, someone should have edited that last part out. For your education and entertainment, then, here is a quick sampling of reviews of *The Inner Swine* and my reaction to them. Can you do better than that for your entertainment money? I think *not*, motherfucker.

THE GOOD

"...this is one of the more entertaining things I've read lately, well thought out articles...all infused with a healthy dose of cynicism and humor, and equal helpings of alcohol and misanthropy. My mom would not like this, but yours might. Ask her." — **Maximumrocknroll, 1998**

I considered using "Your Mom might like this, ask her" as our advertising slogan, but eventually settled on "Just send us the goddamn money", which has worked surprisingly well. MRR is a cool magazine, and I was delighted to get reviewed in it a few times.

"Who in hell doesn't appreciate cynical humor? Nobody I know. I mean, damn, Jeffrey Somers could write about anything (and practically does), and it would be fun to read...Hilarious and interesting to read. I don't know if I agree with some of his sentiments, because sometimes I can't tell whether he is scoffing or really means what he says. Either way, I fucking love this guy, and I think you should check this out." — **Maximumrocknroll, 1998**

It was around this point that I began to realize that seeing my own name in print was the main reason I did anything.

"Here's a true story...Yesterday I settled down...to spend Saturday reading zines...I was halfway through...TIS and got myself a cup of coffee...I took a sip and immediately began choking...after a few minutes my breakfast came up on portions of TIS...I have read thousands of zines in my time but have never barfed on one...I was really upset so I wiped the soiled issue off and put it on the stove to dry and laid back down on the couch...I was able to finish it without losing my innards...I like your brashness and the writing is never boring..." — **Blind Cow Publications, 1999**

I can't count the number of times someone told me they'd vomited all over an issue of TIS. I think it's quite telling—we must be stirring up some serious reactions, to elicit vomit. Generally speaking, vomit is good.

"In the incredibly narcissistic world of zines, The Inner Swine *stands as a* beacon of self-centeredness— here is a zine which, instead of printing reviews of other zines, instead prints reviews other zines run about The Inner Swine ('If it ain't about me, it does not get into the issue, got it?'). Fortunately, Jeff Somers is smart, funny and self-effacing enough to be able to pull it off. . .Just about everything in this 60+ digest-sized publication is hilarious at best, worth reading at worst, and extremely self-referential. And since I know he'll probably print this review in the next issue, I just want to say hello to all readers of The Inner Swine. Highly recommended." — **Shouting At the Postman, 1999**

SATP's review was the first time someone really pointed out the big joke in reprinting our own reviews, and the first to use the 25-cent word 'narcissistic', which impressed me.

"Jeff's main interest in life is clearly Jeff, but he's smart, he's funny, he writes very well and swaggers in style, so his self-infatuation is perfectly understandable. . .Some parts of TIS didn't work for me. . .but hell, maybe that's just me. This remains, however, without doubt, one of the finest zines ever to emerge from Jersey City. Recommended, in case you couldn't tell. This is some serious high-quality shit." — **Zine World, 1999**

For weeks after getting this review, no one could stand to be around me, because I would announce that I was some "serious high-quality shit" at some random point in every conversation. I usually had my copy of *Zine World* in my back pocket to back it up with printed facts. Then again, most people tell me they *usually* can't stand to be around me.

"Hey asshole, I just got the latest TIS in the mail a couple weeks ago. What a piece of crap. Ok, actually, I loved it. I finally feel like I'm vibing with the whole TIS groove. A case in point: Yes, I too was sitting on the toilet at the very moment I was reading in your letters section about how other reviewers were reading it on the toilet. The issue remains in my bookbag, from where I can whip it out at a moment's notice to give myself a shot of self-appreciating Somers-style story-spinning to keep me awake between classes at the University of Minnesota." — **Breakfast, 1999**

Toilets are a strange, disturbing theme in a lot of *Inner Swine* correspondence. People generally seem to read the magazine while sitting in a bathroom, and if they attempt to enjoy it outside the bathroom they tend to suffer some form of gastrointestinal distress. Or vomit, as previously discussed.

"I've read a lot of personal zines, but this is a whole different kind of 'personal'. . .the mantra here, repeated many times in many ways, is that Jeff Somers deserves more hosannas than life has given him, so gosh darn it he'll write his own hosannas. It's quite amusing, and somehow it doesn't even feel self-indulgent. . . There's some non-Jeff-specific material, too, but mostly this is a big celebration of the Joy of Jeffhood, and you'll want to bring a kazoo and join the party." — ***A Reader's Guide to the Underground Press, 1999 (formerly Zine World)***

The last sentence DID become our advertising slogan for some time.

"Great writing is very hard to find in zineland, and you definitely can't make a case against the fact that The Inner Swine *is full of great writing. First, let me quickly dispense the negatives. I dislike seeing the words* 'The Inner Swine' *and* 'Jeff' *a quadrillion million times on each page. Also, long, stupid 'plays' about nothing just don't keep my attention. The same goes for articles like 'Why I Think Jeff Somers Is Real Smart'. Sure, Jeff's long winded, ego-inflated articles could fuel a hot-air balloon convention, but you have to look past all of that. Jeff is a funny and, sometimes, thoughtful writer. As I read this zine at lunch hour, I got an instant glued-on grin and found myself occasionally laughing outloud, spitting out small pieces of Oscar Meyer bologna (or phlegm, it's hard to tell the difference sometimes). Needless to say, my old lady coworkers were staring at me unapprovingly. . .His fiction is decent, and, gasp, his poetry is swell as well. Did I mention that* The Inner Swine *is funny? This zine could certainly grow to be one of my favorites.*" — ***My Moon or More, 1999***

Enjoying *The Inner Swine* when you dislike seeing the words "Jeff" and "The Inner Swine" is almost unthinkable, yet some people manage it. Sort of like enjoying a hot dog despite disliking meat by-products.

"*The closer a zine gets to being really, really good, the harder I tend to scrutinize it to find flaws. About the only flaws I can find with* The Inner Swine *are a sometimes too-self-referential tendency, some pieces that seem arbitrary in their inclusion, and some pieces that could have been improved by a few more revisions. It's really quite good, funny, and engaging, but a little geeky. Remember that guy in high school who was really funny but a little too into the Monty Python thing and would make just one or two too many Monty Python jokes? Not the full-on freak who'd quote you the entire fucking Holy Grail movie in different voices, but someone who was about 30% of that? That's the feeling I kind of get here, but man, it really is pretty funny. . .Bottom Line: Get it.*" — ***Kris Kane, Menace Publishing, 2000***

I've been a little touchy about my extensive knowledge of Monty Python quotes ever since seeing this review. Why must people be so mean! Kris later became my web host and has been serving up swine HTML hot and tasty on the Internet ever since.

"*If you're looking for a jaded, opinionated, aiming-for-humor-lit-mag, put together by a Jersey City drunkard, this is it. . .thematically it's all 'I hate these people. . .these people are stupid. . .I got drunk. . .' etc. . .I guess this is kinda cool cuz usually I really hate things like this, but I thought this was tolerable.*" — ***Maximumrocknroll, 2000***

There's nothing like a reviewer who knows what they like and can sanely express it to you. . .and then there's this guy, who spends 95% of the review telling us all how much I suck (it's true) and then says he liked it, for some reason he's far too complex to be able to sort out. Yes, I see.

"May I say that TIS. . .was a joy!!! and probably the best zine I have ever read. I have never been so entertained by a zine. I read it in the bath and nearly drowned several times from laughter! I believe you are a genius!" — **Blender Children, 2000**

I believe I am a genius too. But then, I also believe I am a leprechaun.

"Jeff Somers is an asshole. So why do I like his zine so much? Is it because of his endless capacity for self-promotion? Is it the fact that he can call for a counter-cultural revolution while simultaneously sitting on his ass watching TV? Is it his rich 'Yugo-slobby-ian' heritage? Is it his hilarious and pointless interviews with his friends? Could it be his enjoyable short fiction? His hatred of consumer culture? Is it the fact that, while most zines print reviews of other people's zines, Jeff reprints reviews of his zine previously featured in other zines? Yup, Jeff Somers is an asshole. Don't buy his zine. Your money will only go toward building his world-wide Swine empire. You wouldn't want to live in such a world." — **Breakfast, 2000**

I was extremely excited to find someone who understands that I'm an asshole.

"What concerns me is this: that there is, at the bottom of certain pages, a little Jeff's head, and the Jeff's head has a word balloon in which are the words 'JEFF SEZ' followed by what Jeff is saying. But: since the words 'JEFF SEZ' are in the word balloon, it would seem that the words 'JEFF SEZ' are, in fact, among the words that Jeff says. In other words, the implication is: when Jeff is speaking, in casual conversation or otherwise, whenever Jeff has something to say, he prefaces it with the words 'JEFF SEZ.' Actually, upon further consideration, this seems very likely. Perhaps my concern, then, was unwarranted. Thank you for clearing that up. P.S. Do you know who Sean Whalen is? He was in 'Twister' and 'The People Under the Stairs.' That's who I think you look like." — **Throwrug, 2000**

JEFF SEZ: How can people be so cruel? I have a speech impediment. It forces me to preface everything I say with JEFF SEZ. I have been treated as a freak my whole life because of this. Now I have to be treated that way in my own magazine! AND NOW EVEN IN MY OWN BOOK! Oh, the injustice.

"It took me well over a week to read the first issue I received of The Inner Swine, *as I was limited to reading at red lights on the way to and from work. When I received the second issue, it jumped to the top of my zine pile queue and I read all 60 text-dense pages in one sitting. A criticism I've seen noted of Jeff's zine is that it is egocentric. Granted, Jeff is Jeff's favorite subject, but it's a subject that is*

presented warts and all, with humor, and never seems to veer into whining self-absorption. Despite the frequency of his issues, the quality is high. His enthusiasm for the written word flows off of the page. The issues I've read are a mixture of well-written fiction and personal pieces." — **Xerox Debt, 2000**

Every now and then we get a quiet, positive review that does not mention toilets, vomit, or my Creeping Assholism. It's rare, and when it happens I like to mark the moment quietly.

"Self-referentialism never had it so good, nor possibly so copious. Many readers shall find this humorous zine merely funny (yes, damn it, there is a difference!). . .Somers' stuff nevertheless floats well with the buoyancy of his eternal self-deprecation and strange, only slightly sophomoric wit. Whether it be long-winded publishing parodies ala the Bard, or late 1970s National Lampoon-esque ego melees, The Inner Swine is worth reading cover to cover. In the end, this endeavor is firmly recommended, even if there is the perpetual push to being in being in being being in the philological rut of tomfoolery." — **Angry Thoreauan, 2001**

Only slightly sophomoric wit? I hate to do anything in half measures. *Angry Thoreauan* published a few pieces of mine in 2001, so they might not have been totally objective, although I doubt they cared enough about the two pages of material I supplied to them to censor their review. Anytime I get compared to the *National Lampoon*, I consider it a Good Thing. We *still* don't know if that last sentence is a joke we don't get or a typo.

"I have just finished killing the better part of the last hour perusing TIS. . .while at work. . .I must say, and I don't mean this the wrong way, I am always surprised that I enjoy reading The Inner Swine. It's combination of outright apathy and vicious cynicism would lead one to believe that TIS was just some dim geek's quarterly exercise in narcissistic vanity passed off on a (limited, I'm sure) public as a joke on its face. But its really more than that. The beauty of TIS is that. . .what's being said does apply to the inner swine in all of us" — **M. Cameron Newell, 2001**

"Some dim geek's quarterly exercise in narcissistic vanity passed off. . .as a joke" came *very* close to being an advertising slogan, but calmer heads eventually prevailed.

"Immediately, as a disclaimer, I should mention that I detest personal zines. That said. . .Somers is sweet on himself, like every other 'per' editor I've encountered, but his slant is that he is so blatant and relentless in this self-aggrandizing that it becomes hypnotic. . .Sometimes I laughed at the geeky wit of this guy. Sometimes I just laughed at him. Not bad." — **A Reader's Guide to the Underground Press, 2001**

Hypnotizing people with the sheer magnitude to which I am sweet on myself—this review rocked my socks when I saw it. The plain truth is, whether you're laughing at me, or with me, I'm generally too drunk to notice anyway.

"For some reason almost every review of this zine I read says something about how egocentric it is. Well, I'd like to know what personal zines these folks are reading that aren't completely self absorbed and egocentric. . .I don't know I just know that Jeff is a funny guy and a good writer. And in his zine he prints every review someone writes of his zine. . .I thought of just making this entire issue one long review of The Inner Swine *so Jeff would then be forced to publish the entire contents of FW/L in an issue of TIS. It would've been pretty funny, but I chickened out. . ."* — **Fish With Legs, 2001**

I actually would do this, but I'd do it by printing his entire issue in type so small and leading so tiny you'd have to be some sort of radioactive mutant to actually read it.

THE BAD

Not everyone loves me. Here are some choice less-than-stellar reviews, most of which are pretty much on the money.

"This is an honest zine, so I will be honest. Most everything in here I didn't need to read. It is written by some guy in Jersey that thinks that he is some self-proclaimed intellectual but seems to only be able to cover topics like 'Great Things About Pornography' and 'Smut-Hunting on the Internet', neither of which were really of any help to me in my smut hunting endeavors. There are a bunch of stories in this, but they made me a little bored since they were mostly a reflection about this boy's life. I read it on the crapper and nearly cracked my head open on the corner of the counter falling asleep, oh!!" — **10 Things Jesus Wants You to Know, 1999**

You can't be loved by everyone, I guess, though lord knows we try. This also continues the toilet theme, which has become the signature of class that *The Inner Swine* wears so proudly.

"The funniest thing about reading this zine is that I was sitting on a toilet when I read the first few pages. Why is this funny? Because they quote a previous 10 Things *review and that reviewer 'read it on the crapper' as well. Hey, at least I got a laugh out of it. There's some interesting (and slightly amusing) writing buried somewhere in this zine, the trouble is that it's surrounded by annoying babble that unfortunately makes you want to put the issue down."* — **10 Things Jesus Wants You to Know, 1999**

Slightly amusing is actually pretty good, as far as I'm concerned. Another *10 Things* reviewer reading us "in the crapper" - makes you wonder what they're feeding their reviewers over there.

"This is really hit-and-miss. The whole gag seems to be utter contempt for

everyone, including readers of the zine. The articles are written well enough, but they tend to go on too long (especially the uninteresting ones). . .The Inner Swine is worth taking a look at, if you can stomach the attitude, but it feels sort of like the zine is treading water" — **Zine World, 1999**

Why does everyone think my utter contempt for everyone is a gag of some sort? Must be my powerful charm and good looks.

"This zine has a huge staff considering that 11 out of 12 articles were written by the egomaniacal Jeff Somers. At least they were well-written. I don't think apathy should be worn as a badge of honor, though, and apathy is entirely different from cynicism, which Somers seems unaware of. . .Basically, I think this would be a really good 40-page zine, if the sophomoric humor is what got cut. The short story at the end, 'Can Open Worms Everywhere' was surprisingly good. It was by far the best part of the zine, and proved that considerable talent lay behind it. This has the potential to become a very good zine, but it's not quite there." — **Maximumrocknroll, 2000**

Some people like the fiction and don't understand the rest of the magazine, some people want nothing but stories about me and Ken West breaking into the White House and kidnapping Jenna Bush for kicks. You can't please everyone. This particular MRR staffer is distinctly not in on our joke, though. For the record, I know the difference between apathy and cynicism. I just wish other people knew the difference between humor and reality.

"Inner Swine is a site about a zine about something or another, and unfortunately tries to be a catalogue for various publications, plus a sampler, plus a web site. There is much that suggests this should be good—audio clips about bad writing and slogans such as "everyone is an asshole, especially us", but it tries too fucking hard to stay on the right side of mass appeal. So what does that mean? It means it's wank. Come on, stick your fucking necks out. You have nothing to lose but your fucking heads." — **Vic Flange, Fleshmouth, 2000**

Ladies and gentlemen, we have a winner! The moment I read this, I knew we had our new advertising slogan. *"The Inner Swine. So what does that mean? IT MEANS IT'S WANK!"* That's been sitting proudly on our web site ever since we read it.

"The Swine is a hit or miss perzine. Some parts are hilarious reading. . .Other parts aren't as engaging and my eyes glazed over. There's enough good stuff that it's worth reading, but with a little more quality control, this zine sure could be something." — **A Reader's Guide to the Underground Press, 2000**

Unfortunately, quality control means work, and we don't "do" work. In a way, though, since we're still getting the same bad reviews seven years later, we do have some form of quality control—reverse quality control, I guess you'd call it.

THE FREAKS

Of course, sometimes the opinions expressed to us in the mail cannot be so easily placed in the "positive" or "negative" categories. Sometimes we read a letter from our friends and then have to get up, pad into the dark kitchen, and place that letter in the freezer to protect us from the eerie freakism emanating from the page. Here are some samples.

DAN B. In 1998 I got a few disturbing letters from Dan B. I wasn't sure how to take them, since they were kind of self-pitying and seemed designed to guilt people into publishing his prose. Here's a sample: *"Dear Jeff, Hope you are having a happy holiday season. I read your listing in Factsheet 5. I am sending these in hopes that you can use them. I am such a fortunate person. Even though I am a diabetic, had cancer, had a couple of nervous breakdowns, I have had a lot of my writing accepted. It makes me feel great and useful. Hope you also feel that your zine is of use. Take care of yourself. Take it easy on yourself over the holiday."* Here's one of the stories Dan sent us:

THE JOKE

After breaking his wife's index finger Jesse gave his mother-in-law an even bigger lip. Women were always against him. They just weren't made right.

Two years later his wife shot him with his shotgun. He squealed and wept till she came closer, then he broke her finger. This time it was her middle finger, so she would have something to look at.

He laughed. The joke killed him worse than the hole in his stomach.

The End

Dan stopped mailing stuff to us after a while. He wasn't the only person who thought we ought to be publishing their work, though.

FAYE L. Your Editor once again proved he is adept at attracting teenage girls when **Faye Lynn** from New Hampshire wrote *The Swine* with some essays back in 1998, which was a banner year for groupies (earlier in the year I'd made the mistake of sending a young girl a letter telling her I liked her zine, which she'd handed to me at a concert in NYC—she tracked me down and called me late at night, expecting me to be some cool dude who would rescue her from her parents, an act which could be described in two words: *statutory rape*). Here's one of Faye's pieces:

For a Good Time Call...

Due to my own admitted weirdness, I do a lot of strange things. Sometimes they are things that could get me into loads of trouble.

OK, I like to put my own phone number in phone booths just to see what will happen. I write: *For a good time call....* I just want to find out if anyone will actually call. I have purposefully left my number in phone booths all over New Hampshire.

One afternoon, I was awakened by a telephone ringing. Upon saying a groggy hello, a slimy, pedophile-ish voice invaded my phone. He stated to me that he was just calling for a good time. I was shocked. Never did I think anyone would really waste their time calling. At first I had forgotten that I had left my number everywhere, but then I remembered, told him to go away, and hung up the phone. If he hadn't sounded so scary I would have talked to him.

I laid there in bed for a while, completely flabbergasted. Then I put on some music and began to go about my usual wake-up routine, which is trying to go back to sleep. About half an hour later, he called back, and his voice was even more slimy this time. He kept asking me my name, and instead of telling him I asked what his was, after all he was the caller. He explained to me that he "just wanted to get off real quick" and that he was not trying to cause a problem, he was only doing what it said to do on the phone booth.

Following his comment about "getting off", I sighed into the phone and hung up. He never called back after that.

Everyday I think about this slimy guy and wonder, he could walk by me on the street and neither of us would know it. I just hope he's not psycho enough to track me down by searching an entire phone book. Then I'd be in for a real treat.

The End

Faye also disappeared shortly thereafter, perhaps because we did not return her love. Ah, the loneliness of the zine publisher. No one writes a book about *that*, do they? But it's true. Listen closely at night and you can hear us on rooftops, croaking out our sad mating calls.

DAN S. Dan S. was Lauren Strutzel's roommate for a few years and became something of a fan of ours. When he moved away to California I kept sending him issues, and he kept sending me bizarre letters in return, which is actually a cool arrangement. Here's the first one I received in 1999:

"Dear editor: Last night I found two women on my bed reading TIS. They were squirming in what appeared to be either pleasure but what could have been the series of death-throes that usually follows ingestion of poisonous legumes. The two women quickly left after I surprised them. -Your most western reader, Dan S."

Dan continues to check in every now and then, and sent this letter to us in 2000:

"Dear Editor: I recently undertook a survey of the magazines in my master bath. You may be happy to know that there are three issues of The New Republic, one issue of The New York Times magazine, and FOUR issues of Inner Swine gracing my can. I love that TIS has a small form factor and is made of low-quality, and thus high-friction, pulp paper, as these attributes help keep it from falling off the slick porcelain that is my throne. I also appreciate the lack of advertisement inserts in TIS, since inserts invariably fall out of magazines and land behind the toilet, and I hate reaching down there to pick them up, especially when they go anywhere near the toilet bowl brush. Keep up the good work."

Dan was also the only reader to respond to a survey I sent out in 2000, although he ignored our suggested answers and checked OTHER for all five questions and scrawled his own:

1. How did you hear about us? **My roommate Lauren inflicted you upon me.**
2. How much of each issue do you usually read? **0%. I "read" the future by interpreting the ashes of burned TIS copies.**
3. Have you ever used this periodical in a manner not intended by the Lord our God? **There is no way to disgrace a copy of TIS, since it has the least grace of anything that exists or that can be dreamed of, or no longer exists.**
4. What would you like to see more of in each issue? **Topless chicks.**
5. When the revolution comes, we can count on you to. . .**Give you up faster than my little ho' cousin gave it up in summer camp in '82.**

LEGAL REMEDY. In 1997 I was thrilled to have someone threaten to sic the cops on us:

"Dear sirs,

This is my second and final request that you remove my minor daughter, Tara X. . .from your mailing list.

If any further correspondence is received from yourself addressed to my daughter I will file a claim of action with the PostMaster General *and the United States Attorney."*

And our response to this snippy piece of mail:

"Dear sir,

Thank you for threatening legal action against us; we are thrilled with the possibility. Your letter. . .was the first correspondence we have received from you; in the future, when considering legal action, may we suggest you send your letters by registered mail, so you will have some proof that you contacted the offending parties."

Unfortunately, nothing came of it, and a priceless potential for free publicity was lost forever. Sadly, no one has threatened to sue or have us arrested since.

JUST WEIRD. *"With all the Swine readers admitting to spending time with your zine while on the toilet, have you ever considered placing the* Swine *in every proctologist's office across the country? Maybe lobbying them to name a disease in your honor, something for those who spend way too much time on the toilet, creating a drooping or malformed butt and having it named the Swine Round Ring Syndrome. Maybe even a marketing deal with Fleet Kit to package a copy of the Swine with every kit." — **Skunk's Life, 2000***

This gave us our third advertising slogan in as many years: "Swine Round Ring Syndrome—catch it!"

POEMS SUCK. For a while we were getting lots of poems in the mail. Here's two from members of our Inner Circle I thought I'd share with you:

From Karen Accavallo: "Hello. I am a charter member of the waiting-to-die crowd and thought you might like to sample some of my poetry for your magazine. I have many more selections for your perusal, in such categories as: **PLAGUE, VERMIN, DISEASE, DISMEMBERMENT, HYPOTHERMIA, WAR, ETHNIC CLEANSING, HANDBALL**. Please let me know. Thanks for your time.

CAULDRON OF ENNUI
By Karen Accavallo

It is raining.
A cold rain, cold as my heart
I stare at the rain
And slowly
I
expire.

And

From Misty S. Quinn, Esq:

TURTLES
By Misty S. Quinn, Esq.

Turtles, turtles, turtles -
they are green and slow
some live in the water
they like to swim real slow
how i love little turtles
all hard and shy
they live in peace
until the day they die

Well, I sure hope you've enjoyed that trip down memory lane with me. That concludes our book.

Contact Info

The following publications were mentioned somewhere in this book. On the off chance you want to check out some of these fantastic publications, here's the contact info we have. Some of it may not be accurate by the time you read this. This is known as *The Way It Is* in zinedom.

A Reader's Guide to the Underground Press. *PMB 2386, 537 Jones Street, San Francisco, CA 94102; www.undergroundpress.org; $4 postpaid single issue.* Formerly known as *Zine World*, this is a fantastic magazine that reviews independently-published material, promotes indy publishing events, and spreads news of interest to anyone who's ever made illicit photocopies of something that would definitely get them fired/expelled if they were caught.

Disquieting Muses. *http://www.geocities.com/SoHo/Lofts/8380/zines.html.* Geocities' web pages get moldy fast, and if the review of *The Inner Swine* is any clue (dating back to 1997) this place hasn't been touched in quite a while.

FactSheet Five. *PO Box 4660, Arlington, VA 22204; www.factsheet5.com; twbounds@pop.mail.rcn.net.* This once-legendary publication has been dormant for years, and went through two new Editors in 2001. Tom Wheeler is currently claiming ownership at the above address, but who knows how long that will last?

Maximumrocknroll. *PO Box 460760, San Francisco CA 94146 ($3).* These guys put out one of the older and more interesting punk publications around.

Blind Cow Publications. *David R. Wyder, 87 Richard Street, Apt. 7, Passaic, NJ 07055 ($3); DailyCow@aol.com;http://members.aol.com/dailycow/indexhcom.htm.* You may not think you can write that much about cows, but boy, would you be wrong.

Shouting at the Postman. *ASKalice art net, PO Box 101, Newtown, PA 18940-0101; http://members.aol.com/satpostman/; kenbmiller@aol.com.* This is one of the more interesting mailing lists you can get yourself onto. Why hesitate? What can you possibly be reading on the toilet now that's so much better?

Breakfast. *Vincent Voeltz, 3621 153rd Lane NW, Andover, MN 55304-3020.* The web site I had went 404 in mid-2001, so I don't know if this zine is still in existence. A zine about the best meal of the day should never die.

My Moon or More. *POB 773, Appleton, WI 54912-0773.* That's all the info I have. Haven't seen a MMOM in a while as of this writing, but continues to publish other things from time to time.

Blender Children. *Lea Ann Martin, 1514 SW Hampton, Topeka, KS 66604; http://www.cjnetworks.com/~mart/welcome.htm*

Throwrug. *Karlos the Jackal, PO Box 29378, Bellingham, WA 98228-1378 ($2).* Karlos is a funny, funny man.

Xerox Debt. *Davida Gypsy Breier, PO Box 963, Havre de Grace, MD 21078 ($2); http://musea.digitalchainsaw.com/xeroxd.html; E-mail: leekinginc@hotmail.com.* A great review-zine with a perzine feel. Well worth the money. Davida can write, too, boyos.

Angry Thoreauan. *Angry Thoreauan MagaZine, POB 3478, Los Angeles, CA 90078-3478; www.angrythoreauan.com; revtinear@angrythoreauan.com.* A nicely delirious publication that has printed one or two pieces by me, so they must be cool.

Fish With Legs. *Eric Lyden, 224 Moraine St., Brockton, MA 02301-3664 ($1.00 or trade).* Eric always has something interesting to say, and his lo-fi zine is always fun and creative.

10 Things Jesus Wants You To Know. *8315 Lake City Way NE #192, Seattle, WA 98115; http://www.10things.com.* Although consistently unimpressed with my zine, this is always interesting.

Fleshmouth. *http://www.fleshmouth.co.uk.* The home of Vic Flange, whoever he is.

Skunk's Life. *DB Pedlar, Skunk's Life, 25727 Cherry Hill Road, Cambridge Springs, PA 16403; http://www.jahitchcock.com/skunk.html; dbpedlar@toolcity.net.* Don't be put off by the odoriferous title, this zine is always filled with good writing.

Well, there you go, kids. The great thing about publishing your own magazine is the community that exists, filled with strange, delightful people who are more than willing to mail you their thoughts and opinions, sometimes about you, sometimes, sadly, about other people. If anything you've read here concerning one of these publications or people seems interesting, I strongly urge you to send them some small amount of money and get a sample issue of whatever it is they produce. Or, send me money and I will then pretend to have never received it.

Hey kids, it's Blatant Self-Promotion!!

Well, Pigs, here is where we beg for your money while trying to maintain an aura of cool, hip, detatchment about the whole thing. The following pages are not for the faint of heart, because they are basically me begging abjectly for about fourteen pages. Do yourself a favor and just mail me some cash, and then you can skip this section without feeling guilty.

In this section you'll find information on how to buy The Inner Swine *retail, like a sucker, how to purchase a subscription, how to access the amazing TIS web site, and an excerpt from my novel. You may be wondering why you should send me even more money after you just defied the laws of probability—nay, the very laws of physics themselves!—by purchasing this book. I don't have a satisfactory answer to that. Maybe in fifty years scientists will be able to explain this phenomenon. For now we must blunder on in ignorance.*

YOU WANT SOME OF THIS?

Where You Can Find
The Inner Swine

Our Motto # 1:
"Fuck you, pay me"

THE INNER SWINE wants your money so badly we're willing to publish this zine just to get it.

RETAIL STORES

• **TOWER RECORDS**: You're standing in one now! Just look for us in their zine racks, we'll be there. If not, write them a nasty letter and steal something.

• If you're a retailer who would like to carry TIS on your shelves, you can contact Jeff Somers directly, or you can contact **Desert Moon Periodicals** (1226A Calle de Comercio, Santa Fe, NM 875005 / TEL: 800-547-0182 / FAX: 505-474-6317 / www.dmoon.com).

• Think bar codes are for Zine Elvis sellouts? You can also order us through STUFF, which is a print catalog of zines and such. You can send $2.50 for the latest issue to: Stuff, 3811 NE 7th, Portland, OR 97212. Contact: phouston46@hotmail.com.

• Quimby's Bookstore in Chicago now carries TIS on their shelves! 1854 W. North Avenue, Chicago, IL 60622; www.quimbys.com, info@quimbys.com

SAMPLES AND TRADES

The Inner Swine's official position on trades is that they fall firmly under the category of free stuff and thus warm our stony little hearts. If you pub a zine or other product, send us a comp and we'll do so in turn. We LOVE trades. Sample issues are available for $2, just drop us a note.

SUBSCRIPTIONS

Buy our magazine, please! *The Inner Swine* offers several subscription packages, and we have actually sold **9** since 1995, believe it or not. We certainly can't.

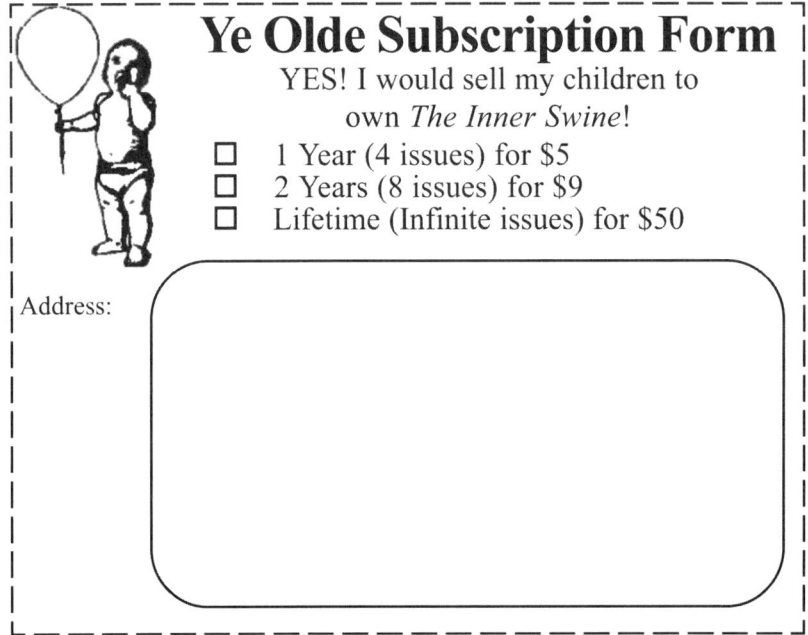

Ye Olde Subscription Form

YES! I would sell my children to own *The Inner Swine*!

- ☐ 1 Year (4 issues) for $5
- ☐ 2 Years (8 issues) for $9
- ☐ Lifetime (Infinite issues) for $50

Address:

We hope you get in touch, read a sample issue, and thus start sending us money on a regular basis. Feel free to drop us a line and tell us what you thought about our zine, this book, or whatever:

The Inner Swine
Jeff Somers, Editor
PO Box 3024, Hoboken, NJ 07030
mreditor@innerswine.com

WWW.INNERSWINE.COM
The Inner Swine's Sinister Web Presence.

It's coffee grounds floating in your mug. It's the subway door shutting in your face. It's the smell of damp socks heating on the radiator. It's getting no buy backs from the bartender. It's throwing up in a public restroom last cleaned in 1983. It's squandered potential, missed opportunities, crushing disdain. It's sarcasm, ennui, bad grammar, and vague disappointment. It's the zine that isn't nearly as good as you hope it is.

Fiction.
Misinformed Opinion.
Bad Poems.
STYLE.
www.innerswine.com

Featuring: Archives of every issue ever published, news, web-only columns, preview articles from the newest issue, downloads of swine-related stuff, and so much more!

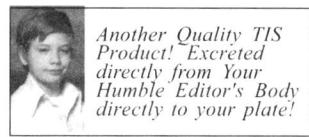

Another Quality TIS Product! Excreted directly from Your Humble Editor's Body directly to your plate!

By the way, **www.innerswine.com** is hosted by the amazing company **Hosting for Humans** (www.hostingforhumans.com). We recommend them to everyone.

MY BOOK.

I wrote a novel titled *Lifers* which was, improbably enough, published by **Creative Arts Book Company**. For money, even. If you'd like to buy a copy and keep me in booze money, you can order it over the Internet, get your local store to order a copy for you, or use the handy order form provided on page 228 to order direct. Heck, send me an e-mail and if you catch me drunk and sentimental one evening I'll probably mail you one for free. Maybe not. I have included an excerpt from the book here, both to fill some blank pages and to try to hawk a few copies. Read it and let me know what you think.

By the way, *The New York Times Book Review* had this to say about *Lifers*: "Midlife crises arrive early for the three young New Yorkers who aspire to lives of crime in this engaging, laid-back first novel. . .Jeff Somers observes these amiable sociopaths with a funky wit that revs up nicely whenever the three friends are companionably abusing one another. . ."

Chapter 10: "Angel-Headed Hipsters"
http://www.innerswine.com/lifers

Dub

alarm went off and I surged up from the pillows into the frigid air of my room, desperate to silence its wail, slapping madly until I hit the sweet snooze button, nine minutes of peace and quiet and I slumped back to the warmth of my blankets, it was seven in the morning and I'd been dreaming of something, something, me and Margaret

alarm went off and I surged up from the pillows into the frigid air of my room and hit the snooze button with deceptive skill, my body dredging up memories of being in shape and taken care I didn't realize it still had access to. I sat, slumped, staring at 7:09AM. I fell backwards into the pillows again, stretching luxuriously and cracking my back, shutting my eyes and wondering what I'd been dreaming of. . .horses? cats? something

alarm went off and I surged up from the pillows into the frigid air of my room and hit the snooze button all wrong, knocked the clock off my night table and onto the floor, where it continued to wail at me, too loud, everyone must hear it, it must be waking up the whole fucking block at 7:18AM with the silken sounds of Deep Purple, Christ of all the stations I had to choose from, why this? I sat in the evaporating warmth of my blankets for a moment, studying the sunlight as it wormed its way into my room from behind the shades, feeling it all seep back into me: It was Thursday, I had to go to work, I had to shower, shave, find clean clothes, tie my tie, make lunch, scrounge for change for the bus, turn the fucking alarm off. . .

Silence. I was beginning to shiver, the bare floor of my bedroom was freezing, the dimmed air frigid, my walls veined with ice. Still, I squatted by my defeated clock and rubbed my eyes for a moment, did some calculations, which led me to believe I'd done this same morning ritual almost seven hundred times.

I walked to the bathroom, scratching my beard, and turned the hot water up all the way in the shower. I stared at myself until the mirror steamed up, and then got naked and dove in, adding cold water to the mix for my own sanity, lathering up and just standing there. The cocksuckers who shared my water supply began to assert themselves: my water went cold, then hot, then settled into lukewarm. I struggled stupidly to bring back the scalding heat in cool water, gritting my teeth against pounding the walls and screaming like Tarzan, a rebel yell that would bring all the local wildlife (pigeons, rabid dogs, feral cats, squirrels, rats, and roaches) to my aid.

Then I rinsed off and turned off the water. I stood there dripping, pushing my hair out of my eyes. I hoped I was burning the skin off of someone.

I shivered back to my room and dressed: thermals, tan khakis, blue workshirt, black socks. Brushed my hair back. Put on my jellybean tie, my black Chucks, tucked a pair of sunglasses in one pocket. I checked my change bowl and grabbed a handful. I picked out a book to read on the bus and grabbed my backpack to shove it into. Back to the kitchen, where I made a sandwich, scooped up my wallet and keys, pulled on a jacket left there conveniently the night before, and left without a glance back.

It was 8:23AM. It almost always was.

The bus was seething with violence and cuss words. The man sitting next to me with the vague smell and the slicked-back hair was muttering profanities to himself, and I was pretending not to hear him, filling up with frustration and cowardice. I was reading *To Kill a Mockingbird* again, a dog-eared copy I'd had for fifteen years. I squinted at it and concentrated, trying to forget all the people around me who seemed poised at any moment to take control of the bus, because they apparently believed they knew how to drive it better.

We stalled in traffic again and mutiny threatened. I sank down into my seat and tried to think about anything but the assholes robbing me of my morning. I thought about the sixty-three dollars I had to my name until payday. I thought about Chick and the sad way she seemed completely unattracted to me. I thought about getting no mail again yesterday, about having no messages on my machine, about all the little mementos I had from the times when I used to acquire mementos, all of them dusty with age. I thought about my mom, and how I hadn't thought about her in days.

Thinking wasn't working, so I went back to grim reading until we were at my stop.

Then I was walking. Sifting through all the cocksuckers who worked in the city with me, the blue suits and tan coats, all of them seemed to know some fundamental rule of life I was missing out on. Then I was at work. I stood outside for a moment, unwilling to go in.

I bought a cup of bitter coffee at the newsstand in the lobby and crawled to the elevators, nodding to whomever I recognized. I took the elevator up and steeled myself for Dame's cheery good morning. Then I was at my desk, the little light on my phone blinking, e-mails on my computer, rock and roll on my radio, kicking my sneakers off and slipping my cracked and aged shoes on. Then I sat there for a minute, catching my breath, which is what I did for the rest of the day.

Trim

Trim woke up at eight o'clock and, knowing full well he had to open the video store by eight-thirty, rolled over and went back to sleep. He noted his pounding head and sore throat with clinical expertise, knowing hangovers better than almost any other subject.

At eight twenty-five, using some internal discipline the naked eye could not observe much less suspect existed, he sat bolt upright in bed and opened his eyes. He was still fully dressed, except for shoes.

For a moment, he sat there and moaned.

Then, he levered himself to the floor, pulled on his jacket, and picked up his backpack, the contents of which never altered. He slung it over one shoulder and left the apartment, a look of grim determination on his face. Outside, in the cold air, he paused to light a cigarette and then walked three blocks to the store. He got there at eight thirty-five, and as usual there was no one waiting to get in.

Opening the store, for Trim, consisted of only three steps: unlocking the doors, turning on the lights, and opening the register. In the employee handbook there were many other such steps, but Trim had taken the time to actually black most of them out, leaving only three sentences behind. Whenever anyone noticed the black marker, he was at a loss to explain why he'd felt it necessary to document his bad work ethic.

He sat down behind the counter, put his feet up, closed his eyes, and entered into a semi-trance that he'd perfected back in school. Ostensibly asleep, the slightest noise or change in air pressure roused him to an almost instant state of alertness.

His first customer didn't arrive until ten o'clock. The old man dropped off some adult videos and shuffled away without saying a word. Trim didn't move except to pop open one eye, and then close it again.

At ten-thirty, the phone rang, and this time Trim kept his eyes closed as he snaked out one arm to answer it.

"Moto Video, this is Damien."

He listened impassively. "Hey, Harry."

Again he listened. "No problem. Jimmy's coming in at three, right?"

He nodded. "Okay then. Yeah. Bye."

Smoothly, he replaced the phone, and was still again until eleven, when he roused himself to order lunch and look the place over. Some of the homebodies were trickling in by then, looking for ways to waste time. Some of them, he knew, came in every day, frittering away endless hours in front of bad movies that hadn't even been released to the big screen. He regarded them with a blank, slightly dim look and a monosyllabic vocabulary that discouraged small talk except in the loneliest and leechiest of them, whom he felt compelled to ignore completely.

As the afternoon wore on, he became more and more animated, until he was walking the aisles and hopping over the counter. When Jimmy arrived at three, Trim jumped up and called out his name with enthusiastic gusto, grinning from ear to ear and chatting amiably as he picked up his jacket, bag, and free videos, walking out the door not even a minute after Jimmy had shown up. He paused just outside to light a new cigarette, and walked home to begin his day.

Dan

There was nothing on TV. As usual. There was nothing in the fridge except ice and baking soda. There was no noise in the place, just the muffled darkness of five in the morning. There were no more cigarettes in the pack on the coffee table, no more magazines unread in the bathroom, no more butane in the lighter anyway, and no more reasons to stay awake.

He flipped the channels anyway: infomercials, dead-head talk shows, commercials, test patterns, old movies, snow. He and Trim had no money for cable so there were thirteen channels to blow through. He did it twice more just in case, and then shut the TV off. The click was deafening, the silence following more so. He sat in the easy chair and stared at the fading glow on the screen for a few moments, breathing heavily and imagining he could see the alcohol leaving his body with every exhalation. He hadn't been very drunk that day: he couldn't afford to be drunk anymore, unless someone was around to buy the drinks.

He glanced at his watch. He knew that Trim set his alarm for eight o'clock every fucking goddamn morning and he made it his business to not be there when the bastard woke up. He hated mornings, and preferred to face them alone, and the worst part of having a roommate, he'd always thought, was having to see him in the morning, fighting for the bathroom, drinking coffee, making small talk.

He considered his options, tracing his fingers over the remote control in the brightening dark.

Pulling himself up from the chair, he twisted himself around until his back cracked. Slowly, he pulled together the remnants of his life: wallet, keys, jacket, shoes. Spare change. Matches. Equipped, he made his way carefully from the apartment, not wanting to wake up his roommate. In the cold air, he allowed himself to make a little more noise as he walked. There was an all night diner a few blocks away that didn't seem to mind him when he nursed coffee there for a few hours in the mornings. He bought an early edition paper on the way and even got a smile from the tired and familiar hostess when he walked into the diner. He ordered coffee and opened the paper, beginning on page one and reading carefully, slowly, taking in every story.

Dub

At four thirty, Wendy from customer service sent me an e-mail suggesting we all go out for a bitchfest-cum-after work cocktail, because she'd had a rough day and needed to decompress. I replied that I'd be glad to join her, but that I couldn't stay late. I liked Wendy. Eight months before I'd asked her out and she'd gently told me no way, and since then we'd managed to remain friendly, and every now and then we had lunch or went out for a drink. I no longer wanted to date her, though I occasionally daydreamed of sleeping with her.

By five after five, we had gained three more socializers, which wasn't so bad. Wendy was a good looking Jewish girl who often found herself with more friends then she knew what to do with, most of them male, and I was used to sharing her with other people; I wasn't the sort of guy that inspired girls who had racks like Wendy's to pay attention exclusively to me. I wasn't sure what kind of guy I was, but it wasn't that type, for sure.

We went to an uptight Manhattan bar, mostly white with a few exceptions, and ordered mixed drinks to show me we weren't proles. I could tell it was going to be the sort of night I really couldn't afford: raucous, later than intended, and with a drink bill the size of the Milky Way. I started off with a scotch on the rocks to prove my manhood and kept trying to keep Wendy for myself despite the obvious futility of the endeavor, and the evening was pretty much downhill from there. The hell of your cubicle friends in the city, I knew, was the amount of time you spent having drinks and talking to people you really didn't like very much. I ended up with Mario.

Mario was in my department but under a different boss, and I had a nodding relationship with him on most days: you nodded hello to each other and left it at that, most days.

This time, however, we found ourselves sitting next to each other in a bar with a few drinks behind us, and it seemed to Mario that it would be good to ask me a few probing questions about myself, since Wendy with the oh-so-delicate features and nice rack was paying more attention to Dan from Finance than to either one of us. I quickly grew to resent this tactic of Mario's, and attacked him with thinly veiled sarcasm.

The joke's on me, though: the guy whose name I can't remember leaves early, and Wendy and Dan leave a few minutes later in a suspicious coupling. Mario and I are left sitting alone in a booth, sipping drinks.

"You ever wonder why you bother, Phil?" He asked in a desultory monotone. I guess he's drunk.

"All the time." I replied.

"Can I tell you something?" He asked.

I tensed up, but what can I say? Besides "Sure."

"I like her." He said slowly. "Wendy, I mean."

I nodded. "Oh yeah?"

"I think I love her."

This strikes me as funny, and I let a short laugh escape. This made Mario angry. He stood up.

"Fuck you, man." He said angrily, and left.

I can't explain what I think was so funny about this. My own issues of unrequited love? The fact that Mario had suddenly decided that a few months of hellos in the hallway meant we were close enough friends for that conversation? Or the fact that he'd stiffed me on the bill? It didn't matter. I left laughing.

I couldn't wait for Christmas.

Trim

After sleeping most of the afternoon and early evening, Trim woke up to shower and make a few calls. The calls were usually to the same people and usually resulted in the same actions. He splashed on some aftershave, pushed his hair out of his face by way of combing it, and put on his usual outfit: worn jeans, white oxford, black sportsjacket. He wore the same clothes more often than not, and had since the age of sixteen when he'd heard that Albert Einstein had done so to conserve his precious mental energies. He pulled on a pair of combat boots he'd had since the age of fourteen, stuffed his wallet and keys into his back pockets, made sure there were cigarettes (most likely stale) in the jacket, and went out to meet his cronies for drinks.

They met at Rue's Morgue, usually, sat in the rear even on

rainy Tuesdays when all the sane souls stayed home to drink. Trim chaired the meetings, which meant he watched everyone intently, doled out healthy doses of sarcasm and insult, and forced everyone to listen to his poetry by sheer force of personality.

As the night wore on and they got drunker, the sarcasm got sloppy, the laughter louder, the poetry much, much worse.

At a quarter after nine, Trim stood on his chair, raised his glass to the ceiling, and said:

"The city regards me with blank, dulled eyes / clouded store windows smog covered lights / it serves me watery drinks in smoky dive bars / which are what it passes as delights."

They broke into wild applause, causing the bartender to glance up and briefly wonder if he should throw them out early this night.

"My God," said Karyn with the bad teeth, "I can't believe it. That one's the worst yet!"

And they broke into laughter as Trim sat down, grumbling. "You idiot bastards wouldn't know good free verse if it crawled up your asses to die peacefully where no one would ever look for it."

She snorted. "I've got more free verse up my ass than you've ever understood, my little Iago."

Trim snorted back. "Fuck you. More beer?"

Dan

Aprici's never had more than twelve customers, and Dan suspected that normally they didn't add anyone until one of the veterans died, preferably of some liver-related ailment. Perhaps they had made an exception for him, a sort of grandchild clause.

He liked Aprici's because it opened at seven in the morning.

Dan thought he was starting to really look a lot like the usuals at Aprici's. He had read once, back when he could amuse himself by reading, that people had a tendency to resemble their spouses and pets, over time. He supposed it was due to the amount of time they spent with each other, and if that were true he was in serious trouble, considering the mugs of his fellow patrons. The thought made him smile, briefly, as he made his way through a beer and the sports page.

Through the murky plate window, he watched normal people walking to work, to the bus, buying papers and coffee and pushing rudely past each other. He studied them for a long time.

"Hey, kid," the bartender said meanly, "you see a ghost?"

Dan supposed he would be known as "kid" until he was seventy in a place like Aprici's. He let his gaze linger on the outside world for a few seconds more.

"Yeah."

There's an ad for the book on the next page -------------->

BUY THE BOOK, DAMMIT.

Okay, now you might wonder what the book's about, especially since you're going to buy a copy, right? It's about ennui, hangovers, desperation, destiny, disdain, and dumbfucks who try to rob their place of employment in a last-ditch effort to alter the slacker course of their meaningless lives, which of course fails. It's an uplifting, feel-good kind of book.

"...a highly entertaining if chillingly accurate reflection of the apathetic work ethics and life disappointments of Gen X postcollegiate dreamers."
- Deborah Rysso, **Booklist**.

"Midlife crises arrive early for the three young New Yorkers who aspire to lives of crime in this engaging, laid-back first novel....Jeff Somers observes these amiable sociopaths with a funky wit that revs up nicely whenever the three friends are companionably abusing one another..."
- Bruce Allen of **The New York Times Book Review**

BUY THIS BOOK AT
www.amazon.com, www.b&n.com, or www.borders.com

OR, order direct:

Creative Arts Book Co. Mail/Fax Sales
Creative Arts Book Co., 833 Bancroft Way, Berkeley, CA 94710
FAX *510-848-4844;* **PHONE** *800-848-7789*

___ copies of *Lifers* (ISBN **0-88739-322-5**) $13.95

Please send me the indicated number of copies of *Lifers* by Jeff Somers.
Enclosed is $_____ (please add $4.00 for shipping and handling, plus $1 for each additional copy; California residents must add 8% sales tax to the price of the book). Mail my order to:

Name_____
Address_____
City_____ State_____ Zip Code_____

Send check or money order--no cash or C.O.D.'s please. Prices and numbers are subject to change without notice. Valid in U.S. only. All orders are subject to availability of books. Please allow 4-6 weeks for delivery.